P9-CLA-833

KIM JONG IL

ON THE ART OF THE CINEMA

April 11, 1973

University Press of the Pacific
Honolulu, Hawaii

On the Art of the Cinema

by
Kim Jong Il

ISBN: 0-89875-613-8

University Press of the Pacific
Honolulu, Hawaii
http://www.universitypressofthepacific.com

CONTENTS

PREFACE

This is the great age of Juche. The Juche age is a new historical era when the popular masses have emerged as masters of the world and are shaping their own destiny independently and creatively.

The popular masses are struggling for Chajusong[1] under the banner of the immortal Juche idea. This is the irresistible main trend of our times. In this very current of the times a new system and order is being established in many parts of the world.

In our country today the Juche idea has been splendidly implemented in all areas of the revolution and construction under the intelligent guidance of the leader. As a result, an epoch-making change has been brought about, and a new period of national prosperity is developing.

Art and literature which represent this new historical age must naturally be Juche-orientated. Juche-orientated art and literature are communist art and literature that meet the requirements of the new age and the aspirations of the popular masses.

In developing communist art and literature, there is nothing for the working class to adopt from the old art and literature which cater to the tastes and sentiments of the exploiting classes. Even the heritage of art and literature which has been created over a long historical course cannot be accepted as it is.

In order to develop Juche-orientated art and literature that can meet the requirements of the period, we must conduct a revolution in the sphere of art and literature.

The revolution in art and literature is an acute class struggle in the ideological and cultural sphere to eliminate outmoded things from all areas of content and form, the creative system and the creative methods and to establish Juche-orientated. new art and literature.

The cinema is now one of the main objects on which efforts should be concentrated in order to conduct the revolution in art and literature. The cinema occupies an important place in the overall development of art and literature. As such it is a powerful ideological weapon for the revolution and construction. Therefore, concentrating efforts on the cinema, making breakthroughs and following up success in all areas of art and literature is the basic principle that we must adhere to in revolutionizing art and literature.

If it is to develop new art and literature, the working-class party must be guided solely by the great Juche idea and solve all problems in accordance with the requirements of Juche.

Proceeding from the requirements of the period and the historical mission of the working class, we shall establish our own theories of art and literature for the creation and development of Juche-orientated art and literature and put them into practice, making unremitting efforts to pave a new path.

LIFE AND LITERATURE

"Truly realistic and revolutionary art and literature show the people the most beautiful and most noble things of human life."

KIM IL SUNG

LITERATURE IS A HUMANICS

Art and literature are important activities which are indispensable to a fully human life. Food, clothing and housing are the essential material conditions for human existence, but man is not satisfied with these alone. The freer man is from the fetters of nature and society and from worries over food, clothing and housing, the greater his need for art and literature. Life without art and literature is unimaginable.

The communist society to which we aspire is a society fully-developed in all fields—economy, culture, ideology and morality; it is a truly popular society in which people of a new type, possessing intellectual and moral integrity and a high degree of physical development are cultivated in a comprehensive manner, and enjoy rich and cultured lives as masters of nature and society. Writers and artists have a significant role to play in building this great society, a unique role, in which they are quite irreplaceable.

If they are to fulfil their mission, writers and artists must first have a correct understanding of the inherent nature of art and literature and be able to create truly revolutionary works which meet the requirements of a socialist and communist society. A profound and accurate understanding of the intrinsic nature of art and literature and the requirements of the times is the starting point for the creation of a new type of revolutionary and popular art and literature, and the basic guarantee of the highest standards in creative work.

Revolutionary art and literature are extremely effective means for equipping people with the great Juche idea and inspiring them to work for the tasks of the revolution and construction. But as yet we do not have many profound and significant works which are of assistance in educating the working people in revolutionary ideas. Some of our literary works move people deeply by describing the beautiful and noble lives of people of the new era, but others neither describe the brilliant lives of outstanding individuals nor convey the live experience of real people. This is not merely a function of the writers' talent, but, more fundamentally, of their understanding of art and literature, and the opinions and attitudes with which they create their works.

Literature belongs to the domain of humanics. The essential characteristic of literary practice as a humanics consists in describing real people and serving man.

To say that literature portrays people means that it describes the lives of people who breathe, think and act as they do in real life. That literature serves man means that it solves urgent and important human problems by describing the way people live, thus teaching them to understand life and influencing them to live in an honourable fashion. Only through an accurate portrayal of people and their lives can literature provide proper solutions to essential human problems, and effectively influence people's behaviour.

Of course, many people in the past have regarded literature as a humanistic activity, but they were unable to give a precise answer as to the fundamental nature of such activity. They only stressed that literature should deal with man as the sum total of social relations and place him at the centre of artistic representation.

The question of the essential nature of man as a social being has only been finally settled by the great concept of Juche. For the first time in history this concept provides a complete answer to the puzzle of man's essential nature by explaining his life and soul in terms of Chajusong, thus also providing the key to the fundamental question of literature as a humanics, the question of how to view man and how to describe him.

Only the concept of Juche allows literature, as a truly humanistic practice, to supply correct answers to the human problems of our time by taking as its starting point the essential nature of man.

We need a humanics, literature, which gives prominence to the principle of Chajusong, the development of independent individuals, and which creates the image of the truly typical man of the new era, thereby contributing to the transformation of the whole of society in accordance with the concept of Juche.

Giving literary prominence to the principle of Chajusong and the development of independent individuals means clarifying the problems which people encounter in the struggle to defend and promote their political Chajusong. Depicting the typical man of the new era means creating images of people who live, work and struggle with the conviction that they are masters of the revolution and the work of socialist construction. In other words, it means creating images of people of a new type who maintain independent and creative positions by accepting full responsibility for solving their own problems without being subjugated to others or depending on the aid of others.

Stressing the principle of Chajusong and creating human images based on the concept of Juche allows literature to make an effective contribution to the education of people as true communists and to changes in every sector of the economy and culture, ideology and morality, in accordance with the concept of Juche.

If literature only deals with personal trivia in describing people's lives, without giving prominence to the fundamental question of man's dignity and intrinsic value, it will be unable to deal with those human problems capable of yielding instruction and deepening understanding.

There have been cases where writers have dealt with matters which were unworthy of literary attention. One example are those literary pieces which, in describing the struggle for socialist economic construction, focus on the subject of production techniques, instead of on human affairs.

A work of literature published some time ago, about the family of a patriotic martyr, concentrated on the question of production, instead of examining in detail the question of how the martyr's family should live, work and struggle. At that time, too, we criticized the value of writing about the martyr's family in a work of literature which is a humanistic activity if the work dealt only with the question of production and not with human affairs. In writing about the life of a martyr's family, one ought to clarify the important problems which arise in the course of people's lives.

Literary work should always deal with human affairs, both posing and answering the question of people's political integrity, that is, it should emphasize the solution to the question of how people can preserve and develop their political integrity. This basic requirement derives from the spirit of independence of each individual.

The people's struggle for the principle of Chajusong is intended to shape their political life and promote their political integrity as masters of the revolution and construction. The efforts of our working people in all areas of social life are all linked to the struggle to shape their political life. Their labour, for instance, is not simply directed to the production of material wealth; it is also a revolutionary struggle to carry out Party policy and transform themselves in a revolutionary manner. That is why the working people always live, work and struggle with a deep sense of their own pride and dignity as revolutionaries.

Since this is the way the people live, writers who deal with human affairs ought to give prominence to questions of people's political integrity and provide insight and guidance in answering them. In this way literary works can set high standards for the people to attain and show them the road of struggle, the road of a worthwhile life, in which every minute can be of lasting value.

The fact that some books give the subject of production priority over human affairs and give unnecessary prominence to production processes, rather than describing people, is due to the writers' failure to understand the essence of literature properly and to balance the relationship between human affairs and production correctly within the framework of a humanistic practice. Even in dealing with productive activities, writers must always concentrate on showing people's attitude to labour and the politico-ideological, cultural and moral relationships which are formed in the course of their work.

Since production is undertaken by man for the benefit of man, literature should naturally make a point of creating artistic images of people as the masters of production, and stress the resolution of the human problems which arise in the course of production.

Not only in representing the struggle for socialist construction, but also in mirroring all other aspects of human life, works of art and literature should raise matters which are urgently important in the struggle and lives of contemporary people, and settle them in accordance with the aspirations of the masses. Only then will these works be of any value.

A human question raised by literature can be settled correctly only through representative human images which can serve as examples for people in their lives and struggles. Therefore, we can say that the value and significance of any human question raised by a literary work is determined by the virtues of the typical character who plays the main role.

Our literature should deal mainly with the masses, including the workers and farmers, and highlight the typical communist individuals emerging from amongst the people.

The masses are masters of the revolution and construction and the makers of history. Socialist and communist society can only be built successfully on the strong foundation of a high degree of political consciousness and creative enthusiasm among the masses. No literature can speak truthfully about history and people's lives and serve the people well, unless it gives an artistic portrayal of the popular masses. In describing the masses as masters of the revolution and construction art and literature must show their independent and creative characters in full. The method of seeing and describing people from the conceptual viewpoint of Juche consists in giving an accurate artistic picture of the popular masses who are performing their role as masters of the revolution and construction.

Literature ought to portray real people.

Literature which does not describe real people is not a humanics in the true sense. If there were no real people in literature, there could be no artistic images; and without artistic images, it would be impossible for literature to preserve its intrinsic nature. The essence of literature which distinguishes it from other branches of social practice and analysis dealing with the same people consists in showing them clearly, as they are in real life, rather than dealing with people and their social relations in an abstract, unreal fashion.

Literature must show people as they are. People are always specific in their thoughts, feelings, will and actions and they have a real existence. Literary images of people, therefore, should always be firm and clear, just as living people are.

If a literary description of a revolutionary were only to show his political conviction and strong will, and not his rich mental world as expressed in the actual context of life, how dull his portrait would be! Of course, staunch conviction and a strong will are noble qualities in a revolutionary, but such a one-sided description of his mental and moral qualities could not be justified. If this conviction and will are to be represented truthfully and memorably it is imperative to give a detailed and multi-faceted description of the source of these qualities. Not only the political conviction and strong will of a revolutionary but also his ideals and ambitions, his temperament and emotions should be shown in depth from various angles. This is the only way to create a portrait of a typical revolutionary which is as vivid as real life.

If a literary work is to represent living people, it must portray people's thoughts and feelings truthfully, as expressed in their lives. These thoughts and feelings are not abstract things, they have definite forms which are expressed in people's actions. Talking about people's thoughts and feelings in isolation from their real lives means that the characters have already been made into abstractions.

In dealing with the courageous struggle of an air force pilot of the People's Army who had survived a crash behind enemy lines, the script of a certain film simply followed his actions in chronological order, merely showing what happened and describing how he was captured by the enemy but fought unyieldingly, maintaining his revolutionary stance, and how he succeeded in escaping and eventually rejoining his unit. The script omitted all the important facts, that is, what he felt when he was dropping into the enemy area, how he fought to keep his revolutionary faith despite the enemy's tactics of torture and appeasement, and the supernatural strength he required to overcome all the difficulties which he encountered on the way back to his unit after his escape. As a result, the hero was made to appear implausible and dull.

If a literary work ignores the world of a person's thoughts and feelings, which ought to be described clearly and in detail, that work will, in consequence, lack artistic excellence, and be reduced entirely to a dull schematic logic.

A lifelike and vivid literary description of people must be coupled with the portrayal of their unique individuality. A literary representation of real people should not be a mere description of people's everyday lives. A narrative of that kind would lack emotional conviction in its attempts to illuminate any significant subject or thought; it would not create a persuasive image of a human being at all.

The more individualistic the depiction of a character in a literary work, the clearer the picture of him becomes. No two people in the world are exactly alike. People are individualistic because they look different, they think and feel differently and each expresses his or her thoughts and feelings in a different way. Literature must show these personal distinctions clearly. A truly creative work provides original solutions to new and important human problems by means of distinctive characters.

In spite of this, we occasionally come across very similar characters in books which have a variety of titles. What is the reason for different writers producing works containing similar sets of stereotyped figures although they are writing about different people and events? It is precisely that these writers do not see people as living entities but describe them according to a set pattern.

Nothing is more monotonous for the reader than a book which lacks lifelike images of individual characters. A work of this kind is inferior to articles on political subjects or news items because it does not show the reader actual people and their lives in a convincing manner.

Literature should describe people's thoughts and feelings truthfully and clearly and in logical terms according to their particular characters, as they are expressed in life. People think differently and act in their own way even when they are confronted with the same problem in the same circumstances. Such characters have individuality. This logic of character is objective and independent of the writers' subjective views. Writers can only portray people naturally and truthfully, and avoid being carried away by their own subjective opinions, when they are well aware of the specific features and logical structure of their characters' lives. In this sense, we say that writers should be interpreters of the human mind and experts in human psychology.

If literature is to create typical characters and solve important human problems, it must mirror life accurately.

Where there are people, there is life. People cannot exist outside real life. Human problems, too, do not exist in a vacuum, they only arise within the context of real life. Therefore, literature cannot describe people artistically nor can it solve human problems properly unless it portrays life skilfully. Only works which contain a rich and accurate description of life are realistic, interesting and instructive.

The humanistic practice of describing life through literature means giving a lifelike description of the process of individual expression of man's essential characteristics. It is only when one thoroughly examines the process by which human thoughts and feelings are translated into action, that one can see the true character of real people, understand the human relationships formed in the course of living and the human problems which arise, and then solve them correctly.

Works of art and literature should always give a rich and detailed description of typical lives, in which people are shown as they really are.

A typical life means one which embodies the essence of the times and the law of historical progress. The typical life of our people today is expressed in their noble struggle for an independent and creative existence. Indeed, a revolutionary life is the most typical life, one which is lived in the main current of historical progress. It is only through a rich and detailed description of this kind of life that a literary work can both create lifelike human characters and correctly depict the essence of the times and the law of social progress.

When writing about the anti-Japanese guerrillas or the People's Army, some writers tend to dwell unduly on their military activities and when describing workers and farmers they over-emphasize their productive activities. Not only does a representation of this kind fail to conform with these people's real lives, it is also not relevant to the literary purpose.

By their very nature, the lives of those who work for the revolution are rich and varied. Revolutionaries are not people engaged only in military activities or production. They have a political life, a cultural life and also a home life. That is why writers must not merely depict people involved in combat and production work, but must describe their lives in a complex manner, from various angles. Even when they do deal with military actions and production work, they should provide insight into people's psychological world, the thoughts and feelings which find expression through these activities.

Of course, one should not write about everything in the attempt to depict this or that kind of life on the grounds that life should be described in a varied way. But in any case, literary works should represent life in its totality by probing beneath the surface of the facts and describing them in a variety of ways.

The film *The Story of a Nurse* is a detailed and skilful portrayal of the life of the heroine, who is taking wounded soldiers to a hospital behind the lines. The process of evacuation is shown from several viewpoints; a stage in the life of the wounded soldiers, who are distressed at the idea of going to hospital and leaving their embattled units; an episode in the lives of the Party members, who hold a meeting where they criticize themselves seriously and decide to help the young nurse; a portrayal of noble revolutionary comradeship displayed by the heroine who gives a transfusion of her own blood to a wounded man; and also the many beautiful features of life resulting from the strong unity between the army and the people. Although this is a simple story of wounded soldiers being taken to hospital, it moves people deeply because the process of evacuation is described in this varied manner. Works of art and literature should thus explore, from different directions, those areas of life where people's thoughts and feelings are given concrete expression and where human relationships are established and developed.

To achieve an authentic and striking literary depiction of people, life should be described in detail. Only deep study and detailed depiction of the concrete aspects of life, in which people's thoughts and feelings are expressed and through which human relations take shape and develop, enables a literary work to create realistic human characters.

A bald recital of facts is insufficient to show living people in detail, nor can it give a clear picture of life itself. A writer cannot show life as it really is if he simply assembles together great socio-historical events or restricts himself to describing a magnificent struggle for production in an attempt to present a theme of high political import. Nothing could be less like an artistic portrayal than the lumping together of events without examining the details, or a description of life which is centred on events, not on people, or the mere description of the outcome of actual events.

Bearing in mind that a single detail neglected or carelessly handled can spoil the whole picture, writers should strive to select those details of real events which will plainly express people's thoughts and feelings and clearly delineate their characters, and then describe them carefully.

After all, a skilful literary and artistic description of life is intended to give a clear and accurate picture of the characters. So writers must focus their attention on showing the characters as they are, no matter what aspects of life they are dealing with. Even when they are describing a fierce battle or a complicated production activity, they must accentuate the human voice rather than the roar of guns or machines.

Regardless of their historical background and the nature of the events they deal with, literary works must introduce and examine in detail subjects of urgent importance to the lives and struggle of our people today, and thus provide them with insight and instruction from life, as well as the confidence and courage to fight on staunchly.

Our literature must become a communist humanics which sets the masses in the forefront as the strongest, noblest and most beautiful of human beings. Our literature must serve them. A communist society is the highest ideal of mankind, and a Juche-type man is a man who typifies the noblest and most beautiful ideal. The humanistic practice by which we wish to create a representative man of the Juche type and promote the revolutionary education of people, can only be developed by true patriots, honestly revolutionary writers and artists who love their people ardently and dedicate all their energies and talents to the struggle for the common good.

A writer who has no love for the people cannot write sincerely for them, and an artist who is not devoted to the struggle for the people's cause can never create art for them. Our writers and artists must strive to equip themselves through revolutionary training and education as writers and artists of the Juche type, securely armed with the great concept of Juche, ardent love of their fellow-countrymen and devotion to the people's revolutionary cause.

THE SEED IS THE CORE OF A LITERARY WORK

If a writer is to produce a good piece of work, he must first select the right seed, which is the core of a literary work.

If we compare a written work to a living organism the question arises. What is the core of the life with which the organism is imbued and where is it located? In order to build the organic structure of a literary piece, it is necessary to have a clear vision of the fundamental principle which permeates all the elements of an artistic image and welds them into an integral whole.

There used to be lengthy arguments in literary circles about what it was that formed the basis of artistic images, determined the direction of the creative process and impelled it forward. But no clear-cut answer could be found. This question has only been correctly answered by our Party's theoretical concept of Juche-oriented art and literature.

A long time ago, the great leader Comrade Kim Il Sung said that a literary work must contain a core of convincing ideological substance.

This core of a literary work is the main factor defining the content of the work and determining the basic structure which gives life to the image.

Even in writing a scientific treatise, the author can only arrange his discourse into a system and develop his arguments when he has a core of distinct ideological substance to express. For instance, it was not until his discovery of the law of surplus value, which constitutes the core of his economic doctrine, that Marx was able to write *Capital,* which analyses the whole economic structure of capitalism. Marx needed to study an enormous amount of material on the capitalist socio-economic system, which is full of contradictions, before he discovered the core substance of *Capital.*

In the same way, in the creation of literary works, scientific studies and in other new undertakings, it is necessary to recognize the essential core by distinguishing it from other factors. This is what is meant by discovering the seed.

In art and literature the seed means the core of a work; it is the ideological life-essence which contains both the writer's main subject and the soil in which the elements of the image can strike root.

Life as described in a literary work must deal with a definite subject drawn from human experience. A writer does not take everything from real life, but only those aspects of it which are the expression of urgent and vital problems, as seen from his class and ideological standpoint. The seed means the living embryo of the work and the ideological essence which the writer has discovered for himself in real life, in the course of his search for human subjects.

The seed is the basis and the kernel of a literary work. It integrates material, theme and thought in an organic relationship.

If a writer is to create a fine work, he must first gather valuable material about life. This material serves as the life-giving soil which nurtures the seed as it grows and matures into an artistic image. So it is of the greatest importance in guaranteeing the ideological and artistic qualities of a work to choose from life material which is appropriate and fresh. But the mere recital or rearrangement of these facts, no matter how valuable they are in themselves, cannot ensure the ideological and artistic qualities of a literary work.

Actual life-events can only serve as the basis for the realization of the concept and theme of the literary piece once they have been analysed, appraised and artistically reshaped by the writer. In this context the material constitutes the basis provided for the seed by life.

A writer must select and fully understand the right seed on the basis of which to define the theme in concrete terms.

The theme is determined and restricted by the seed. So it is impossible to discuss any themes effectively without selecting the correct seed.

It has always been a simple waste of time and energy to attempt to write randomly, and usually no substantial result is produced when the act of creation is not linked to a correct understanding of ideological essence—even in cases where straightforward questions have been dealt with, to say nothing of those cases where the themes included a general discussion of matters such as revolutionary traditions and revolutionary transformation. In the final analysis, it is clear that failure was inevitable where any question, concrete or abstract, was made the basis of creative effort without the ideological essence being fully mastered.

The idea of a literary work is also derived from the seed. So a valuable idea can only be clearly expressed when the seed has been fully grasped. Only an outstandingly worthy seed can serve as the source of a clear and meaningful theme and idea. If a work has been produced without a distinct seed, simply in order to depict the heroic struggle of the People's Army or the beautiful spiritual world of the Chollima riders, the author will find it impossible to deal with important social questions and, therefore, to express his idea correctly.

A writer can only do justice to a valuable theme and idea and create a suitable artistic image which is capable of expressing them when he has discovered and fully understood a valuable seed from life.

This seed is the basic factor ensuring the ideological value of a work.

This value depends in turn on the strength of the artistic image which expresses the essence of life. The ideological qualities of a literary work, therefore, are only assured when it raises important questions and depicts them perceptively in accordance with the logic by which life itself develops. The ideological substance which has been acquired by the writer in his quest for the essence of life can serve him as the core of a literary work which clearly depicts the typical features of the historical period and society and also helps people to develop their own outlook on the world, encouraging them to make positive innovations in their own lives.

Attempting to improve the ideological level of a literary work without mastering the ideological substance would be as absurd as wishing to harvest good crops without planting seeds. Some works contain suitable themes and interesting incidents but still fail to move people. This shortcoming is often due to the fact that the presentation of the themes lacks ideological substance. Only images which have been accurately created on the basis of sound seeds are capable of incorporating noble and profound ideas.

The seed is the basis which blends the ideological and artistic qualities of a literary work, and the decisive factor in assuring its value.

Since the seed is the ideological essence which has been grasped from life itself, it has the fundamental capability of welding together the ideological and aesthetic qualities of a literary work. A writer does not envisage his seed as an abstract idea, but as a living entity, so that the ideological substance not only provides the main content of his literary work, it also constitutes the basis of its form and is the essential factor which integrates the two.

The seed also provides the ground in which the constituent elements of the image can strike root.

Once he has mastered the seed, the writer can discern the outline of the image he is going to create. Until he is inspired with a clear picture of the basic elements of the image, including the context of life and its ideological essence, the character of the hero and his relationships with other people, the scope of his life, and the plot of the story, the seed cannot yet be said to have matured, even if the writer claims that he has discovered it.

A seed which gives the writer a clear artistic picture, that is, the prototype of the image, is a real seed. Only a seed which has a clear and vivid ideological essence can give rise to a clear and vivid picture of the elements of the image.

The seed provides the writer with the basic impulse for creative work as well as a source of artistic vision and creative enthusiasm.

The writer is stimulated to worthwhile creative activity by a highly developed awareness of the noble mission entrusted to him by the Party and the revolution. However, if he has not thoroughly understood his seed, he cannot go on writing smoothly.

The writer can only be fired with creative zeal and develop his artistic vision to the full when he has chosen a good seed. He will only manifest enormous strength and talent and apply himself to his work night and day with indomitable energy, when he has grasped a seed which fires his heart with an unquenchable flame. Indeed, the seed is the force which both drives and leads his creativity throughout.

Excellent seeds are not only the prerequisite for an effective campaign for the accelerated production of art and literature, they are also the basic factor which guarantees the quality of each work.

Selecting the right seed is the most important thing in the process of creation.

A writer must always concentrate on the quest for the right seed, one which is in accord with the requirements of the specific time and the revolution. If the cognitive and educational role of a literary work is to be maximized, the author must discover and clearly define a valuable seed which can contribute effectively to advancing our revolution and construction.

The object in reality to which attention is directed, and the aspect of social life from which the seed is selected, are two major factors in determining the character and quality of a work of literature. They play a major role in the solution of all theoretical and practical questions arising in creative work. Since all the artistic elements of a work are chosen in accordance with the requirements of the seed, the correct selection of the seed is the key to successful creative work.

Above all, the seed must be chosen in accordance with Party policy.

Our Party's policy scientifically determines the requirements of the developing situation and the way to meet them. It teaches people how to understand life correctly and change it for the better. Therefore, writers must first of all understand our Party's policy completely, and then examine reality.

Only those writers who approach reality in the light of the Party's policy can see all the questions which arise in life correctly. What is important here is that they maintain a revolutionary stance in the selection of seeds to write about, in order to champion Party policy firmly, rather than that they study Party policy for the purpose of selecting good seeds.

If they only study the Party's policy from the viewpoint of some specific question related to the particular aspect of life from which they intend to select their seeds, they will be unable to grasp Party policy in its totality. In that case they will see even that particular aspect of life superficially and fail to find the right seed. Writers and artists involved in creating revolutionary works will only be able to effectively manage the ideological substance of their works in the manner required by the Party when they accept Party policy as their own conviction and their guide to creation, and reject the superficial tendency to regard Party policy merely as something to be learned.

Writers have to equip themselves effectively with the monolithic ideology of our Party, the great Juche idea, and seek out the seeds which are of greatest significance in our people's life and their noble struggle for the victory of socialism and communism.

In the selection of living ideological material, writers should never exclusively emphasize artistic qualities at the expense of political requirements on the pretext of observing the specific requirements of the creative process, nor should they seek out only that aspect of life which is typically political in expression, under the pretext of choosing seeds of political significance. Seeds of social significance selected from various areas—the struggle for economic construction, cultural life or questions of morality—can be treated politically to any extent they wish. The main thing is the way in which new socio-political, cultural and moral problems arising in our people's lives are explained in accordance with Party policy.

The seed which was initially selected for the film *A Worker's Family* was that a man who is a miner is not necessarily a worker and that a man who has worked in a mine for a short time does not necessarily belong to the working class. On the basis of the general intention—to produce a film which would show the process of the revolutionary transformation of a worker's family—the question could only be dealt with in this way.

We helped the author to understand life from a fresh viewpoint in accordance with Party policy, to delve deeper into life and discover a more serious and vital new seed defined by the socio-historical status of the working class and their revolutionary cause. As a result, he was able to grasp that the ideological substance of his work lay in the fact that members of the working class must not forget their origins and that, should they remember them but become conceited only continuous personal revolutionary transformation will prevent their deterioration.

This seed is of tremendous importance, in that it teaches people that the workers and everyone else must continuously revolutionize themselves at all times. In the light of this concept people can clearly see how the immediate requirements of the situation are met by the Party's policy of improving the leading role of the working class through revolutionizing that class, which is to be an example for the revolutionary transformation of the whole of society and for its modelling on the working-class pattern.

A seed must conform to the requirements of Party policy and also be capable of being expressed artistically.

The seed which is the core of a literary work must be such that it can mirror Party policy artistically in accordance with the intrinsic nature of humanics. Even when the task is to present the Party policy on economic and cultural construction, the seed must always include within itself the problems of the people who are carrying out the technical and cultural revolutions.

If a writer has discovered an ideological essence which fails to provide him with any idea of the characters of the principal figures, their relationships, the compositional elements and the mood of his literary work—all of which are fundamental to his creative endeavour—then he must have selected a seed which should be dealt with by philosophy or political economy, not literature.

In fact, there are occasions when some writers work on literary pieces dealing with ideological problems which cannot be the seeds of literature. They will not be successful with such seeds, no matter how hard they may try to create excellent images. Even valuable ideological material cannot touch the people's hearts unless it is expressed through an artistic image.

In the selection of the seed, its politico-ideological qualities must not be given absolute priority at the expense of its artistic significance. Anything which does not permit artistic description cannot be a seed of art, no matter how politically and ideologically relevant it is. That is why the seed is referred to as the basic factor which guarantees the artistic quality of a literary product. A writer without the right seed can provide neither ideological nor artistic quality.

If they are to choose a seed which has political significance and artistic value, writers must study a wide spectrum of life and experience it to the full.

In this respect, it is most important that they should be in the thick of life, see for themselves the noble lives of the working people, listen to them, feel and understand them. Living in the midst of real life, they will be able to discover the seeds necessary for their creative work, while at the same time educating themselves politically and ideologically. But they will be unable to write anything good if they merely gather those facts which please their eyes and ears, material based on a superficial view of things. When they seek experience in real life, they must pursue new seeds with definite objectives in mind and must not fail to return with excellent seeds.

Needless to say, it is impossible for a writer to gain firsthand experience of everything, nor does he write solely from his own personal experience. Sometimes he has to write about something which he has not experienced himself, because of the circumstances of his present life, or because he is writing of life in former times.

When he has to write about the past of which he has no personal experience, he must make a greater effort to study and analyse events in that period and discover the seed which represents the essence of those times.

The seed of the film *Five Guerrilla Brothers* could never have been discovered without studying the life of the Os, including O Jung Hwa and O Jung Hup, those indomitable fighters dedicated to the revolution.

Even when one is involved in real life, one cannot discover a valuable seed unless one approaches life with a high degree of political awareness and a keen eye.

Writers must know how to observe real life in its breadth and its depth, they must sense in their hearts the aspirations of the times, and their noble spirits must be unquenchable in their ardour to fight for the realization of those aspirations. Only then will they be able to discover the seeds containing new and essential subjects which can contribute to the people's revolutionary education.

The seed must always be new and have its own unique features.

Selecting a characteristic seed from real life is the prerequisite for the creation of an original image. The primary selection of the seed which serves as the ideological and artistic basis of a literary work is the starting point for the creation of an original image. The choice of a distinctive seed will enable the writer to deal with new and important subjects in his work and create a forceful and interesting image.

A new and distinctive seed means a seed which is original and contains in a novel form a new shoot for the development of life. Such seeds are not easy to find, not because they are as rare as specks of gold on a wide, sandy beach, but because it is not easy to recognize their quality correctly, although there are plenty of them to be found in life.

In order to uncover a seed with these distinctive qualities, it is necessary to explore new areas of life. New artistic sensibilities and original images stem from a new and distinctive seed. Therefore, writers should explore new areas of life in order to avoid banal repetition, although they should always also seek distinctive new seeds in the environment with which they are familiar. The choice of the environment from which seeds are selected is of great importance, not only for the creation of original works, but also for catering to the high level of the working people's artistic tastes by mirroring their lives in a variety of ways.

Careful cultivation of the seeds will bear excellent fruit in creative literary work.

The selection of a good seed does not, by itself, guarantee the successful completion of a literary work. The seed can only serve as the prerequisite condition and basis of literary creation. Even when a good seed has been found, the creative endeavour will be certain to fail if the seed is not properly cultivated. Having chosen a good seed the writer must concentrate all his skill and artistry on it in order to develop its narrative potential in depth.

A correct realization of the writers' ideological and artistic aims will only be achieved by carefully tending the seeds throughout the whole course of the narrative after they have been selected in accordance with Party policy.

In the cultivation of seeds, it is most important to define the characters of the figures appearing in a work accurately and to describe them clearly.

A seed's potential finds its expression through the portrayal of the characters of the hero and other figures. If they are not chosen properly or their characters are portrayed illogically, the seed will prove worthless, no matter how interestingly the story is written, and no matter how meticulously the dramatic structure is built up. The principal character in whom the seed's potential finds embodiment is the hero. For this reason, writers should pay especial attention to describing him or her skilfully, although they have to describe every character in a work well.

If the seed is to develop into an image, the situation must also be described well.

In art and literature, people are only deeply influenced by ideas which are expressed through the flow of life.

Life is complex and varied. Writers should choose from its varied features only those aspects which meet the requirements of their seeds; they must not include anything which has no connection with them. If aspects of life which have no bearing on the seeds are included, these will obscure the ideas which should be expressed in the works, and consequently prevent the writers' artistic intentions from being interpreted correctly.

Artistic creation requires not only clear ideological intentions but also the creative skill capable of expressing them. Without this skill it would be difficult for a writer to succeed in his creative work, even though he had selected a good seed.

After selecting a seed, a writer must subordinate characters, events, anecdotes, conflicts and every other artistic element to it by correctly following the basic line of narration developed from the requirements of the seed. He must not ignore these requirements even in the wording of a dialogue or in the setting and treatment of a scene.

Literary creation is a process through which writers produce clear images by representing, in accordance with the nature of their seeds, the experiences which have made a deep impression on them. Therefore, writers have to be able to experience life and to reflect on it, to apply their enthusiasm and imagination at all times, even in the process of developing their seeds.

Works crudely expressing ideas which are not clearly described in accordance with common sense, and show life as it is without adding any artistic elements, are the result of a low level of creative skill.

If they are to affect people deeply and provide powerful inspiration for their new endeavours, literary works must include valuable seeds which have been chosen from life and expressed through highly artistic images.

The correct selection of seeds and their skilful cultivation are the decisive factors which ensure success in creative work and guarantee a valuable outcome. In the selection and cultivation of seeds, writers must study seriously and comprehensively and think deeply. Those who devote their time, energy and thought to the selection of good seeds and their skilful cultivation, will always harvest excellent fruit.

THEMES SHOULD BE TREATED IN SUCH A WAY AS TO ENHANCE THEIR POLITICAL IMPORTANCE

A writer begins his creative work from the moment he receives a strong ideological and emotional impulse. But this impulse arousing the writer to creative activity does not simply occur of itself at any moment or in any phase of his life.

A proper seed which is of vital importance in real life may be grasped by a writer who zealously explores new revolutionary subjects by closely examining the valuable life-experience of the working people, who are fighting to create a new society and a new life based on their high ideals. But a writer who does not get into the thick of things and study life will never experience a truly creative impulse.

The writer who is guided by the Party's ideology in his thinking and acts on the Party's will, constantly devotes his attention to the Party's problems and makes every effort to solve them. Such a standpoint and attitude on the part of the writer are directly reflected in the Party spirit, working-class spirit and popular spirit of his work.

The writer's standpoint and attitude towards life are expressed above all in his choice of seed from life and his development of it. The discovery of a good seed is the initial guarantee of ideological and artistic quality in his work, but the good seed does not develop into a good literary work by itself.

If the writer is to embody the seed's potential artistically, he must treat the theme properly. The theme is the main topic with which he has to deal. When he has selected his seed, the writer determines the basic subjects he is going to deal with, and in the course of solving the problems which these pose, the seed's artistic depiction is unfolded. The ideological and artistic quality of his work, therefore, depends on how he solves the problems involved in developing his theme.

Themes must be dealt with so that they assume political importance.

All human questions arise in the context of man's social life, and as such they always assume a social character. Just as no human being can exist outside a social relationship, so there can be no human question which is not social in character. This means that literary questions must be dealt with on the basis of people's social relationships and in such a way as to assume political significance.

Dealing with subjects from the point of view of their political significance is the major requirement for improving the ideological quality of literary works. The more sharply you depict all the artistic elements from a political angle, in particular the characters and their lives, the events and conflicts, which are subordinated to the overall expression of your theme, the higher will be the ideological quality of your work. Of course, the degree of political significance of the facts, events and conflicts in question may vary considerably. But likewise, the degree of political content expressed through a particular subject may vary with the standpoint and attitude of different writers. If a writer who follows the Party's stand analyses every single detail of life accurately from the political point of view and portrays it in depth, the political import of the theme will be conveyed much more strongly.

The political meaning imparted to the theme by dealing with it in the correct way is also a major factor contributing to the artistic quality of the literary work. This quality is not something which arises spontaneously, still less can it be attained by cunning and artifice. Since the artistic quality is defined by the clarity and emotional force with which a given ideological content is represented, the significance of the ideological content itself must first be absolutely clear. If a writer regards technique as everything and ignores substantial ideological content, he will tend to follow the path of art for its own sake.

It is only easy to describe a theme artistically when its political import is defined correctly. If a writer gets bogged down in dealing with this fundamental aspect of creation, no matter how good his artistic project may be, it will come to nothing.

The political significance of the subject is also indispensable to the educational function of literary works. If people are to be educated to acquire a correct politico-ideological attitude and a higher class consciousness and to display greater revolutionary enthusiasm, the political meaning of everything must be clear to them. When the subject of a work has been treated correctly, it can do a great deal to impart a correct understanding of the urgent problems arising in life and to rouse people to struggle to solve these problems.

If the subject is to assume political importance through its representation in the work, it must be treated in accordance with Party policy.

Our Party's policy gives correct answers in concrete terms to all important social problems which arise in real life. By means of its scientific guiding ideology and theory, our Party correctly clarifies problems in every area of life, indicating the specific approaches and methods required in order to advance the revolution and construction. Thus our Party organizes and leads the masses to victory in their fight. That is why writers must solve questions raised in real life in accordance with Party policy. Only in this way can they be sure of correctly fulfilling their task of meaningful artistic representation.

Our art and literature are directed towards clear and exalted ideological goals. They represent life correctly and profoundly because they solve the problems of life on Party lines. Therefore, in order to impart political meaning to their themes, writers require not only a good theoretical understanding of the essence and validity of Party policy, but also a heartfelt personal commitment.

The theme of a literary work must be treated naturally through the artistic structure rather than through direct commentary by the writer. All the elements of the narrative must therefore play their part in highlighting the political significance of the subject.

To this end, one must first of all clearly define the ideological and spiritual state of the hero and other characters, which is to be expressed through their actions.

The human relationships formed in implementing the Party's policy for the final emancipation of the working people from the burden of backbreaking work may involve people who know the Party's intention and work zealously and also shortsighted people who only rush work through under the pretext of heavy pressure, paying little heed to solving the problems of working and living conditions or postponing the fulfilment of these tasks. The ideological view of such people should be given emphatic treatment, and the problems raised should be solved in accordance with the requirements of the Party's policy.

If a writer approaches problems from a strictly technical position, without a profound study of the ideas held by the people, he will be unable to treat the subject politically. When a socially important issue taken up at the start of a work fades away and is reduced to a matter of production technique, that is, a question of whether or not a new technical innovation is made, or whether or not a production plan is carried out, it is entirely due to the fact that the theme has not been treated politically, in terms of human relationships.

If the subject matter is to be treated meaningfully, the development of events and the conclusions to which they lead should be imbued with political significance.

The action of a literary work reveals the ideological views of the hero and other characters. People cannot remain indifferent to events in their society. They evaluate them in one way or another in the light of their own interests, attempt to influence them and adapt to them in order to achieve their own aims in life.

Therefore, great care should be devoted throughout the work to the literary construction of the main events, which clearly demonstrate the people's views and attitudes to life, and events of secondary importance snould be made to support the main events. This is the only way to give correct emphasis to the political significance of the main events, while treating the theme with insight and sensitivity.

In order to invest events with a political significance, it is also necessary to show them in a way which convincingly demonstrates the correctness and the great vitality of Party policy. A dramatic event, no matter how interesting and impressive it may be, cannot affect people profoundly unless it is introduced and developed from the point of view of Party policy.

The settlement of conflicts in accordance with the Party's class and mass lines[2] is also a major factor in the depiction of the theme's political significance.

Conflicts have to assume a political character because they represent the contradictions and struggles between different ideas in the course of people's social relationships. For this reason conflicts can only be settled justly and meaningfully on the basis of the Party's class line and mass line.

The revolutionary transformation of people and their training as communists constitute the basic content of revolutionary works of literature, and a theme of such great political significance naturally raises the question of how the line of political organizations should be treated.

The lives and destiny of those who have been awakened to class consciousness and embarked on the road of struggle, those who are already engaged in the revolutionary struggle, and the working people who are actively building socialism, are all linked to their political organizations. Everyone who wants to lead a truly worthy life and advance towards socialism and communism can only realize his aim and attain his ideal under the leadership of the Party. It is impossible for a man to make a valuable contribution to society if he is divorced from his political organization, nor can he develop his political integrity fully.

In a work which deals with revolutionary life, the question of the line of political organizations assumes special importance. Needless to say, the line of political organizations may or may not be set depending on the characteristics of the seed and the requirements of the theme. Where the theme of a work requires the portrayal of the people fighting under the leadership and influence of a political organization, it is imperative to show the role of their Party organization or their working people's organization. If the line of the political organizations is not shown in such a work, it will be impossible to provide a correct political solution for the particular problem under consideration, and the picture of life itself will be distorted. But this does not mean that by simply depicting stereotyped

Party workers or a political organization one automatically solves the problem. If Party officials are not to be presented, it is important to describe the role of rank-and-file Party members well, in order to show that a Party organization exists and is active.

Political workers who represent the line of political organizations in literary works must be shown to play distinct roles in relation to the main characters who are involved in the theme. They must be presented as men or women who play the leading role in organizing people in their struggle, breaking down all barriers in their way in order to ensure the victory of the positive forces.

If a serious issue arises between the conflicting characters and sharp criticism and a decisive blow are needed to attack the negative forces, the question must be settled politically and organizationally. Any deviation from this principle will obscure the real nature of people's relationships, emphasize a tendency towards personal feelings, and dull the edge of criticism and struggle.

The artistic qualities of a written work must not be sacrificed to an exclusive emphasis on the political aspects on the pretext of stressing the political significance of the theme. The political and ideological factors in a literary work can only find their true artistic expression and make a profound impression on people when they are artistically and emotionally integrated.

The theme of a literary work is not fully expressed at the beginning, nor is it simply stated once or twice during the narrative. It is developed throughout the course of the work and is fully revealed at the conclusion of the story.

In the artistic presentation of the theme, it is important to describe life naturally, gradually increasing the scope and depth of the depiction in step with the development of the hero's personality and the main story line. A theme will only make a really deep impression on people when it is developed with the current of life, growing through the tortuous course of struggle, and stands fully revealed with the dramatic resolution.

The Sea of Blood is a classic because it moves people deeply by its clear exposition of the theme. The theme of this masterpiece is presented clearly through the tortuous life-history of the heroine until the point when she takes the road of armed struggle after realizing the fundamental truth of anti-imperialist revolutionary struggle, that blood must be repaid with blood and that violence must be countered with violence.

A literary work will be dull and monotonous if it starts with a big problem but drags on tediously and fizzles out without any ideological development. The introduction of a pretentious theme at the beginning of a work is, in itself, an indication of the writer's attempt to state some sort of ideological question in a few words of narrative or express an immature thought on his own behalf instead of raising and solving problems in the context of people's lives. This is not a true depiction—it is tantamount to literary coercion. It does not convince people by the portrayal of distinctive behaviour, but amounts to preaching to them on an abstract idea.

Nor is it advisable to stretch the subject over many story lines on the excuse of broadening the theme. A literary work must concentrate its treatment of all the characters and all aspects of life on developing the main subject.

All literary works need to develop a well-defined plot for the presentation of the theme, in particular those works involving many characters who are associated with the hero, and this demands meticulous planning. The merit of the story will increase in proportion with the clarity of definition of the task of each character in the dramatic structure, the clear presentation of the ideological content of every incident and the precision with which they are arranged to support and express the main subject.

A large number of characters who do not contribute to developing the theme, and complex events and incidents which are not integrated harmoniously with the narration of the theme, will only result in confusing the hero's story and complicating the plot. An artistic work must always introduce a variety of characters to meet its purpose and to elaborate human questions which are as profoundly entangled with each other as they are in real life.

Writers must deal quickly with the new problems which arise in socialist life and answer them decisively, while at the same time continuing to explore the wide variety of themes in our revolutionary art and literature. To this end they should immerse themselves in the revolutionary events and thrilling developments of real life, devoting all their energy and talent to working in company with the Party and the people towards the brilliant completion of the new tasks.

THE PROCESS BY WHICH A REVOLUTIONARY OUTLOOK ON THE WORLD IS ESTABLISHED SHOULD BE CLEARLY DEMONSTRATED

The choice of a hero and the portrayal of his character is a fundamental problem related to the social character of art and literature, and, therefore, this question is constantly being raised and resolved in various ways in different social systems and by different classes.

Our Party has consistently taught that the working class, the master of the new age and the unique human model for the communist future, should be set in the forefront and that the process by which ordinary people acquire their world outlook and mature into revolutionaries should be shown in detail. This very important guideline indicates the way in which our art and literature can correctly fulfil the basic tasks of the communist movement, the working-class movement and the national-liberation movement of our time.

If one is to succeed in the revolution in one's own country, one must have a force of competent revolutionaries who have established their own Juche and are therefore capable of solving every problem through their own efforts and on the basis of their own convictions. This indicates the need to prepare a large force of communists by intensifying ideological education for the working class, the main force of the revolution, and for the rest of the working masses.

Even after the victory of the socialist revolution, every member of society must be firmly equipped with the revolutionary world outlook if they are to storm and capture the ideological and material fortresses of communism.

Only when people are equipped with the revolutionary world outlook can they understand life correctly, analyse and evaluate everything from the point of view of the working class, and devote all their energies to its interests. People equipped with this revolutionary outlook can fight unwaveringly against the influence of all unhealthy ideas which run counter to the revolutionary ideas of the working class, and devote themselves to the struggle to overthrow the capitalist system and build a socialist and communist society. Therefore, the most important task of art and literature dedicated to the revolutionary education of the popular masses, is to provide a detailed description of the process by which people establish a revolutionary world outlook.

It is also in the nature of literature, a humanics, to study people's inner spiritual world and show the process by which their ideological consciousness develops. Since works of art and literature must portray real people who mature as their lives progress, writers must give a true picture of this process, following the course of events through which the revolutionary consciousness of the characters awakens and matures. An accurate portrayal of the process of people establishing their revolutionary world outlook will enhance both the ideological and artistic quality of literary works and increase their cognitive and educational effectiveness. When they see the process of growth by which the hero is awakened to class consciousness and takes up the struggle, imbued with bitter hatred for the enemy, the audience will realize clearly the true meaning of revolution and why the revolution is necessary, and they will be convinced that everyone can work for the revolution if they are determined, indeed, that they must do so.

No matter what aspects of life our works of art and literature may deal with, they must give a true picture of the process of the growth of people's revolutionary consciousness, the process of change and development of their spiritual world.

The presentation of images of people acquiring their revolutionary world outlook is indispensable, not only in large works which deal with typical men growing into fighters over a long historical period of revolutionary struggle, but also in short works which tell simple stories covering a relatively short historical period. It does not necessarily take people a long time to acquire revolutionary consciousness, nor is it always necessary for them to participate in large-scale struggles. The process by which revolutionary consciousness is formed in the minds of people may vary with the circumstances in which they grow up and with the influences which affect them. This implies that the depiction of the process of growth of people's revolutionary consciousness is a principle which can, and must, be realized not only in large-scale works but also in simple ones.

Literature which is to serve the people in their revolutionary transformation and assimilation to the working class [3] must show in detail the process by which people establish their revolutionary world outlook at the same time as it depicts the revolutionary struggle and the fight to build socialism. People acquire the revolutionary world outlook in the struggle for socialist transformation, in the course of their creative labour to conquer nature and develop the economy, in the revolutionary struggle to overthrow the exploiting society and in revolutionary wars to defeat imperialist aggressors. Therefore, the process by which people revolutionize themselves and become fully integrated into the working class has to be shown in the works of our art and literature which deal with the great contemporary themes of socialist life—its pulsing energies of innovation and creation, and the worthwhile lives of our people.

In this regard it is important to describe the process of re-education of negative characters who are involved in reconcilable conflicts, as a process by which their consciousness is reformed in a revolutionary manner. The re-education through criticism of people who lack class consciousness and revolutionary awareness is, in essence, the process through which they establish the revolutionary world outlook. If they have discarded outmoded ideas, become convinced supporters of the new revolutionary ideas, and embarked upon a new life, then it means that there has been a change in their ideological consciousness.

Since the process of re-educating backward people is always a process of equipping them with the revolutionary world outlook, the detailed description of the development of their revolutionary consciousness, in conjunction with images of men of a communist type who are emerging as masters of the new era, plays an important role in people's revolutionary education.

This comprehensive and profound representation of the establishment of people's revolutionary world outlook is a fundamental requirement and an essential element of revolutionary literature.

How, in specific terms, is the people's revolutionary world outlook to be formed and what is its essential constituent? In literary work it is important to understand this problem correctly and provide a solution in artistic terms.

The process by which people establish their opinions and their attitude to the world is very complex, but the process of shaping their revolutionary world outlook is governed by a universal law.

As the great leader Comrade Kim Il Sung has said, a person's revolutionary world outlook is shaped, consolidated and further developed through distinct stages of the development of his consciousness. He has also explained the stages in concrete terms.

In the initial stage of shaping the revolutionary world outlook, the main thing is to understand the basic nature of the exploiting classes and their society. Hatred for them stems from an understanding of the reactionary nature of capitalist society. After this stage comes the revolutionary determination to fight to the end to overthrow the outdated and corrupt capitalist society and build a socialist and communist society which is free from exploitation and oppression.

Only when people have acquired the noble ideological and spiritual qualities of communists who are guided by their revolutionary understanding and determination can they say that they have completely established their revolutionary world outlook. If one wants to become a true communist, one must cultivate strong willpower which cannot be broken by any adversity, acquire a rich experience of revolutionary struggle and master its methods through constant ideological self-improvement and practical struggle. Moreover, one must learn to love one's country and people ardently, to value one's political organization and comrades and strictly observe organizational discipline.

There are no born revolutionaries, nor are there any perfect revolutionaries. A person's revolutionary world outlook is formed, consolidated and developed only through patient education and practical struggle. Even after one has established one's revolutionary world outlook, one can scarcely claim to be a perfect communist. One may suffer momentary frustration and doubt during the complicated course of revolution, and then gather one's strength and courage again, in order to harden oneself still more and continue with the struggle.

Since the purpose of describing in books the process by which people establish their revolutionary world outlook is to train revolutionaries, the process of acquisition of the ideological and spiritual qualities of communists must be clearly shown. In this way readers receive a lasting impression of real people who are shaping and developing their own revolutionary world outlook.

Literature cannot deal with the various problems which arise in the establishment of people's revolutionary world outlook in the orderly chapters and sections of a textbook. It can only solve these problems satisfactorily when it creates vivid pictures of people who are shaping their revolutionary world outlook in the course of their rich experience of life, ideological self-improvement and revolutionary practice.

To provide an elaborate picture of the development of a person's ideological consciousness, writers must probe the essence of each particular phase of his or her innermost development.

It is possible to reach an understanding of society and revolution through the real experience of life. When literature fails to show explicitly the process by which people shape their ideological consciousness, it is liable to treat it as an abstract concept.

In order to give an accurate description of people's innermost lives it is essential to show clearly how they form and develop their class consciousness through their experience of varied and complicated social situations. Class consciousness gives a definite direction to hatred, hostility and resistance to the exploiting society, it intensifies all these feelings and strengthens them. When spontaneous feelings are given direction by class consciousness, they become a purposeful and powerful force in life and in battle.

People's class consciousness finds its clear expression in their political life. People who participate in the revolutionary struggle eventually find themselves as members of their organization and collective, in the theatre of fierce class struggle, no matter how complex a process they may undergo. In the course of this process they develop into true fighters capable of totally subordinating their own lives and future to the interests of their class. A literary work can give people a proper understanding of society and revolution and inspire them with enthusiasm for the struggle by means of accurate descriptions of political life, in which the heroes develop their revolutionary consciousness.

If a true picture of the process of people shaping their revolutionary world outlook is to be given, it is necessary to describe their innermost thoughts and feelings in detail, in accordance with the logical course of their lives and their own characters.

Revolutionary consciousness is not an inborn human quality, nor does it spontaneously spring into being anywhere. The revolutionary world outlook has its own social and class basis. If the process of its formation is to be presented accurately, it is imperative to establish properly the various social situations in which the revolutionary consciousness can germinate and mature and, starting from this basis, to describe the subtle changes in people's inner world and their process of development.

People shape and consolidate their revolutionary consciousness according to their various class origins and social status, through their experience of life and under the influence of their environment, school education and various other factors.

The revolutionary world outlook is formed in the minds of workers and peasants when they suffer exploitation and oppression, experiencing at first hand the true nature of the exploiting classes and their system. Even people who have not experienced exploitation themselves, can gradually learn to hate capitalist society when they see capitalists and landlords bleeding the workers and peasants white and experience indignation at this brutality and disgust with the system of exploitation.

When people can clearly see the reactionary nature of capitalism in books on politics and in revolutionary works of art and literature, they can rid themselves of illusions about class society and make up their minds to destroy the system of exploitation.

Outstanding revolutionaries and the environment also have a great effect in persuading people to embark on the road of revolution. But, in the shaping of their world outlook, their social practice, including activities in political organizations, is more important. People's ideological consciousness takes firmer root, gathers strength and advances to a higher stage in the course of practical struggle.

Generally speaking, the social conditions under which people's revolutionary consciousness grows vary according to their class background and economic situation, and are involved in a complex and varied manner with their concrete experience of life. Take, for instance, the poor peasants who till the land for landlords, and are subjected to other related forms of social exploitation. Their social, class and economic conditions find different forms of expression according to the specific circumstances of various contexts.

People who begin to realize through experience the true nature of the exploiting classes and their system, grow into stalwart communists by acquiring a profound knowledge of the laws of social progress and the essence of the class struggle, whereas those who have come to understand the corruption of the capitalist system and the inhumane nature of the exploiting classes through their education or by observing them, can only become genuine communists when they train themselves through incessant struggle. Neither firsthand experience of exploitation, nor the reading of revolutionary books is sufficient in itself to make a person a true communist. Revolutionaries must, without exception, regard study as their foremost task and work hard to make themselves well-informed, while at the same time toughening themselves through practical social activity. Only in this way can they acquire the ideological and spiritual qualities worthy of a communist.

It is important that the situations in a book should provide an accurate picture of the process by which the revolutionary consciousness of the hero germinates, takes root and gradually develops to a higher level. A description of a young farmhand having a fight with his landlord because he is enraged at the man's cruelty, or an intellectual watching or being involved in a workers' strike, and suddenly deciding to embark on the road of struggle, would not only contradict the logic of real life but also fail to give people a correct idea of the character of revolutionaries. A person does not become a revolutionary on the spur of the moment, following the impulsive urge of one morning nor does he simply jump over a fence onto the revolutionary path. Since everyone nurtures his class consciousness gradually and becomes a revolutionary through the experience of life and struggle, a literary work must give an accurate picture of the tortuous course of this struggle. This is the only way to win people's sympathy.

The stimulus which shapes the revolutionary consciousness differs from person to person and so does the process of acquiring a world outlook. The individual motives on the basis of which people form their world outlook differ from one person to another according to their family background, environment and position in life, and the process of maturing into fighters also varies between workers, peasants and intellectuals. It is not possible for everyone to revolutionize himself in the same way. Some do it quickly, and some slowly, overcoming on the way many tempestuous difficulties.

It is not right to ignore people's characters and their particular living conditions and describe every character in a stereotyped manner by smoothing out various uneven features, on the pretext of presenting the universal law according to which a person's world outlook is shaped as he develops into a typical revolutionary.

In depicting typical characters, writers must portray the individuals in bold relief and draw attention to their essential characteristics, instead of rounding them out in one way or the other.

Characters develop as life changes. In the course of life hatred for the enemy, revolutionary conviction and fighting spirit gradually acquire strength. The correct course for a literary work, therefore, is to select a typical life in which the revolutionary world outlook is established, and describe it carefully. A writer must not waste all his creative efforts by the careless positioning of a single brick in building his tower of world outlook. If he omits a single link in the changes and development of the hero's ideological consciousness or substitutes one for another, he will fail in his attempt to portray accurately the process of formation of the revolutionary world outlook.

Once the framework for the growth of the world outlook has been established, the writer must give a detailed account of what the characters see, hear, feel and accept as the truth. When we say that in dealing with the hero's innermost thoughts and feelings it is important to delve into the process by which the revolutionary world outlook is shaped, we mean that it is necessary to give a true picture of the acquisition of this experience.

In any case, it is impossible to give a rich and varied ideological and spiritual portrait of the characters if the writer fails to probe beneath the surface of life into the world of the characters' experience. If in describing people's gradual attainment of a higher level of ideological consciousness he simply traces the course of events, instead of following the development of their spiritual world, he will be unable to represent the essential process of the development of their characters or arouse sympathy for their actions and experiences. So, once the conditions for the shaping of the revolutionary world outlook have been established, it is imperative that the hero's changing feelings and beliefs should be carefully described. The proper fulfilment of this task will carry people deep into the world of the hero's experience and persuade them to resolve to work for the revolution.

If the picture of the development of the hero's ideological consciousness is to be accurate, his psychological beliefs must be expressed through his actions. A man's ideological consciousness cannot be seen or measured. His actions provide the only yardstick by which to judge his ideological standpoint, or his attitude and views in general; and you can only confirm the degree to which he has been ideologically reformed when you have observed how he lives for a certain period.

A careful description of the stages which mark the tortuous progress of ordinary people towards an understanding of the meaning of the revolution and a commitment to the struggle, is also required to give people a correct understanding of the revolution

A revolution is not something beyond the comprehension of ordinary people, nor is it something reserved for a special kind of person. Everyone can take part in it if he or she is determined to do so, but it is not so easy to shape a firm revolutionary world outlook and develop into a good communist. It would be impossible for people to acquire a satisfactory understanding of revolutionary ideas merely by participating in the struggle once or twice or by studying for a certain period. They can only establish a revolutionary world outlook by overcoming various difficulties in the course of arduous struggle. A bold description of the tortuous course of the revolutionary struggle is required in order to teach people this fact and inspire them with an indomitable fighting spirit and confidence in victory.

It is most important to present the process of the revolutionary struggle as emerging victorious following great tribulations, not only in order to instil the spirit of revolutionary optimism in the minds of people but also to demonstrate convincingly to them the immense creative energy of people who possess a firm revolutionary world outlook.

A true and clear picture of all the twists and turns in the process of the hero's growth also increases the artistic interest considerably. The whole content of a literary work would be clear at a glance if it were to condense the process of a man's development into a simple concept. A work of this kind would be uninteresting. When the process of a person's development is sincerely and clearly described as it is in real life, showing how the characters emerge victorious after a long struggle to overcome difficulties, the audience will see themselves reflected in the characters and take note of the lesson.

The image of the mother in the film *The Sea of Blood* is an excellent example of a character whose growth into a revolutionary is conditioned by life's vicissitudes. Her character clearly demonstrates that a person's revolutionary world outlook is not formed in a day or two, nor is it acquired in smooth stages, in the way that a first grader is promoted to the second grade in school. The mother leads a tragic life before she stops being afraid of the enemy and takes the first step on the road of revolution. Such is the course of revolutionary development which slowly but steadily brings into being a new type of person.

In the final analysis, writing about a hero who is developing his or her revolutionary world outlook means describing the birth of a new type of communist man.

A communist possesses not only the ideological and moral virtues which make him or her honourable, noble and fine, but also a high degree of cultural attainment of a rich humanity. A gem can be flawed, but a communist as a human being cannot be. Steady growth and development through struggle represent the natural course of life.

A flower is beautiful when in bud, but it is more beautiful when it is in full bloom. When we say that there are no perfect revolutionaries, we are not suggesting a height of attainment which is beyond the reach of ordinary people, but merely indicating the exalted goals and profound modesty of the communist, who is never satisfied with his or her own spiritual and moral self-improvement.

LIFE IS STRUGGLE AND STRUGGLE IS LIFE

Art presupposes life. Without life there could be no artistic creation. An artistic work which does not mirror life honestly is useless.

An artistic work which mirrors a noble and beautiful life truthfully and richly, gives the people great strength in their practical struggle to transform nature and society. People acquire a better understanding of the way things are through the noble lives described in art and literature, and from this they derive greater strength and courage in their fight to build a new life.

The intrinsic nature of art and literature requires that they should describe life fully and accurately. Only by presenting a true and full picture of life can art and literature give people a correct understanding of the law of historical progress and show them the way to a sincere life of work and struggle. And only by describing life accurately and from various angles, can art and literature solve important and urgent problems and express great ideas in a moving and artistic fashion.

What matters in art and literature is how life is observed and described. The stand one takes in viewing and depicting life determines the nature of one's creation, that is, whether it is a work of realism or anti-realism, a work of revolutionary art and literature or a counter-revolutionary work.

Life, in short, is the people's creative efforts to conquer nature and transform society. Life, which includes every aspect of people's relation-ships and their activities, is very rich, varied and complex. But a writer cannot undiscriminatingly approve of and love any life.

A writer who is to serve the people must naturally have a deep interest in their lives, and be quick to recognize the urgent problems which can be used to raise the level of their class consciousness and to advance society, and must strive to solve them in the interests of the revolution.

Our art and literature must create rich and detailed pictures of the fine life of our people who are battling heroically for socialism and communism.

Real life consists in our people's struggle to create what is new, progressive and beautiful. A life which develops through intense struggle is most ennobling and beautiful. A life which develops through the struggle to eliminate what is old, conservative and reactionary and to create what is new and progressive, is not only ennobling in its aspirations but also militant, optimistic and beautiful in itself.

If art is to show a meaningful life, it must seek that life in the struggle of communist people of a new type and depict it in all its depth.

No one is so sincere and loves life so ardently as a communist. Communists are revolutionaries who always know how to create a new life wherever they are. Their emotions are more profound and humane than those of other people. This is why, wherever the communist people of the new type are growing up, life is always vigorous, vibrant, overflowing with revolutionary optimism, diverse and rich.

Some authors, however, tend to write exclusively—and boringly—about military combat actions in an attempt to portray the struggle of revolutionaries. This is a mistake. Revolutionaries are not the kind of people who regard their struggle and their lives as two separate things. Life and struggle always mean one and the same thing to revolutionaries who are devoted to the revolution and construction and whose belief in communism is firm.

As the great leader Comrade Kim Il Sung has said, the life of a revolutionary begins with struggle and ends with struggle. For revolutionaries, life consists of their struggle and the struggle is their life.

For example, the struggle of the anti-Japanese guerrillas in the 1930's involved not only battles against the Japanese imperialist aggressors, but also many other interesting aspects of life—the creation of guerrilla bases, the establishment of the people's government, democratic reforms, the preparation of textbooks and notebooks for the Children's Corps, political work among the general population, entertainment and recreation, and so on. For the anti-Japanese guerrillas this revolutionary life was no less important than fighting the enemy with weapons. Through this complex and diverse unity of life and struggle, revolutionaries develop a strong will and realize beautiful ideals and aspirations. In fact, there can be no revolutionary life which is not associated with the ennobling moral world of the revolutionaries, nor is the aspiration to a fruitful and worthwhile life conceivable apart from the struggle to bring about their beautiful ideals.

Nothing can break the will of communists, and nothing can halt the life of revolutionaries. The body of a revolutionary may be chained, but not his noble ideals. He never wastes his time even when he finds himself alone on an isolated mountain or a secluded island. Wherever he is, he always remains single-heartedly loyal to the revolution, striving to awaken the masses to class awareness, and whenever he finds himself among them, uniting them around his organization and leading them in the struggle. Such is the life and struggle of revolutionaries. Writers must describe these practical activities of communists whose lives and struggles are integrated into one truthful and rich totality. Only then will they be able to give a clear picture of the revolutionaries' ennobling spiritual world and correctly illuminate the essence of human activity.

A literary work may deal with battles. In this case, the attention must be focused on the description of the fighting people's ideological and spiritual world and their experience, rather than exclusively on military actions.

Literary works must provide comprehensive and profound pictures of typical lives. To this end, it is important to distinguish correctly between the essence of life and its particular phenomena. A life depicted in a literary work can only be typical when it incorporates the characteristics of the period and the essence of the social system. A life lacking characteristic social and historical dimensions cannot be typical, no matter how interesting and moving it is.

Some writers tend to construct an abnormal and deformed view of life in their attempt to show the optimistic life of our contemporaries. But artistic interest and laughter must always spring from the true essence of life, not from some vulgar deformity.

Our literary works must truthfully mirror the healthy and revolutionary life. Only works of this kind can contribute powerfully and effectively to people's revolutionary education. Describing a revolutionary life does not mean dealing with a single aspect of life. The essence of life and the typical characteristics of the period manifest themselves not only in politics but also in economic, cultural and moral life. So the essential elements of various aspects of the life of society must be described in full.

The characteristics of a given social system and a given era are revealed most glaringly in the way of life. If the life of our people living in a socialist society is to be depicted truthfully, it must be described in the context of the socialist way of life.

The way of life is the mode of living, the mode of activity of people as social beings. It is expressed in different ways according to the social system and the level of people's ideological consciousness. In a socialist society all the people work and live in harmony as masters of the country. In our society, today, all the working people jointly manage state and social property and take good care of them. They voluntarily maintain public order, helping each other and leading each other forward. This is their natural practice. This is precisely the new way of life based on the socialist system under which the means of production have been socialized and unity and cooperation between the working class, cooperative farmers and working intellectuals are the basis of social relationships.

In our society the Party's committed and determined struggle to transform the whole of society on the pattern of the working class is accelerating the establishment of the socialist way of life on a wide scale. Art and literature, therefore, must create and publicize examples of a fine and ennobling way of life which conforms to the intrinsic nature of a socialist society, and thus help towards the revolutionary transformation of the whole of society and its assimilation to the working class.

Art and literature must also concentrate their efforts on meeting the needs of the times by a proper description of the noble and cultivated traditional life of our people.

Writers and artists should truthfully portray the uniquely beautiful life of our people, while at the same time elaborating on the frugal and cultured practices of the true patriots, the communists, who, armed with extensive knowledge and an ardent love of their national history, geography and cultural heritage, fight devotedly for the prosperity of their country and nation.

Traditional life should always be dealt with in such a way as to promote in people a greater sense of national dignity and pride and imbue them with the spirit of socialist patriotism. In dealing with the life of the past, which is dominated by national custom and tradition the principles of fidelity to historical truth and acceptability to modern sensibilities are most important.

It would be wrong to misrepresent the life of the people in the past. If a writer were to rewrite it in modern terms, distorting it in order to cater to modern ideas, feelings and tastes, he would distort the historical truth. Writers should seek out and portray progressive and beautiful subjects from the past which are acceptable to our contemporaries, instead of trying to update them. What must be borne in mind here is that the manners and customs of the past should not be given too much emphasis in order to depict a way of life which is rich in national colour.

Manners and customs also depend on the period and the social system. So it is necessary to show these aspects of life as representative of the essence of the period and the social system, so that they harmonize with the content of the work. If, instead, practices which are backward, vulgar or superfluous are revived by description, simply for the sake of preserving distinctive national characteristics, then the result will be a return to the past. On the other hand, if an alien life-style which does not correspond to the sentiments and tastes of the Korean people were to be introduced into literary works, this would distort both history and life, cloud national sentiment and—a serious consequence indeed—dull the sense of national independence.

Artistic works must mirror a life which has a rich ideological content and, at the same time, describe it movingly in an artistic fashion. Even a life imbued with rich content and profound meaning will lose all effective value if it is not described well artistically.

A work must describe a well-chosen life which conforms to the seed and it must present it naturally. If subsidiary lives which have no connection with the seed, are included, then it will be impossible to develop the story along the correct line and keep to the point of the matter.

One book which dealt with the people's struggle in the period of the temporary retreat during the Fatherland Liberation War[4], failed to concentrate primarily on the requirements of the seed. In the main it described how the hero and his wife had led a terrible life as farmhands in the past and how they were now fighting to protect their happiness. As a result, it omitted a number of most important subjects, such as the organization of guerrilla units, how weapons were obtained, the activities of the underground organizations and the establishment of contact with Supreme Headquarters, all of which are essential for the people to acquire a correct understanding of war and to learn how to fight. If a writer fails to discover the right seed and to concentrate on a life which conforms to its requirements, he will be sure to stray from the line of his work and obscure the thoughts which he should be expressing.

Life should always be shown in detail. The essence of life can only make an effective emotional appeal to the people's hearts when it is expressed through detailed descriptions. A clear image of life can only be derived from a human relationship which is firmly established, reflecting the times and the social system, and from a careful description of people's psychological world.

The Sea of Blood shows the poverty-stricken life of the mother's family, and describes very clearly and painstakingly the clarity and purity of their psychological world. What a complete and clear picture is given of the relationship between the mother, Won Nam and Gap Sun, of their thoughts and emotions, in the scene which develops around nothing more than a bowl of rice cake!

Let us examine the description of this event which begins when Won Nam, who has been crying for supper because he is hungry, devours his few lumps of cake in an instant. He peers into the bowl of his younger sister and says regretfully, "You've already eaten everything!" His sister has, in fact, eaten only one piece of cake and put the rest on the shelf for her mother, who always goes without food for the sake of her children. She gives the rest of her share to her mother when the mother is in bed. As she silently watches her daughter, the mother's heart is filled with pain and grief for her children who are always hungry.

This scene, though simple, accurately portrays the thoughts and emotions, the tender-heartedness of the mother and her children who are trying to live bravely and honestly, caring for one another, loving, helping and leading each other forward, in spite of grinding poverty and hunger. Thus, *The Sea of Blood* is an excellent example of a fine and detailed description of thoughts and feelings expressed through the relations between the characters.

In art, emotions and sentiments have to be expressed clearly, earnestly and enthusiastically. The more forceful and enthusiastic they are, the greater the effect the work will have. Art derives its great power from noble thoughts which are inspired by fine feelings.

If one is to describe life persuasively, one must investigate the fine and subtle nuances of the psychology of people who accept what they see, hear and feel.

People see and react to things and events in terms of their own ideas and attitudes. Writers must have a keen eye for the characters' emotions such as love, hatred, approval, rejection, praise and condemnation as these are expressed in their views and attitudes to people and life. They must describe their characters' psychological reaction to their experiences truthfully and carefully from the class point of view. In fact, in order to create an impression when describing people and their life a writer can do no more than show the delicate stirrings in people's innermost world, which occur as they see, hear and assimilate their experience.

An impressive picture of well-drawn images and correctly-chosen details which reveal the essence of life is extremely effective in rousing people's emotions and passions.

The selection of essential and characteristic details of life and their precise description is the secret of creating clear and concise images and the key to the convincing depiction of characters and the representation of life's essential meaning. People's complex and intricate psychological feelings can only be expressed by showing their lives in minute detail. The deeper you probe the details of the essentials which reveal people's thoughts and feelings, the better able you are to portray their mental state and, accordingly, exert a positive emotional influence on the minds of your audience.

Characters can also be convincingly represented through the description of their personalities. Even in the same circumstances, people reveal their personalities by expressing their thoughts and feelings in their own distinctive ways. So it is essential to discover the specific characteristics of the man or woman you are writing about and describe them skilfully. This is the way to create a striking character.

If you fail to identify the correct details of life you will not be able to create an accurate depiction in your work. In artistic creation, neglect of the smallest detail can seriously damage the accuracy of the whole piece.

Art and literature must not describe a meaningless life simply out of idle interest, nor should they overstate or exaggerate. Books and films should never be created simply for the sake of entertainment, nor should their themes be exaggerated.

Writers must not try to make themselves appear superior by creating works dealing with many notable events and the colourful lives of flamboyant characters. They must focus their efforts on the characters of worthy people drawn from real life. Inventing boastful individuals or writing about them unconvincingly, will distort the truth, misrepresent the characters and make the works themselves unbelievable. The tendency to make life appear excessively glamorous and luxurious or to caricature people in a way which is contrary to the simple cultured yet militant aesthetic tastes of the working people, is the exact opposite of the kind of art which the people need.

In order to understand our working people's ideals correctly and portray life from the viewpoint of the working class, creative artists must emphasize the revolutionary content of their characters' noble life. If they deliberately exaggerate by writing pretentiously, they will obscure the class line and distort the picture of life and the era they are writing about.

If a writer who is dealing with life during the war were to describe the People's Army as if it were always fighting hard under difficult conditions and portray the enemy as though he always lived comfortably in luxurious surroundings, then he would, of course, be distorting the truth. What is important in this regard is the class attitude of the writer who attempts to depict as grand and splendid the despicable enemy mercenaries, whose characters are utterly degenerate, desperate, dissolute and brutal. Our writers and artists must adhere firmly to their class stand in describing the enemy and clearly demonstrate his reactionary nature, his vulnerability and the inevitability of his destruction. Enemies must be shown as they are and portrayed honestly.

A writer who cannot correctly see the beautiful and noble spiritual and moral qualities of the working class and who lacks the dignity and pride of this class, is unable to describe worthy people properly from a high ideological and spiritual point of view, and even when he does so, he is doing it without personal conviction.

Only writers who have a sincere love of life can really understand the revolutionary life. Only those who understand it thoroughly can describe it accurately and naturally.

WHICH MAKES A WORK A MASTERPIECE—ITS SCALE OR ITS CONTENT?

This question actually resolves itself into the question of form and content in art and literature in general, and their relationship in a masterpiece in particular.

In works of art and literature, as in everything else, form and content are in dialectical relationship. Just as form is inconceivable without content, so is content without form. The content determines and restricts the form and the form follows and expresses the content.

In the relationship between the two, the content is decisive, but the primary of the content does not mean that the form can be ignored. The content can only be expressed correctly through an appropriate form, and a good form that suits the content positively reacts back on the latter by expressing it clearly.

Good art and literary works are marked by a perfect unity between elevated content and pure form, with the content satisfying the requirements of the period and the people's aspirations. Only works whose content and form are well harmonized can rouse people's sympathy and make an effective contribution to their ideological and emotional education.

A correct adjustment of the relationship between content and form is one of the essential elements of realism in art. It can be said that the history of art and literature, when viewed in the context of content and form, is a continuous process of seeking and creating new content and new form. Fixing the relationship between artistic content and form in accordance with correct principles is precisely what distinguishes realism from formalism.

But, in practice, this relationship is sometimes handled contrary to these principles and this is the essential expression of formalism. A preference for large and complex works over those which have a valuable and profound content is also a manifestation of formalism.

For example, in describing the anti-Japanese revolutionary struggle[5] or the Fatherland Liberation War, there is a tendency to deal with the whole course of the hero's struggle, from its beginning to its victorious end, in a single work, as though it was a biography or a chronicle. There is also a tendency to collect a number of apparently good story lines from here and there and put them together as one work. The fondness for colossal blockbuster films also springs from the desire to seek fame by producing a huge work which opens with a pretentious title announcing an epic theme, then goes on to introduce problems of revolutionary strategy and deal with turbulent historical events with an enormous cast of characters.

In fact, it is wrong to attempt to produce a film which contains the whole history of a revolutionary struggle or to show people everything that they need to shape their revolutionary world outlook. It is perfectly possible to single out one event from the armed struggle against the Japanese or the Fatherland Liberation War and write a fairly large piece which can be highly influential in people's revolutionary education. If a literary work tries to deal with the whole process of a revolutionary struggle, it will be compelled to do no more than assemble facts or simply record them, and the result will be a large piece devoid of content. All these tendencies are a far cry from the writer's basic duty and mission, which is to deal seriously with socially important problems in order to further people's revolutionary education.

Works of art and literature must express profound content if they are to instil revolutionary thoughts in people's minds and portray the experiences and methods of struggle. When the *Five Guerrilla Brothers* was being filmed, I asked the writers: "Which makes a work a masterpiece—its scale or its content?" I pointed out that if they wanted to produce a masterpiece they should treat the content with philosophical depth rather than focus on slickness of form.

A masterpiece is not something with a special form. There is no special form for a masterpiece in art and literature even in the areas of characterization or plot. When people say that a certain work is a masterpiece or a great work, they are referring to the high level of its ideological and artistic qualities, and not to the special features of its form.

A masterpiece is distinguished essentially by the philosophical depth of its ideological content. So we can say that a masterpiece is a work which provides a complete solution to a socially important problem on a high ideological and artistic plane and makes a substantial contribution to people's revolutionary education.

Into the category of masterpieces fall such multipart works as the films *The Sea of Blood* and *Five Guerrilla Brothers,* which, following a sequence of historical events, depict the essence of the revolutionary struggle through the images of heroes who grow up in the course of that struggle, as the revolution itself develops. The category also includes shorter narratives like the film *The Flower Girl* which creates a profound image by examining the broader implications of a small event. In each case the value of the work is assessed on the basis of its content. No matter how great an event and how wide the scope of life depicted in a work, it will not be a masterpiece unless its content is profound and rich. On the contrary, a work with profound and rich ideological content is fully entitled to be called a masterpiece even if its dimensions are small.

The Flower Girl is a masterpiece even though it is a small-scale work. By means of an extensive and detailed description of a commonplace situation in the Korean countryside in the old days—the misfortunes and sufferings of a servant's family—and through the life-story of the warm-hearted heroine Ggot Bun, it states the important idea that the revolution is the only path to survival. This is a perfect example in that it unfolds an important problem and develops a momentous idea from a small event, plainly demonstrating the inevitability of the revolution through the growth of an ordinary person.

A writer can create a great work which runs into many volumes and deals with an enormous number of facts, following the course of historical events over a long period, or a masterpiece which sketches one phase of a revolutionary war or economic construction—it depends on the requirements of the seed and the particular events to be dealt with. The scale and form of a great work must always be determined by its content.

If he is to write a masterpiece in terms of content, a writer must choose the appropriate seed, one which will have a great revolutionary impact on people, a seed which will germinate into an important philosophical idea. If he fails to select the right seed, not only will he be unable to develop the work's ideological content in a comprehensive fashion, he will also have to rely for effect on the work's bulk and his creative endeavour will degenerate into formalism. This is the failing that produces works dealing with the events of life on a huge scale through ostentatious forms devoid of any substantial content.

A seed capable of expressing an important idea can be found in the context of typical events which express the essence of life's development at a particular time. Therefore, writers who wish to create masterpieces must be able to identify the main current of the revolution, which destroys every outmoded, conservative and reactionary, aspect of social life, replacing it with something new, advanced and progressive.

In general, works of art and literature can deal with a diversity of problems arising in the course of the revolutionary struggle. They can deal not only with the basic problems of social revolution but also with contingent problems. In other words, they can deal with any problems at all which, although they may not be basic to the revolution, are nevertheless important for its advancement. However, since masterpieces have to show people the revolution's development and impart the experience and methods of revolutionary struggle, they must always deal with basic problems arising in the course of the revolution.

The films *The Sea of Blood* and *The Fate of a Self-defence Corps Man,* which were adapted from literary classics, provide detailed and highly artistic solutions to the vital problems arising in the revolutionary struggle which the masses are waging for their national and class emancipation. These works pose the basic problems of social revolution in an original way and demonstrate the great truth that where there is oppression, there is always resistance and the oppressed people can only liberate themselves and secure a happy future through armed struggle.

This shows us that a masterpiece ought to concern itself with the indispensable theme of the basic problems of the revolutionary cause of the working class. This principle concerns the content of literary works, not their form. It is one reason why the content, and not the form, makes a work a masterpiece.

The basic problems of the revolution dealt with by a masterpiece can only be correctly resolved by describing typical lives which express the nature of society. Masterpieces have to provide comprehensive and profound accounts of many aspects of life which represent the essence of the society of a particular period. Only then will they be able to clarify the nature of the developing revolution, and the basic problems arising from it.

In order to produce a masterpiece in terms of content it is also necessary to represent the nature of the developing revolution truthfully and clearly through the development of the characters and, in particular, the process of the shaping of the hero's revolutionary world outlook.

It is impossible for works of art and literature to describe the process of revolutionary development clearly, except through the development of their characters. The basic problems of a work become more clearly defined and acquire greater depth and richness of ideological content as the characters grow and develop in the course of the fight, gradually acquiring a deeper understanding of the truth of the revolution and the inevitability of its victory. The process by which a work's basic problems are comprehensively developed into a great ideological content is intimately linked with the process of development of the hero's revolutionary world outlook. The hero deepens his or her understanding of the nature of the revolutionary struggle as the struggle itself develops, and he or she battles on with a clear sense of purpose and an optimistic belief in the future. The true content of a masterpiece consists of a broad and comprehensive depiction of the ideological consciousness and emotions of the hero as he matures with the development of the revolutionary struggle.

The film *Five Guerrilla Brothers* is a masterpiece because it reveals the essence of the armed struggle against the Japanese through the process by which the heroes establish their revolutionary world outlook. If its authors had not illustrated the essence of the armed struggle through the images of the heroes maturing into revolutionaries as the struggle proceeded, the work would not have been a masterpiece, despite all the tremendous events it contains and its epic time-frame.

One of the principal methods for creating a masterpiece based upon content is tightly-focused description.

Unless a work focuses attention on the fundamental motive power which gives impetus and direction to a person's ideological progress and the revolutionary movement, it will be impossible to depict correctly the formative process of the hero's revolutionary world outlook or the law of development of the revolution, nor will the work fulfil its role of equipping people with the concept of the revolution and educating them to work consciously and actively in its cause.

It is important, therefore, to focus on a single character or event, examine it in depth and create a detailed picture. In practice, penetrating into the content means creating a profound and exhaustive depiction, from various viewpoints, of the event, the life or the character the writer has chosen.

The requirement of a broad and profound elaboration of content cannot be used to justify the weaving of a complex web of events, constantly drawing in innumerable new aspects of life and new characters. Some writers have a tendency to grapple simultaneously with many events and lives, describing none of them profoundly, often producing works which are complex and rambling, almost devoid of content that actually moves people.

If a writer is to concentrate on the description of events and lives, he must intermingle the strands of action well so that they will be welded dramatically into the structure of a human relationship, and he must carefully define the characters' attitude to life-events so as to reveal their disposition. If he is to develop his plot in depth, without enlarging its scope, a writer must ensure that events are carefully interlinked as the dramatic expression of the formation and development of relationships between people. He will only be able to create interesting characters, without extending the action so far as to become boring, if the plot is carefully constructed so as to reveal the characters' deepest thoughts from various angles. He must not include events which have no dramatic impact, nor lives devoid of content. These will only increase the scale and extend the form of the work.

The intensification and close concentration of descriptive elements means that every single event or life which is dealt with must be portrayed in depth from various angles without over-extending the story-line, so that many different things can be sensed and understood through that single event. In fundamental terms, the essence of description lies in presenting vivid and profound pictures of people and events exactly as they really are, so that people can see these pictures with their own eyes and feel their meaning in their hearts. The more intense and precise a portrayal is, the more profound will be its ideological content, and the more deeply will it move people, though the story-line may be neither complex nor long.

If a work is to be a masterpiece, the form, as well as the content, must be concisely realized. The dramatic concentration of description enhances the harmony of the work's form, whereas flat, inflated description can result in undesirable complication and length. But this does not mean that a work of great dimensions cannot be well-constructed or that it is devoid of harmonious form. There are many films in which content and form are in perfect harmony, despite their great dimensions.

People who judge masterpieces solely by the criterion of form, give it priority over content and consider that works dealing with small events will suffice, even though their content is so much simpler and smaller.

Writers have to present a diversified picture of our people's revolutionary struggle and constructive endeavours, based on a correct understanding of what constitutes a masterpiece.

At the present time, some writers pay no attention at all to our working people's present struggle and their everyday lives, because they believe that masterpieces must necessarily deal with the lives of people who fight battles against the enemy, with the armed struggle against the

Japanese or the Fatherland Liberation War. Our art and literature must produce masterpieces based on both the revolutionary struggle and socialist construction. To be masterpieces, works need not necessarily deal with revolutionary wars or class struggles, nor are these all that is required.

Our Party and people are still engaged in the revolution. The struggle to eliminate the vestiges of outmoded ideas from people's minds and re-educate them to become true communists of the Juche type, the struggle to free people once and for all from backbreaking toil, to make work easy and pleasant and increase production, and the struggle to build socialist and communist culture—all these are difficult but important revolutions. Describe the noble lives and inspiring struggles of our people properly, and you will be creating genuinely revolutionary works and masterpieces.

The relationship of content and form is also of vital importance in the creation of small-scale works, indeed, it is a matter of fundamental principle for all works of art and literature. It is also important to represent the ideological content positively and in detail, even in shorter pieces dealing with events and lives on a smaller scale.

Writers must produce masterpieces, but they must not follow the practice of searching for what they consider to be large-scale works. If they do, they will be unable to produce successful works of high ideological and artistic merit, nor will they be able to respond adequately to the needs of the people.

If scriptwriters were to follow this practice, then directors would clearly tend to seek still more tempestuous events, larger crowds and more colossal subjects, and camera-work would be concentrated on the shooting of literally large-scale films, for the wide screen. The artistic results would be minimal compared with the large amounts of manpower and funds expended on the production of the film.

COMPOSE THE PLOT CORRECTLY

If one is to make oneself clearly understood, one has first to work out a logical plot and then express it cogently. A good speaker leaves no opportunity for his audience's attention to flag, he holds their attention focused on what he is saying, making them wait for what follows until they are convinced unawares that his message is an immutable truth.

If a writer is to blend several different real-life stories into an interesting and meaningful drama to give people a convincing picture of life, then an original formal resolution is essential. And that, precisely, is the plot.

A film can only develop its ideological content with depth and clarity, and show life truthfully, if it has a good plot.

The great leader Comrade Kim Il Sung said that in order to ensure a high degree of ideological and artistic quality in works based on fact, scriptwriters should be efficient in their treatment of events, instead of just jumbling them together. He cautioned that the latter practice would devalue their work.

Any writer who intends to provide a proper solution for the problems he raises in his work and emphasizes important ideas, needs to be highly skilled in the meticulous development of the plot structure. Without this skill he will be unable to achieve his goal. This is why drama is called the art of plot-construction. It is very important, therefore, that the plot of a film be planned carefully and correctly, and that it deal adequately with all problems arising in the composition of the drama.

Even though a writer may select a very worthwhile seed, in order to express the idea of his work clearly he is still obliged to devise a plot which suits the seed. The plot is the basic form integrating the characters, conflicts, events and other elements of dramatic description into a harmonious framework which clearly expresses the seed. That is why the writer can express nothing adequately unless he has planned the plot correctly.

Works of art and literature need tightly-drawn plots. Untidy plots are not only inadequate to the writer's intention, they also diminish the truth of descriptive elements and further obscure the ideological content of the work. So writers must not forget that even the smallest gap in the plot will cause the whole work to crumble.

A film with an untidy plot cannot grip the audience and define their emotional response. Only when the story-line flows naturally and logically can the film rouse the ideological and emotional sympathy of the audience, and make their hearts beat faster. If it does not convince the audience of the truth through the natural flow of the story, it is not art.

The plots of works of art and literature must be planned according to the requirements of the seeds, in order to meet the needs of real life.

A writer's guiding criterion in constructing his work must be the seed, which provides the principles for the organization of content and the unification of all the formal elements of the work in conformity with the content. Only by working from the requirements of the seed can the writer select certain aspects of real life and blend them into a well-knit story and an organically harmonious work. The writer must never work out his plot irresponsibly, ignoring the requirements of the seed.

Some writers seem to think that they can construct the plots of their works in any way they please. But they could only do that if they were to collect various kinds of material before selecting their seeds. They can consider all kinds of plots because, not having chosen their seeds, they have not yet defined their themes properly. But it would be a great mistake for them to think that they can work like this once their seeds have been selected.

A writer can never judge the value of the form of his plot without reference to the seed he has selected. The plot structure of a work can only be determined correctly according to the standards of the seed. Which plot structures will develop the content most efficiently in the light of the requirements of the seed? That is the way the question should be put. So writers must endeavour to work out the plot which best meets the requirements of their seed.

The plot of a literary work should be designed in such a way as to conform with the logic of life, since its structure has to develop the seed gradually and comprehensively through the interaction of diverse and complex life-stories. Only a work in which the plot is logically constructed is capable of representing its ideological essence truthfully. The ideological content of the work can only be depicted truthfully when the events basic to the structure of the work and the human relationships formed around these events develop logically.

Each literary plot must have its own distinguishing characteristics. Since every work has its own individual seed and, accordingly, its own theme, and every work deals with different people, there is no reason why they should all follow the same pattern.

In creating new works, writers must not cling to existing structural forms but create a new structure for every new piece they produce.

Art and literature have a number of established structural forms which have been developed in the course of history. Writers need not regard them as absolute ideals just because they have been polished through use. These forms change and develop and are steadily enriched as society changes with the times and man's artistic understanding develops accordingly. Writers must constantly explore, develop and perfect new structural forms which are in keeping with the changing times and the intrinsic nature of revolutionary art, while at the same time choosing from amongst the existing forms which have been historically refined those which mirror life truthfully and accord with our contemporary aesthetic taste.

Plots must be taut and consistent without any gaps.

If a well-knit plot is to be worked out, all its constituent parts have to be dovetailed together. As for the relationships of the various characters, all of them must be subordinated to giving prominence to the hero's line of development. In the development of conflicts, the various secondary conflicts must converge on the line of the main conflict, and in the sequencing of events, all the secondary lines must be linked to the main line. Furthermore, all elements must be subordinated to the interpretation of the theme and the idea.

The most important thing here is to ensure the consistency of the hero's line of development, while at the same time organizing the characters in such a way that each of them will have his own distinct share of the story-line.

In a dramatic plot, the most important thing is to establish human relationships correctly. The correct definition of the relationships between characters largely determines both the artistic clarity of the work's content, and the adequacy with which the major social contradictions are depicted, as well as the strength and dimensions of the plot structure.

If the characters are to become dramatically embedded in the story-line, each of them must occupy the correct position within the structure, each with his own share of associated description, and they must all contribute to the expression of the theme and the idea. Even where they might seem to have a value of their own, individual characters and events will prove worthless unless they have a definite place and descriptive task in the context of the plot.

The hero must always occupy the centre of the stage, fulfilling his role of linking together the other characters and leading them forward. The clarity and suppleness of the relationships between all the characters depend on how consistently the hero's line of development is maintained.

For the hero's line of development to be clearly defined, he must play the leading role in the resolution of the work's fundamental issue and occupy a central place in relation to the other characters, so that they will move in tune with him. If the hero does not occupy his rightful place and play his rightful role, other characters will dominate the plot.

The hero's place and role are determined by the active and decisive influence he has on the resolution of the major issue. If other characters come into contact with each other and weave a story-line as a result of being drawn into the situation created by the hero's dramatic actions, then the hero can remain quite distinctly present through the images of the other characters, even if he does not appear in the foreground himself. The hero can create the strongest dramatic impression by appearing in only those scenes where his presence is required.

It will not do in attempting a clear presentation of one character's line of development to allow that character to develop quite independently, sidetracking the story or fragmenting it, instead of subordinating it to the hero's line. Any character's line of development is valuable only insofar as it fulfils the dramatic task of highlighting the hero's line and widening the scope of the story. The various characters' lines must each have their own distinctive features and develop in a neat fashion, so that they are easily understood.

The question of the development of characters is directly related to the relative position of the characters in the structure. There should be no gaps in their distribution, nor should there be a duplication of similar characters. Characters must have their own particular positions, where they can play their proper roles. Typical characters should be selected from different classes and backgrounds in accordance with the content of the work and organized in a structured relationship which can be settled with clear political implications. This character-set serves as the basis of life through which the theme and idea are defined.

If characters are created simply to make an interesting story, or relationships are formed between them merely in order to produce moving episodes, then these characters and their relationships will not develop consistently, nor will they contribute to the clear expression of the work's ideological content.

Considerable care is required in establishing the relationships between characters, even with those whose role is to establish links between the main characters and to intensify conflicts and disagreements.

Any lacuna in the disposition of characters is a pitfall to be avoided in the telling of the story, and the creation of a superfluous character is a snare to be avoided in description. Both the pitfall and the snare are equally harmful in their destructive effect on the narrative. Nevertheless, some writers, claiming that this character is suitable for this scene and that character has a particular charm, tend to duplicate or triplicate characters or create separate characters who can only be included in a single scene. This results in the indiscriminate involvement of superfluous characters, usually producing situations which lack some truly essential character, or, where he does exist, fail to make him play his proper part in his proper place. These writers attempt to win fame through the great number of their characters, rather than their intrinsic charm. Their indiscriminate creation of characters renders the story-line discursive and loosens the plot and in the final analysis it blurs the focal point, the essence, of the idea.

The relationships between characters in a drama are formed and developed in the course of the story, and they are, therefore, inseparable from the development of the story-line. The central place in the dramatic structure is held by the story-line, which takes shape as contacts are established between characters, culminates in the climax, and then proceeds to the denouement. If the story-line is not closely-knit, the overall structure will not be compact. A careful analysis of a work in which the content is obscure and discursive will show that the defect is mainly due to a vague and loose story-line. A rambling story-line will also be incapable of showing the process of development of life in a clear and interesting way.

Once they have appeared on the screen, scenes in a film cannot be viewed again immediately, so that a scene which was not clear to the audience remains so until the end of the story. A vague story-line will introduce ambiguous scenes into the film, and the audience will ultimately not be certain of what they have seen. The close weaving of the story-line is therefore always a matter of great importance.

The story-line of a work includes the general stages of narrative development usually beginning with a specific event, gradually advancing to a leap to the climax, which is followed by the conclusion. So if the structure is to be well-knit, the story-line must be planned to include these distinct stages—the initiation of events, their development, climax and conclusion. The development of events can be defined with a coherent logic when the writer identifies the most essential links in the internal relations of human life and dovetails them firmly together.

In developing the story-line it is impossible to carry along every line of events and every episode evenly. The major requirement, if the central points of the structure are to be given prominence, and the story-line is to remain closely-knit, is that priority must be given to clarity in the development of the basic events, which link and direct the narrative-lines of various secondary events, episodes and details.

A literary work has no room for meaningless and unnecessary events, episodes and details. Incidents and episodes which prove merely to be interesting in themselves will not simply be useless, but a positive nuisance. Even if a writer has a bundle of very interesting episodes, these will only cause him a great deal of trouble unless they contribute effectively to the composition of the drama and the portrayal of the characters' distinguishing features. Episodes must be in the right place if they are to support the characterization, advance the story-line and clarify the theme and idea.

Some writers attempt to ornament the story by tactfully inserting a few interesting episodes. However, episodes which have been added merely for the sake of interest, without regard to the demands of the events and the characters, are usually taken out at the polishing stage. So writers should think very carefully before deciding to add supplementary episodes in order to fill gaps or link disjointed story-lines.

New developments in the plot must advance the story-line steadily and maintain the dramatic tension. Only the literary work with a well-knit plot is capable of holding the attention of the audience, alternately tightening and loosening its grip by means of a stream of incidents with rising and falling emotions.

Tension is maintained through the combination of deep sympathy for the hero, anticipation of the development of events and interest in the noble lives disclosed in the story-line. This tension must be motivated on the author's part by the need to deepen the audience's understanding by presenting them with a clear and forceful impression of life.

The constantly changing current of life is an uninterrupted flow of inexorable logic, by which a cause produces an effect which in turn becomes the cause of a new effect. The audience will naturally be drawn into the current of life when the writer recognizes the most essential line of these logical connections, and follows it faithfully, highlighting it by eliminating those elements which obscure or weaken it, and skilfully focusing attention on its necessary implications.

However, the audience should never be roused to a state of tension simply by the introduction of exciting incidents. The psychology of the people in the audience should also be taken into consideration in stimulating the feeling of tension. It is not possible, nor is it necessary, to maintain a high level of tension from start to finish.

The plot of a film must not be a mere grouping of events; it must be a sequential process of stimulating emotions.

Since characters' thoughts and emotions find concrete expression in the events of life, it is important when dealing with these events to have a proper understanding of the ideological and emotional state of the characters, and to describe it clearly. In working out the plot, close attention to the flow of emotions is essential, not only to maintain a correct balance in the development of the characters' feelings, but also in order to control the emotional response of the audience.

In the writing of a work, the characters' emotions must be treated as their response to the subtle development of their lives, their feelings should grow in intensity, culminating strong in explosive outbursts which are the natural result of this development. Discovering noble, honourable lives and portraying the rich and complicated emotions of the characters, so as to stimulate a profound emotional response—this is the secret of writing a plot.

The organization of events must correspond to the organization of emotions. The emotions of the characters and the feelings of the audience are roused, converge and unite in response to the same sequence of events in the work. The audience can only be drawn into the compass of the work when there is a logical match between the harmonious flow of events and the process by which the emotions of the characters are roused, expressed in action and communicated to the audience.

If the crucial scene is introduced before the conditions required to rouse the characters' feelings have been adequately developed and the situation properly prepared, or if the events reach a conclusion before emotions reach their full pitch, then the flow of the characters' emotions will be interrupted and the audience's excitement will also subside. Dull events lacking emotional support will not excite the audience, even though they follow a logical idea.

A film must deal naturally and concisely with the events and emotions which develop in the course of complex lives. The distinctive character of a film is largely determined by the conciseness with which it sets forth the major, prominent points. Individual events and stories, even if valuable in themselves, will be of no use unless they are presented dramatically.

This is even more true of a work which is constructed on a large scale, involving many major characters and weaving together numerous events and lines of development. In such a work it is essential to establish the main story-line correctly, subordinating the secondary lines to it and eliminating all vague and confused elements.

Even the structure of a work which recounts a simple event does not automatically emerge well-knit. The brevity, depth and compactness of a film which deals with simple story-lines also depend on how the plot is designed.

The construction of a good plot requires skill in combining several diverse and fully-rounded lives into a compact and interesting story. It is advisable to be bold in discarding those events and episodes which, while appearing valuable when viewed individually, do not match the story-line and result in gaps in the plot. Amputation is always the least desirable remedy. It is wiser to apply effective preventive measures and avoid an excruciating operation on a critical case, from which the patient might take a long time to recover. Writers are sometimes obliged to cut out an event which, judging it to be good, they have included in the plot at the outset and have kept throughout, as too good to discard. In such cases the amputation disrupts the story-line and sets the plot off balance. The author then has to spend a great deal of time on repairing the defect in the plot and this causes the film studio a great deal of trouble. There should not be such painful moments in creative work.

CONFLICTS SHOULD BE SETTLED IN ACCORDANCE WITH THE LAW OF CLASS STRUGGLE

Nowadays the question of conflicts is generally considered a difficult one by both writers and critics. One day, at a seminar to study Comrade Kim Il Sung's Juche-oriented ideas on art and literature, a questioner asked whether there were any conflicts in the film *We Are the Happiest* and if there were, how they should be explained. This question demonstrates the lack of a correct understanding of the nature of conflicts.

In the case of this film, there is no obvious focus of struggle, no character who is directly opposed to the hero. Therefore, no specifically negative characters appear on the screen. This point caused some people to have doubts about its value.

In order to have a correct understanding of conflicts you must know life, and if you want to know life you must know the law of class struggle. Conflict in art is the reflection of the class struggle in life. The contradictions and the struggle between opposed class positions and ideas in real life are the basis of artistic conflicts. The conflicts in revolutionary art and literature are always based on the class struggle, and as such they can only show the law of historical progress and truth correctly when they faithfully mirror the life in which the class struggle takes place.

Our revolution is the struggle to destroy everything that is outmoded, and to create things that are new. The struggles between the progressive and the conservative, between the active and the passive, between collectivism and egoism, that is, the struggle between the new and the old, between socialism and capitalism in general, are the basic content of our revolutionary struggle. This acute struggle undergoes constant development in all fields of politics, the economy, culture and morality.

Just as the real revolutionary struggle is diverse and rich in content, so the artistic conflicts which mirror the class struggle through specific life-stories must also be diverse in nature.

Conflicts in artistic works are diverse in their nature, their substance, their forms and their lines of development. Artistic conflicts are clearly marked by the nature of social contradictions, and by the way these change at each stage of the revolution, requiring different forms and methods of struggle.

But the diversity of conflicts does not alter their essence, which reflects the class struggle. The apparent diversity of conflicts in artistic works is based on the diverse forms of the class struggle, and is permeated with the unifying principle of class struggle. This is the very reason why questions concerning conflicts which reflect diverse and complex contradictions must be solved in accordance with the law of class struggle.

Solving the conflicts as required by the law of class struggle provides a powerful stimulus to the social functions of revolutionary art and literature. In reflecting the class struggle, the conflicts in literary works expressly show the essence, vitality and validity of the Party's class line and mass line. The correct solution of the conflicts in literary works can thus provide people with a proper understanding of the law of social progress and the inevitable victory of socialism and communism, clearly demonstrating the vitality and validity of the class and mass lines followed consistently by our Party in forwarding the revolution and promoting construction.

Conflicts are important in that they mirror life accurately and clearly demonstrate the essence of revolutionary struggle. Since life consists of people's attempts to realize their ideals and purposes through action, struggles form an inevitable element of their lives, and they find expression in the form of class antagonism and class conflicts. Clashes between the interests of the exploiting class and the exploited class, and the antagonism between the socialist and capitalist ideologies, are clearly expressed in life. Conflicts therefore constitute the basic content of life as mirrored in literary works, and the truth of the conflicts represented is the factor which guarantees the faithful representation of life.

In the representation of life in a dramatic work, dramatic relationships between characters are established on the basis of conflicts, and the story line unfolds and develops in accordance with these conflicts. In the drama all structural elements are intimately related to conflicts, so these conflicts must be correctly defined and resolved if the characters are to be drawn accurately and their relationships and story lines described in a natural manner.

The important thing in describing conflicts correctly is to treat them in conformity with the distinguishing features of socio-historically defined contradictions and forms and methods of struggle.

The class struggle is continually changing and developing. This means that the character and content of class contradictions and the forms and methods of struggle also change. The character of class struggle is determined by the nature of the contradictions on which the struggle is based. The forms and methods of struggle are determined by the character and purpose of the struggle and by the specific socio-historical circumstances under which the struggle takes place. This is why the conflicts in literary works should be defined and resolved in accordance with the changes taking place as the class struggle develops.

A correct solution of the question of conflicts requires, first of all, a correct understanding of the nature of the contradictions determined by the basic social relationship, and, based on this, a clear definition of the character of the conflicts. In the exploiting society, antagonism and struggle between the exploiting class and the exploited class, between the dominating class and the dominated class, constitute the basis of social relations. Accordingly, the conflicts in any artistic work which mirrors this social relationship are antagonistic. But in socialist society, which is free from exploiting classes, comradely cooperation and unity between the working class, cooperative farmers and working intellectuals form the basis of social relations. So the artistic conflicts which reflect this social relationship are reconcilable. Conflicts in art must therefore be correctly defined in accordance with the character of the social relationship which they reflect. Only in this way can they be defined in accordance with the law of social progress.

Through the correct resolution of conflicts, art can also depict the true essence of social systems and the law of the development of life, and teach the people the principles and methods of class struggle.

Artistic conflicts which reflect antagonistic social relations are acute and extreme from the outset, and they end in confrontation. But artistic conflicts which mirror the life of the working people in socialist society should not be portrayed as extreme nor should they lead to hostility. They should be settled through the overcoming of the negative element and the strengthening of comradely unity.

If a work of art deals with the struggle to overcome the remnants of outmoded ideology still surviving in the minds of working people in socialist society by measures of liquidation, namely, the putting-down of hostile elements, on the ground that this is an impressive and serious way of handling the issue, then not only will people be given an incorrect idea of the ideological struggle, but the constrained atmosphere which will develop in society will, in the final analysis, hinder the consolidation of unity and solidarity amongst the working people. If, on the other hand, the class character of contradictions is presented vaguely in dealing with the struggle against hostile elements, then people's class consciousness will be dulled, reactionary elements will be revived, and the revolutionary forces will be weakened. The result will be dangerous.

It is important in creative work to define clearly the essential content of contradictions which are determined by basic social relations and resolve the relations between the positive and the negative sides of conflicts in a correct manner.

A writer who deals in his work with the national and class contradictions of the Korean people during the period of Japanese imperialist colonial rule or the current anti-US struggle of the south Korean people to save the Korean nation, may be faced with the following situation. Although the kinds of conflict he has to describe will depend on the requirements of his seed, he will find it imperative, in the course of his attack on foreign aggressors, to hit out at the comprador capitalists and landlords who are totally unscrupulous in their collaboration with the aggressors, serving them as guides, selling out the country and undermining the national interest. The national and class contradictions reveal themselves most sharply in this area. In fact the contradictions between the non-comprador capitalists and the workers must also be antagonistic, since they stand in the relationship of exploiter and exploited. Nevertheless, the non-comprador capitalists stand by the revolution, whereas the comprador capitalists are a target which must be decisively destroyed in the national-liberation revolution against the aggressors. Therefore, the non-comprador capitalists, though antagonistic from the class point of view, must not be defined and described as the target of the revolution in the struggle to solve national contradictions.

In the period of socialist revolution, the character of these contradictions and the way in which they are solved will, of course, change in accordance with new socio-historical conditions. This is because the main elements of the contradictions change in accordance with the basis of social relations and the circumstances of each historical period of revolutionary development.If this law of class struggle is not implemented thoroughly in creative work, the Party's class policy will be distorted.

The question of the role and significance of the positive and the negative in a work is settled in various ways, depending on the social relations dealt with by the work.

The positive holds the predominant place in socialist society because in this society, in which the politico-ideological unity, solidarity and cooperation of the people, the masters of the country, have been fully achieved, there are no hostile classes and, therefore, no oppression and exploitation. Of course, there are negative elements as well as positive ones, but in socialist society these have already been relegated to a secondary role. This means that conflicts which reflect the lives of the working people in socialist society should be settled by giving prominence to the positive and overcoming the negative by its influence. If, in dealing with the situation in socialist society, the negative is strongly emphasized and the positive is accorded a secondary place, then that is already a distortion of the truth, for in socialist society the positive is the basic factor.

In capitalist society the positive cannot be the basic factor because the exploiting classes such as the capitalists and landlords hold the dominant position and oppress and exploit the working masses, the overwhelming majority. It is precisely this domination of the negative which determines the reactionary nature of the social relations of capitalism. The working class wages a life-and-death struggle to eliminate once and for all the outmoded, corrupt and negative factors which dominate capitalist society. Therefore, artistic conflicts which reflect capitalist social relations can only portray the relationship of positive and negative as sharply antagonistic, and productive of extremes of opposition and confrontation.

Since class contradictions and antagonisms in society constantly change and develop and the methods of struggle also undergo change, literary works must always concentrate their descriptive efforts on highlighting and resolving the main conflicts, which accurately reflect the relations of social contradictions. Confusing basic and secondary conflicts and obscuring the relationship underlying the main conflicts will not only render the theme and idea vague, but also distort the truth. When many targets of the revolutionary struggle are involved in the various lines of conflict, you must hold firmly to the main line of conflict connected with the main target of struggle.

Conflicts should be settled politically from the point of view of the working class. In revolutionary works this means that all contradictions must be viewed from the viewpoint of the working class, and settled in their interests in clear demonstration of the law of historical progress that the new triumphs and the old perishes. If you do not see and describe the subject from the angle of what the working class is going to achieve through the struggle, you will be unable to resolve the conflicts in a politically significant manner.

The relationship between the positive and the negative in the situation under socialism should also be defined with keen political understanding, in accordance with the law of class struggle. The struggle to overcome the remnants of outmoded ideas which survive in the minds of people in socialist society is also a serious class struggle, because it is a struggle between the socialist and capitalist ideologies.

Even blood brothers can act out of different ideological beliefs. As the film *When We Pick Apples* shows, there is a serious ideological contradiction, which cannot be ignored, between the two sisters. The younger sister considers it shocking to see so many fallen apples rotting and makes up her mind to save more of them for the people, as required by the Party. The elder sister leads an easy-going life, and seems unperturbed, as if she could not see the apples. In our society a far-reaching class struggle results from contradictions between socialist ideology, expressed in the attitude of treasuring and taking good care of public property, and the selfish attitude of regarding as paramount one's own interests and personal comfort, and paying no heed to the waste of property belonging to the country and the people. These contradictions can only be resolved through an ideological struggle, so they must be resolved politically, in accordance with the law of class struggle, which continues to apply in socialist society.

When attempting to resolve conflicts in accordance with the nature, purpose, content and forms of class struggle, some writers find it more difficult to describe reconcilable conflicts than irreconcilable ones. In particular, they often prove unsuccessful in their attempts to deal with negative characters when describing the struggle amongst working people in socialist society.

In order to solve this problem correctly, they should depict the negative characters well, making of them a typical example suited to the socio-historical circumstances and the specific situation. The careless description of negative characters, simply because they are negative, will not result in an accurate representation of the conflicts involved.

With the exception of actual hostile elements there are no negative people in socialist society who find fault with Party policy or oppose it, nor could such people exist. The negative elements in our society are largely represented by those people who lag behind the developing situation because they still retain vestiges of outmoded ideas or fail to accept Party policy promptly and understand it correctly. These people differ from the members of the reactionary classes, who accept the ideas of the exploiting classes as absolute and apply their energies to the resurrection of the old system. The negative elements in our society are typified by people who, in spite of their subjective desire to follow the Party, are influenced by the remnants of obsolete ideas which linger in their minds and therefore reveal various shortcomings in their work and their lives. Therefore, the struggle against the non-hostile negative elements in our socialist system must not be conducted in such a way as to brand people as negative, to punish and alienate them, or make it impossible for them to raise their standards from the level to which they have fallen. The same applies to works of art and literature, in which the opponents in the struggle are not the negative people themselves, but their empiricism, conservatism, passivity, and other remnants of outmoded ideas and outworn habits. The content of the conflicts represented must be the struggle between advanced ideas and the residual attitudes and habits which oppose them, and these conflicts have to be settled through the struggle for the re-education of the negative by means of the positive, for improved comradely cooperation and stronger unity.

In conformity with the law of class struggle in socialist society our Party considers it to be the basic method of mass education to put the emphasis on the positive as the most important factor and re-educate the negative under the influence of positive example. Education by means of positive influence accords fully with the essential nature and requirement of the class struggle, which is conducted in the form of ideological struggle amongst the socialist working people. This is the most adequate method of struggle, since it demonstrates the way forward by holding up an example which guides people in acting against the negative, and criticizing and re-educating it thoroughly, without weakening or giving up before the struggle has achieved its aim. Conflicts in works of art must also be resolved according to this principle.

The criticism expressed in revolutionary art and literature must be serious, thorough and sharp. In revolutionary art and literature the edge of criticism must never be blunted, for they are called upon to contribute to the elimination from people's minds of remnants of outmoded ideas to assist in the revolutionary transformation and assimilation to the working class. Blunting the edge of criticism of the negative will only result in weakening the militant revolutionary character of art and literature. Revolutionary art and literature must confirm the victory of the new ideology in its fierce struggle against the negative and clearly demonstrate its immense vitality.

When the conflicts concerned reflect internal contradictions amongst the working people of socialist society, it is important both to make the social origin of the negative quite clear, and to ensure that its disposal is correctly managed. It is not acceptable to dispose of the negative element by simply stigmatizing it as old and knocking it down. A negative person must always be led to repent of his mistake and take the right road.

Literary works which deal with the situation under socialism can create excellent images based exclusively on positive facts, images which really move people, depending on the nature of the seed and the material.

Dramatic conflicts are an expression of the confrontation and struggle of opposing factors in life. It is only natural, therefore, that a work which deals with life without showing the direct confrontation and struggle between the positive and the negative, will not contain any conflicts which are expressed in direct clashes.

As well as combating the remnants of capitalist ideas which linger in the minds of working people, socialist society is also involved in fierce struggles against external class enemies and the remnants of the liquidated hostile classes. In works which reflect these struggles the dramatic conflicts must convey their sharpness and momentous significance.

But in socialist society, where the unity and solidarity of the people forms the basis of social relations, and where the positive holds the dominant place, people can be profoundly moved and inspired by the beautiful lives of people who love their comrades and collective and devote their all to the struggle for the country and their fellow countrymen, and by the uncompromising struggle against all that is outmoded and reactionary. This changed situation requires art and literature to reflect life through new forms of dramatic composition.

In fact, the most beautiful and ennobling picture of our time is provided by the estimable and worthy lives of those who devote all their energies and talents to working to repay the warm benevolence of the Party and the country. Writers whose sympathy with these people fires them with the desire to affirm this fact are capable of composing beautiful songs in praise of the socialist motherland and creating noble artistic images of the beautiful people of the new era by depicting life itself.

In the socialist situation in our country, emphasis on and praise of the positive imply of themselves an attack on and criticism of the negative, and the affirmation and defence of socialism signify of themselves the denial and criticism of capitalism. Thus, when writers express their ardent admiration of the socialist reality in works dealing with life in which there are no conflicts reflecting a direct clash between the positive and negative, they must underlay these aspirations with a powerful yearning for the renunciation of what is opposed to the reality.

Here we have the answer to the question of dramatic conflicts in the film *We Are the Happiest,* concerning which some writers and critics had their doubts.

The possibility that works dealing with socialist life can either deal with conflicts or dispense with them according to the requirements of their seeds and the nature of the material used, must not be interpreted one-sidedly to mean that works depicting our socialist reality and the lives of the working people of our time may avoid all mention of negative themes, or avoid criticizing them sharply when they are raised and attempt to represent them in a tolerant or approving fashion. This mistaken practice would result in a distortion of the essence of ideological struggle in socialist society and an artificial weakening of conflicts.

If they are to resolve conflicts in accordance with the law of class struggle, writers must base their handling of them on the positions of our Party's class and mass lines. The conflicts in literary works directly reflect these lines. The resolution of conflicts according to the requirements of Party policy is the absolutely correct way of resolving social contradictions and substantially enhances the cognitive and educational role of literary works.

Our Party scientifically defines the motive force of the revolution and the enemy to be destroyed by the revolution in accordance with its character and tasks and then adopts correct class and mass lines. Writers must therefore correctly define the focal point of a conflict in the light of the lines and the policies of our Party, and state quite clearly the relationship between the positive and the negative from the political point of view. If they stray from the Party's class and mass lines, imagining pure conflicts and ignoring the class relations of their characters, they might even find themselves depicting as enemies the class and social group which are the motive force of the revolution, or describing as an ally of the working class the reactionary elements that must be kept under control by the proletarian dictatorship.

In order to guard themselves securely against the expression in their work of any prejudices or ambiguous attitudes, writers must adhere firmly to Party policy and solve the people's problems correctly in the interests of the revolution. Our Party's lines and policies provide concrete solutions for the problems of people from all classes and social groups.

Writers are only able to portray and resolve conflicts involving questions of great socio-political significance correctly, when they depict all the human relations which they have drawn from life in detail, according to the Party's revolutionary theory.

EACH SCENE MUST BE DRAMATIC

A film has to compress a considerable amount of narrative into a small space and yet express a serious content. The continuous flow of shots which depict the essence of life, building up into scenes, can produce a work of profound and significant content. A film will do little to stimulate emotion or learning if its scenes lack the essential quality of life and simply narrate a commonplace story. The film as a whole will only express a profound and rich content if the content of each scene is substantial. The creation of a film therefore requires that particular attention be paid to the framing of the scenes, the basic units of film-making.

Each scene in a film must have its own element of drama. This is an essential requirement of the art of film-making, which reflects the drama of life. If every scene lacks drama, the film as a whole can have no dramatic structure and dramatic description will be impossible.

If a drama is the representation of the confrontation and struggle of life's opposing forces, then every scene must, in effect, represent a small part of the process of that struggle. A scene must contain characters who oppose each other in their efforts to achieve their goal, thus forming their dramatic relations which must develop through the constant appearance of new dramatic elements. Thus each scene must be a drama in itself and a link, or stepping-stone to the further development of the drama.

In planning the action of a scene it is important to have a clear idea of what the key point is and how it is to be highlighted.

Every scene must be made to deal with only one clearly-defined main task, whether it has an independent significance of its own or serves as a link between other episodes. The central purpose of a scene is to expand the theme and idea of the work according to the requirements of the seed. If a scene is diverted to the pursuit of other matters which have nothing to do with this central purpose, the point of the scene will be obscured and the overall structure of the film will even be destabilized. The dramatic tasks must be clearly defined if the backbone of the plot is to be strong and the theme and idea of the work are to be clearly expressed.

The characters, events and details in a scene must all be directly involved in the fulfilment of the basic task. The fulfilment of this task at the level of organization of a scene is often referred to as focusing. Just as a lens focuses rays of light in space to a point, in order to magnify the image, so the descriptive elements of a scene must be directed to the basic task in order to amplify it in depth. Brevity and clarity of composition can be assured by clearly defining the lines of development of characters, events and conflicts, drawing them to convergence on a single central focus and concentrating on the scenes which describe the phases of their development.

The task of each particular scene can never be absolutely in-dependent. A scene can only make a worthwhile contribution when it is gradually developed in depth and scope matching the development of events and the advance of the drama while maintaining internal coherence and obeying the representational requirements of the ideological sub-stance of the work. The functions assigned to scenes cannot be simply repeated, still less can they be gradually diminished in importance. They should always be raised afresh and extended in greater depth as the line of the drama develops.

Since the basic function of a scene is intensively fulfilled through the actions of the characters, it is essential that the objectives of their actions are clearly defined and carefully related to the fulfilment of this function.

The objectives of the characters' actions are defined by the aspira-tions which they strive to realize and are expressed most clearly in their dramatic relationships. As the dramatic relationships of the characters take shape and develop, the new events which occur determine the position and the attitude adopted by each of the characters, which thus clearly express the function of the scene. The positions and attitudes of the characters must therefore be clearly portrayed, while their relationships must be defined in sharp relief. In this way the function of the scene can be clearly expressed.

The dramatic relationship between the characters in a scene develops content and definition as they gradually become more committed and confirmed in their positions and attitudes to the events taking place. This is inevitable, both for the logical development of the characters and for the development of the dramatic line.

If a character's attitude to life as shown at the beginning of a film remains completely unchanged until the middle or the end, it means that the theme and idea have not been developed in depth in accordance with the line of dramatic development. A character who does not develop in step with the line of dramatic development is not a real person whom one might encounter in everyday life, but an artificial character deliberately concocted by the writer. The dramatic point of a scene in which he appears will therefore not be clear.

The writer must give close attention to the thoughts and feelings, the psychological states and relationships of the characters, attempting to see and feel for himself the actual circumstances of the scene. Characters appear in a scene at a specific dramatic moment for a definite reason, they participate in events and enter into relations with one another, acting in accordance with their own convictions. The characters' actions can only contribute to the fulfilment of their dramatic tasks if their behaviour is represented truthfully. The more incisive and subtle the depiction of their thoughts and actions, the more powerful will be the effect of the scene.

If the characters' behaviour in a given situation is determined by the whim of the writer, and not by their own will and conviction, they will not seem like living people and will fail to arouse a genuine emotional response. Actions which have no basis in logic or the characters' rationale are no more than the imposed movements of marionettes. The functions of the scenes are then not performed naturally by the characters' actions as the events unfold, but are merely explained or demonstrated by the author. If a writer attempts to emphasize the features of a character by artificial means, he will have to underplay the other characters and even the character on whom he intends to focus attention will not be realized properly. Without his vivid counterpart it is impossible for a character to manifest his or her own spiritual and moral features to the full. The characters' behaviour must be consistently directed towards the fulfilment of the basic task, and must correspond to the requirements of the situation in the scene.

One of the basic requirements in assuring the philosophical depth of film images is that each scene of a film must be presented on three levels. Even if each scene already dramatically expresses the essential nature of life, its image will not possess philosophical depth unless the scene is presented in three dimensions. Although a literary work may acquire philosophical depth through a generalized statement on the essence of life, the profundity of its artistic images cannot be assured by treating the essence of life as an abstract concept. This philosophical profundity can only be achieved if the essence of the human characters is presented through a broad and skilful depiction of their lives, if the profound content of events is presented analytically at various points in their development, if the characters in a scene give a genuinely convincing impression of having past and future lives, and if they convey through small details the whole picture of human life.

In studying the dramatic content of each scene, a writer must carefully consider the links between all the scenes and their development.

Although each scene is comparatively independent by virtue of being a relatively complete segment of events, it will have absolutely no value if it is not properly dovetailed into the flow of the developing drama. Every scene, as a link in the whole structure, must naturally be directed towards the presentation of the theme by embodying and advancing the dramatic line. If each scene does not blend naturally into the next, they will not move the drama along steadily, but will actually interrupt the natural, consistent flow of emotions.

Although each individual scene must fulfil its function by playing its own part in its own legitimate place in the structure, the scenes must all be linked together without any gaps in order to be really effective. There is a Korean saying that even three *mal* of gems only become a treasure when they are linked by a chain. The links between scenes must therefore be developed and presented with great skill, while at the same time giving prominence to the dramatic impact of each scene.

In the planning and linking of scenes, the main task of the work as a whole should be emphasized. While contributing as necessary to the development of the theme and idea, each scene must proceed logically from the preceding one and prepare the way for the one that follows. This series of scenes must form a single sequence which develops in a rising curve, continuously heightening the spectator's interest.

Scenes which are not directly concerned with the centred event may be included as necessary. These scenes are usually introduced immediately following intensely dramatic scenes, as a means of giving the audience some emotional respite. The audience are able to review and absorb the previous scene, on which they have been concentrating tensely, and relax for a moment as they prepare themselves psychologically to concentrate on major events still to come.

Scenes which are inserted between powerful dramatic scenes in order to relax the tension of the audience should contribute to a correct understanding of the work by serving as emotional bridges between the main scenes and varying the pace of the dramatic flow. These interpolated scenes must not become simple explanations, and they must certainly not make the drama dull.

The scene which is the keystone in the construction of a film is the climax, in which the dramatic tension that has developed in the course of the previous scenes, comes to a head. The dramatic climax is the point at which the maturing events and conflicts reach their peak and the hero's line of emotional development reaches its highest point.

The correct presentation of the idea underlying the theme, and also of the conflicts and events of the narrative depends upon the proper planning and successful realization of the climax.

The climax must be the inevitable result of the development of the events, conflicts and characters. As the inevitable result of the development of these lives, it can only be introduced when the characters and events have matured to their highest point and when the essential motive for the explosion of the conflicts and the situation for a decisive action have been established.

The event precipitating the climax in the film *The Fate of a Self-defence Corps Man* is the shooting by the enemy of the hero's father. The death of his father is the fuse which ignites the hero's long-accumulated grievances and hatred for the enemy.

In the unfolding of a man's destiny, his moral growth may not bring about a radical change unless an immediate motive is provided for such a change, and the specific motive may vary widely from one character to another.

The reason for Gap Ryong's revolt and subsequent struggle is the death of his father, whilst the reason for Man Sik's desertion from the camp is his realization that he is involved in criminal activities.

A particular incident can trigger the explosion of one man's resentment, whilst it may not produce a similar response from someone else. The extent to which a person is affected is determined by the direct effect of the incident on his or her interests.

The dramatic stimulus which finally triggers the explosion of the critical mass of contradictions at the climax must be directly related to the most vital question of the hero's life. Even the victimization or physical abuse of a person cannot be the cause of the climax if it does not stir the hero to decisive action.

The death of Gap Ryong's father robs him of the mainstay of a life which is filled with dreams. In other words, it destroys the last real foothold which supports him in enduring every hardship and humiliation. Gap Ryong no longer has a parent to whom he can fulfil his filial obligations, even if he should wish to; he can no longer take comfort in the warmth of a home, no matter how much he may desire happiness. Deprived of everything by a ruthless enemy in a contemptible world, his patience is finally exhausted; he can no longer restrain the upsurge of his resentment and hatred for the enemy. At this point his revolt and determined resistance to the enemy become inevitable.

The situation provides specific conditions for the development of events as well as a real basis for a clear delineation of the characters. The circumstances of the climactic scene must provide a basis for the final resolution of the development of the characters and the course of events.

The situation in this scene must impel the characters on opposing sides towards an unavoidable, explosive confrontation. Their differences can only finally come to a head in the course of simultaneous struggle by both sides. The negative and positive components of a conflicting relationship eventually arrive at a critical point where the conflict can no longer remain unresolved, and in this confrontation the new triumphs and vanquishes the old.

The dramatic purpose of the climax is the final and complete resolution of the theme and idea. If a writer fails to accomplish this in the climax, he will not get another chance. The conclusion which follows the climax can only confirm and clarify the theme and idea which have been fully unfolded in the climax. If the climax fails to present a full picture of the seed, then the seed will remain a bud which never blossoms.

Since the key to the successful dramatic realization of the climax is the image of the hero, his mental outlook must be thoroughly explored and the theme and idea must be exemplified in his life.

Although the climax is the scene in which the final clash occurs, it cannot simply present the external intensity of the action, resulting in the defeat of the negative by the positive. Even if a battle is fought during the climax, it is imperative to describe the development of the hero's ideological consciousness and the resultant improvement in his ethical and moral qualities. In this way the idea of the work will be represented in every detail.

It is also important for the climax to provide a summary of the fate of the other characters but this element must be subordinated to the emphasis on the correctness of the idea expressed in the hero's actions. At this point the drama must concentrate on the hero and not allow any other characters or emotional factors to obscure the portrayal of his temperament.

Exploring a dramatic theme is absorbing, but an artist must not allow himself to become its prisoner. An artist who is captivated by the drama cannot fully appreciate its real value and will end up by writing a play for the sake of the play itself.

BEGIN ON A SMALL SCALE AND END GRANDLY

First impressions are important in a film. The subsequent development of events can only be properly understood if the opening scene offers the audience a clear picture of the time and the place, the social background of the story, the characters of the people appearing on the screen and their relationships with each other. The opening scene must also hint at what the subject will be. If the beginning is too complicated, it will be difficult to follow the development of the story as the picture progresses.

A film must also come to a clear and intelligent conclusion. At the end of the work, through the development of the life of the hero, the seed flowers and bears fruit in the final presentation of the theme and idea. A great effort will have been wasted if the conclusion of the story is not well managed after an interesting start and good progress.

A film must begin on a small scale and end on a large one. Beginning small and ending large is the general form of the development of life. Any event usually begins with small things and gradually expands.

Since it reflects life in the very form of life's own development, a film should portray the process of human life and struggle in an accurate manner, beginning with small things which lead on to large-scale results. Only then can the portrayal be natural.

This form also fully accords with the tastes of our people. From olden times our people have never been fond of things that begin flamboyantly and end in no substantial result; things which, as the saying goes, start like a dragon's head and dwindle to a snake's tail. This is also true of art.

Films usually begin with ordinary lives, and they generally indicate or hint at their basic subjects in the opening scenes. Whether a story line follows the chronological sequence of events or they are dealt with in retrospect, it must begin in an interesting manner, setting the audience at their ease and firmly planting the seed of the subject.

If it is to give the audience a feeling of tranquility in the opening scene, a film must begin its story in a simple and straightforward manner, with small things, so that everything will be as familiar and natural as in real life. Only then will they willingly enter into the world of the story, and really believe in it.

Some screen writers, however, attempt to startle their audience from the outset. They try to gain people's attention by means of a tedious silence which is shattered by the sudden sound of shots or some strange incident. This is not a good method.

Of course, one should not lay down a strict pattern here. The more diverse and original the beginning of a film is, the better it is. But, although the beginning must give the audience an impression of novelty, it must not disturb them. From their initial undisturbed emotional state, the audience must gradually be drawn deeper into the serious world of the film.

The beginning must be quiet, and yet interesting. Artistic interest must always be provided by fresh insight into the profound meaning of everyday life and one's own involvement in the uplifting endeavours of the real world. Such an interesting start to a film can grip the hearts of the people watching it.

It is impossible, in art, to ignore interest in events for their own sake or the attraction of the novel. But this interest or attraction must be expressed through genuine artistic sentiment, mingled with the ardent aspiration to the beautiful and the noble; there must not be any unnatural interest aroused by a surprising event or an unusual situation. Introducing some stunning occurrence or the total impact of something completely strange and unheard-of, in the hope of evoking meaningless exclamations of wonder, is a vulgarity which is incompatible with art created for the people.

When the emotional tone has been established, the film must move quickly on to the main topic so that the audience will not become bored.

A work and its drama need not begin at exactly the same moment. Films can begin with a long shot of a town, or a forest landscape, or the sea, or with scenes of ordinary life which do not yet possess any dramatic elements. They can also choose to show the stages of dramatic development at the outset, or even begin the story with its climax and follow it in reverse order. Thus the beginning of a work does not necessarily coincide with the start of the drama, and there are many ways of beginning.

The descriptive structure of a film normally begins with the explanation of backgrounds and the introduction of the characters and then gradually develops from there. It is clearly inappropriate to devote too much attention to the explanation of the backgrounds and characters, and their relationships in order, thus burdening the opening scene with a boring presentation of things which could be shown in the course of the development of the film. As soon as the environment and the characters have been introduced, the main topic must be quickly taken up in order to indicate clearly the basic subject the writer intends to present.

The structure of drama inherently requires that the work be started in such a way that the writer's main topic can be guessed. The initiation, development and conclusion of a dramatic event correspond to the statement, development and resolution of an important human question. The beginning of a drama means that characters who are involved in this theme are beginning to form their relationship. Something which happens between people who have no involvement in the matter at hand cannot be regarded as the beginning of the drama. The beginning must either hint at or directly indicate an urgent issue, which is the main subject and substance of the work, while at the same time clearly indicating the dramatic relationship between the characters.

If no clue is given as to the subject of the story until the end of the first, second or third reel, and if it is difficult to guess the main subject while the characters are being introduced, the audience will feel uncertain and their interest will evaporate. The interest of the audience will only be gradually engaged, step by step, when they can guess the question that the writer is raising and anticipate its solution through a story which begins simply and naturally with no pomp or flourish.

The first part of a film must also provide a clear, well-defined picture of the times and the relationships between the characters. The introductory scene of a film is thus required to provide an overview of the period, the social backgrounds of the main characters and their relationships, the theatre of their activity and the events to come. This clear picture of the times, the characters and their relationships is very important in giving the audience a correct understanding of the basic question and drawing them quickly into the world of the film.

The period, the social backgrounds, the theatre of activity and the major events which will make up the main story line must all be established simultaneously at the start, centring on the introduction of the hero and the other leading characters. A novelist is in a position to explain all these facts, but a scriptwriter is not. Subtitles and narratives are sometimes used, but they are not always possible. The introductory part of the film would become prolonged and boring if all these elements were introduced separately, that is, if the period were related to the characters by subtitles, if the social background were filled in by narratives, if the place were established by the signboard on a building, and the events by the words of the characters. A clumsy beginning will spoil the effect of the subsequent development of the story.

The beginning of a work must be clear, without giving away the end. However, there is no need to deliberately hide the end at the beginning in order to keep the audience from guessing it.

For the form of the work's beginning to be fresh and original it must conform to the content and mood of life as shown in the film. It would be boring if different works all began in the same way, without any individuality; but there is no justification for using forms which are incompatible with the content, purely for the sake of originality.

Generally speaking, there are certain ways of introducing films according to the mood of the work, and these can be used if so desired. But it is advisable for creators to invent new forms whenever possible. Some writers and directors, however, do not pay much attention to the beginning of films, and treat it casually, even though they admit that the impression made by a film's opening is important. They do not realize that such carelessness actually does great harm to the work.

The ending of a film must be convincing and comprehensive. A comprehensive ending means that the result of the struggle has been clearly demonstrated and an understanding of some great idea has been achieved through an extensive and detailed review of the matter which was raised.

A fine conclusion does not require the invention of some high-flown grand finale. The concluding part of a film must always express the work's idea clearly and profoundly. In order to have great educational significance a film must come to a clear and significant ideological conclusion.

If a film is to make a deep impression on people and assist them to accept the facts of life and the law of struggle, it must confirm the settlement of the question arrived at by life and through the development of the characters in the light of a great and clear idea. A work would seem dull and pointless if it made no progress in developing ideas and left unanswered at the close all the issues raised by the large-scale events set out at the start. The closing scene must therefore clearly demonstrate the outcome of the struggle of the hero and other positive characters, while at the same time answering the question posed in the body of the work by means of a great and clear idea which provides a true picture of life. It is not enough simply to say that the struggle is honourable and worthwhile. Only when the real value and nobility of the revolution are confirmed through the act of living will the audience be roused to a high level of artistic excitement. In art no one will accept an idea as life experience unless the idea springs naturally from life.

Depth and clarity in the exposition of ideological content require the proper handling of the destiny of all the characters who contribute to the presentation of the theme. It hardly needs to be said that in all this the hero occupies the most important place. However, the proper treatment of the negative characters who are in direct conflict with the hero not only increases the significance of the positive, but also has tremendous educational importance in itself

An explicit emphasis on the inevitability of the defeat and collapse of the hostile classes who undermine social progress can give tremendous encouragement to people in their ardent love of justice and truth and their admiration for the revolutionary struggle.

In a work dealing with the situation under socialism it is desirable to show the new, noble lives of the backward characters after their re-education, rather than to end the story with their repentance. This will give the audience a natural understanding of the beauty and nobility of the revolutionary way of life. With the exception of class enemies, the negative people of our era have to be re-educated. It should therefore be shown very clearly how re-educated people attain new levels of achievement in their work and their lives, through their own efforts. This sharp criticism of negative facts and clear demonstration of the way in which the negative characters should follow the example of the positive is a very important method of encouraging people to lead noble and beautiful lives.

Dramatic works usually resolve every issue at the climax and rapidly conclude the story; but the story must not end abruptly if the subsequent lives of reformed negative characters are to be clearly depicted. A vivid picture of events, providing further confirmation of the solution to the basic question which has been clarified in a work, is more effective than a hundred words.

In revolutionary works writers must not refrain from providing absolute conclusions, on the assumption that these should be left to the imagination of the audience. In particular, those works which deal with the question of people's revolutionary transformation must provide powerful motivation for backward people to re-educate themselves and join the general advance along the revolutionary road. If they only expose people's shortcomings to criticism without motivating people to lead a truly new way of life, their work does not conform to the spirit of the present revolutionary era.

It is advisable to treat the concluding part of a work in a way that gives its political message strong impact and appeal.

A film should always demonstrate that the revolution is continuing and that the struggle is being pursued ever more vigorously. If it concludes with triumphant cheering and the determination to lead a comfortable life now that the struggle has triumphed and success has finally been achieved, it will have no power to inspire people with revolutionary enthusiasm and fighting spirit.

Even if the struggle is arduous and the sacrifice is great, even if the hero has been taken captive by the enemy, the film must emphasize that the future of the revolution is bright and that justice and truth are bound to triumph. In other words, it must inspire the spirit of revolutionary optimism and a firm conviction of victory. Only if the hero is able to look forward to the happiness of victory and the promise of a brighter future as the result of his struggle, will the audience feel a strong desire to fight as zealously as he has done on the road of revolution and be drawn into the world of revolutionary optimism.

If the end of a work is to have a strong political impact and a long-term ideological effect, it must clearly indicate to people the road of future struggle.

In the film *The Flourishing Village* the reporter closely examines the process of revolutionization of those who, under the influence of egoism and selfishness, have not lived their lives as they should, and he comments that the struggle for the revolutionary transformation of such people and their assimilation to the working class should be developed in depth in the future. In this way he convincingly underlines the Party's policy. The revolutionization of people is not a task which is undertaken one morning and completed a few days later. It is a task requiring unceasing struggle by everyone until the complete establishment of communist society. By emphasizing this idea in the natural context of the closing scene, the film makes a profound impression on the audience. A descriptive conclusion of this kind provokes people to deep thought and gives them the great strength required to lead a more sincere and worthy life.

If the ideological and emotional impact of a film is to be long-lived, it must not drag on monotonously, but come to its conclusion neatly and quickly. If the film drags on tediously when it has finished telling the story and has nothing more to add, it will dissipate the emotional excitation which has cost so much effort to arouse. The stronger the long-term effect, the greater the real influence of the film on the audience.

THE BEST WORDS ARE FULL OF MEANING AND EASY TO UNDERSTAND

Language is the most important means for describing people and their lives. Language is extremely important in literature, which uses it as a means of description, and particularly in the art of drama, which does not permit direct explanation by the writer.

In a film, several descriptive methods—the actors' performance, the music and the visual designing—contribute significantly to the description of the characters and their lives. But these are not as effective as words are for the direct and vivid expression of the characters' thoughts, feelings, psychological state and mood, nor do they express the ideological content of the work in such breadth and depth as words do.

It is usually said that a film should contain less speech and more action, but action is not capable of completely replacing words. The fewer the words that are used in a film, the better those words must be.

Words play an important part in enhancing the ideological and artistic qualities of a work. As the expression of the characters' thoughts, feelings and psychology, words directly reveal the ideological content of the work. This is evident if we consider what a great effect a few apt words spoken at the right moment can have on the clear expression of the ideological content. In contrast, an inappropriate or badly spoken word can have more serious consequences than several imperfect shots. A single ill-chosen word can distort the character or obscure the theme of the work. One inadequate word can create a corresponding gap in the film.

Words must be filled with meaning, and should always be clear and easy to understand. A lengthy, crude or intricate jumble of difficult words which lack real meaning is quite useless. The best words are full of meaning and easy to understand.

Good words only flow from a rich experience of life and deep thought. People's emotions can only be stirred by truth which has been learned through experience and spoken clearly and simply, in terms which suit the context.

In that immortal work *The Sea of Blood,* the underground political worker from the Anti-Japanese Guerrilla Army explains to Won Nam's mother that a revolution is not something reserved for a special kind of person and that the ill-treated and oppressed poor can only win back the country and avenge their blood when all of them work for the revolution. These words are easy to understand and they have a very deep meaning. The political worker speaks truthfully, from the heart, in plain, convincing language to the mother who, having been deprived of her country and even her husband, finds herself at a critical moment of choice; she can sit and drown in the cruel sea of blood or stand on her own feet and fight. His words are important because they penetrate the very depths of her experience.

A character without a wide experience of life can never use the best words and no fine words spoken without a basis in experience can convey deep meaning and move people's hearts.

The words used in a film can only carry real conviction and substance when they are supported by experience and appropriate to the occasion. Words must always be used sparingly and at the right moment. In this way they become useful and valuable.

In the search for suitable words one should not try to invent some smart ringing phrase or use witty expressions. Even words which are used frequently in everyday life may or may not be good, depending on whether or not writers use them where they are appropriate to the characters and the situation.

At a given moment and in a given situation there is only one appropriate thing for a character to say. Writers must strive to create words which clearly express the characters' individual features, are appropriate to the action and the situation, and ring as true and clear as in real life.

A man's speech is the man himself. His thoughts and feelings, preferences and his tastes are all expressed through his speech and so, too, are his profession, the extent of his education and the level of his moral and cultural development. Workers and farmers use different words, and so do the young and the old, because there are differences in their jobs, their ages and the extent of their education, and therefore also in their ways of thinking.

In literature, too, the words must be appropriate to the characters and the particular context. A man's speech must always be appropriate. Words can only sound genuine and contribute to the clear description of people when they are in harmony with the characters and the way they live their lives.

It is important in personalizing characters' words to concentrate on the expression of their ideological state, while accurately portraying their psychology and emotions and correctly reflecting the circumstances of their lives. Words which are unsuited to the characters and their lives cannot be the speech of living people and therefore will not carry conviction.

Clear, correctly-chosen words can also reflect the characteristics of the period and society. Since people are influenced by contemporary ideas, culture and morality, their way of speaking reflects the spirit of the society in which they live. Language, which is the product of labour and mirrors social life, changes and grows richer as times change and society progresses. So words must express the socio-historical features reflected in the people's linguistic style.

In order to give a clear and accurate picture of the distinctive features of life in a particular era it is necessary to reflect the linguistic life of the period correctly. If the characters speak a single word which is inappropriate to the period, this will detract from the accuracy of the whole picture, even though the environment, events and objects of the time may be skilfully depicted.

When establishing the linguistic practice conforming to a particular period, special attention should be given to the careful selection and use of words which express the period's socio-political system, economic relations and cultural and moral standards. These vocabulary sets constitute the basic content of the language of the period and reflect the essence of the social system and the people's lives. A single word which does not suit the occasion would distort the picture of the period and the life of the time.

A writer who describes the heroic life of the People's Army and the people during the Fatherland Liberation War, must choose the most typical words from their contemporary vocabulary. Of course, he must understand the life of those times and depict it properly from the viewpoint of today, but he must not create something out of nothing, nor departing from the historical principle, alter the facts.

The words must suit the context. Even words of profound meaning will sound ridiculous or nonsensical if they conflict with the occasion. The same idea and the same feeling may be expressed by different words, according to the situation in which the characters find themselves, and different things may be described by the same words. As the saying has it, a word may convey different meanings depending on the way it is spoken.

A remark which is apt is also logical. The logic of speech is the primary factor which makes it comprehensible. To speak logically means to say things which are reasonable in the context, and consistent with one's life, ideas and actions. A man's thoughts and feelings arise from a particular cause, and when they are firm in his mind they are expressed in words. Words, therefore, are not spoken without a setting of time and place, nor are they used carelessly, without reason.

Before he speaks, a man has to assimilate certain ideas and feelings from life around him and his own experience. A man who thinks and acts in a normal fashion is in the habit of speaking logically in this sense, so he does not pay particular attention to the logical process of speaking. But everyone uses his own sense to convince the hearer that his words are consistent with the facts, that they are reasonable and accord with the precepts of morality.

Words should be colloquial, brief and filled with meaning.

In a film. which is a form of dramatic art. words. actions and other means of description used to express the ideas and feelings of the characters, must be correctly chosen and aptly used. Words, in particular, must be used only when they are essential, that is, when their functions cannot be performed by the characters' actions or any other descriptive means. Repeating things which can be understood without explanation or dealing at length with something which requires only a single word, will only detract from the point of an idea and its impact.

A word has connotations beyond its obvious meaning. The talent for conveying the greater meaning, beyond the obvious, is only seen in writers who understand the significance of every aspect of life and can express each one briefly. It can be said that the single word capable of standing in place of ten and the simple expression capable of throwing fresh light on the truth are the basis of excellent language in art.

Even a single word which the characters use in their daily life must suggest a great deal. A work may need to explain an event or an action by words. In that case it is advisable to speak in a way that suggests people's inmost feelings, their past and their future, rather than give a direct explanation of what can be seen. Writing in this way can convey a great deal of meaning.

One word of great substance, spoken after deep thought, is more powerful and impressive, and has greater impact than ten or a hundred casual words. A diffuse expression contains few useful words. A verbose man is apt to use empty words, and empty words will prove false and result in making the character pompous. In a film commonplace, senseless words slacken the dramatic tension and detract from the content.

The careless use of archaic or vulgar words or crude expressions, even though they may be colloquial, degrades the quality of the work. The words of the positive characters in any work must express their thoughts and feelings elegantly and accord with the aesthetic tastes of the period, as well as sounding morally uplifting.

Communists are revolutionaries who continuously eliminate everything that is outmoded and create new things and as such they are sensitive to the spirit of the times and are always exemplary in their speech. Since they value justice and truth, they do not use empty words. Since they are frugal and cultured by nature, they do not use vulgar and senseless words.

Describing workers and farmers, without reason, as crude or rough in their speech, indicates that an author is ignorant of the beautiful and noble spiritual world of the working masses, the real masters of the new era, and that his own cultural standard is low.

Generally speaking, language, more than anything else, retains outmoded remnants of the past, and these do not disappear in a few days. These remnants of outmoded language, and the surviving elements of obsolete ideology, can only be removed through tireless education and effort. So archaic words, though colloquial, must be identified and eliminated quickly.

As a result of the thorough implementation of the Party's policy for the development of our socialist national language, the work of replacing ideographic and borrowed words with our own words, and refining our language to make it more beautiful, is proceeding successfully. Language is making rapid progress particularly in step with the establishment of a new socialist way of life in accord with the basic character of the working class in all spheres of the economy, culture, ideology and morality. Therefore, if writers are to use words which suit their characters and their way of life, they must rely on the rich and diverse linguistic practice of the working masses, the builders of socialism.

It is the popular masses who create and develop language. They are the genuine masters of language who create and develop the most beautiful, elegant and forceful of words. The people's speech is easy to understand, clear, profound and rich in meaning. Words which are unintelligible and distasteful to the people are the creation of ignorant men. These words cannot rouse the sympathy of the people nor will they last for long.

Writers can only create excellent structures of words, which can be understood and accepted by the masses, when they discover and select noble and beautiful words from the unfathomable source of the popular language.

Words of Korean origin are basic to the popular language.

As the great leader Comrade Kim Il Sung said, our language has distinct rising and falling inflections and a clear intonation; it is fluent and sounds very beautiful to the ear. Our language is so rich that it is capable of expressing any complex idea and delicate feeling, and can move people to laughter or to tears. It is also highly effective in educating people in communist morality, because it can express questions of courtesy with great precision. In their work, therefore, writers must preserve and use more of our own words, which are beautiful and elegant and rich in meaning, so that people will come to appreciate the fact that those who have a good command of their national language are highly cultured and patriotic.

The words of the heroes and other positive characters in works of art must be derived from the cultured language which is in accord with the norms of the new era and the new life. The words which are used not only help people to understand life, they also have a great effect on their linguistic education. Writers must pay particular attention to each word used by their characters and create beautiful new words which accord with the aesthetic feelings of the period, so that the working people can follow their example.

The task of coining new words requires the greatest prudence and responsibility. An impolite or preposterous word may invade the lives of many people, dull their minds and induce them to perform unpleasant action, whereas militant, beautiful and cultured words may contribute greatly to raising their ideological and moral level and establishing the socialist way of life.

In creating new words, it is important to hold firmly to the working-class line, and thoroughly implement the principle of serving the people. New words which will serve as examples for the people must be in harmony with the tastes and emotions of the working class, be easy for the masses to understand, and simple to use. We must never tolerate the indiscriminate use of words which are obscure and complicated in meaning and undermine the people's sound ideology, or the introduction of such words in literary works, simply to satisfy the writers' own tastes.

Writers must always remember that they are communicating with the people. When they write even a single word, they must stand where the people stand. The best words are excellent because they are liked by the masses and are effective in enlightening people. Good words can be found in the lives of the people. That is why writers must adopt a humble and earnest attitude to the popular language, examine life and learn their lessons diligently.

THE MOOD MUST BE EXPRESSED WELL

Defining the mood of a work is always a problem in artistic and literary creation.

Works of art and literature depict life by means of real characters with feelings. They therefore have different emotional tones, because different works represent different lives in different forms and their authors differ from one another in their personalities.

The mood of a work means the specific shading of the various images which give a clear picture of the true emotional tones of life.

The distinctive impression of an image is mainly intensified by its mood. The clearer the mood of a work, the more unmistakable the specific features of the life it represents. A work without the individual stamp of the image cannot make a deep impression even when the content is excellent.

Mood is an element which cannot be ignored in the truthful representation of life. The truth and naturalness of images depend on how the mood is set for the description of life. The more accurate the mood, the more clearly apparent the features of life and the clearer their expression.

Writers who deal with the present-day situation ought to describe the lives of our working people in a bright, cheerful and hopeful light. The pulsing spirit and emotions which fill our people's lives spring from their fine, uplifting thoughts and feelings and their happy and noble lives.

In the exploitative society, the working people, the overwhelming majority of the population, live in low spirits, plagued by worries and anxiety because they are poor and have no rights, whereas in socialist society, where the people are masters of the country, the working masses display their Chajusong and creativity at all times and their lives become happier and more prosperous with every day. Therefore, describing the lives of the working people of our time in gloomy and unsettled emotional terms would be a distorting of the real situation.

It hardly needs to be said that the emotional colouring of life cannot be defined in general terms because it is both concrete and delicate. Even under socialism, different works depict different aspects of our life, so their moods must be different. But works depicting today's happy and worthwhile lives must be filled to overflowing with happy feelings.

Mood is also a factor in the realization of rich and multi-faceted images. Rich and colourful literary images grow as writers portray life from various angles, in different forms and by different methods. Even in dealing with the same life, different writers describe its different aspects in their own distinctive ways. In this way new works are produced.

A writer who is incapable of clearly expressing a mood is not a true creative artist. Mood can only be correctly expressed by artists who have attained a high level of creative skill. However, some artists do not pay much attention to the mood of their works. Their products are coarse, offensive to the eye, vague in content, and incapable of rousing a deep response.

The definition of mood is related to the basic attitude adopted by writers in their understanding of the life which they intend to show, even before they choose the means and techniques of expression.

The mood of works of art and literature must first be defined in accordance with the actual nature of life.

Mood is not something which a writer adjusts according to his own wishes. His own individuality must also be based on real life and find its expression in an elegant and vivid description of that life. If he wishes to gain a deep understanding of life and depict it in a particular mood, he must therefore pay due attention to recognizing its essential nature and clearly defining its characteristics.

Basing the mood of a work on life means that the characteristic elements of the mood should be derived from the essence of life. In any form of work, writers must clearly portray the essence of life and the main current of its development. They must not blur the main trend of development of the life of their period and its essential characteristics by vague psychological or lyrical arguments.

The mood of works of art and literature must be based on life, but it does not automatically find its proper expression even if life is presented factually. A writer re-creates life artistically in his work, by means of a descriptive process in which he eliminates from the story all that is inessential and vulgar and gives prominence to what is typical, beautiful and noble. In the course of this process the unique tones and shades of the life with which he is dealing, acquire clear emphasis.

He will not be able to represent any mood if he depicts life exactly as it is, on the pretext of preserving its natural colours. He can only describe life in a specific mood and emphasize its essential nature when he correctly understands the gamut of hues in life's emotional radiance and draws on them to unify all his images. A mood based on life is only enduring when the writer has rendered it distinct and vivid.

Mood must be determined on the basis of real life and in accordance with the educational purpose of the work. The mood is not required to point up qualities of form, but in order to express the ideological content of the work correctly and enhance its educational value. Without a definite educational creative purpose in mind it is difficult to define the mood correctly.

However, there is a tendency to play down the need to express a mood which supports the educational purpose of the work being created.

Suppose that one intends to produce a film which deals with the re-education of an official, who regards himself as exemplary both in and out of work, when in fact he is not. The problem arises of how to define the mood of the piece. If the work is simply defined as a comedy because there is something comical in a man whose actions are at variance with his intentions, there will be considerable disparity between the creative purpose and the image actually produced.

If the work is to deal with the revolutionary transformation of people, and particularly of an official in a responsible position, the story line must unfold in a thoughtful fashion. The mood must be defined in such a way that the audience will learn an important lesson from the picture of an official who commits a serious error in his work and his life because of his complacency. If the writer tries, instead, to trigger off laughter at important points in the narrative, the image will be diverted from the correct course and the work will not achieve its educational purpose.

In the hands of our Party art and literature are powerful weapons for ideological education and discussion of the mood of works is inconceivable in separation from this noble mission. The task of each work is determined by the specific features of real life and the requirements of the revolution and only the correct artistic fulfilment of this task throws the ideological and artistic characteristics of the work into prominence and enhances its instructional and educational role.

A writer whose view of life is politically informed, can direct his attention to the important matter of people's revolutionary education even when depicting the vigorous struggle on the labour front; he can instil sound ideological consciousness in people even when describing the world of human feelings; even in a humorous outburst he can emphasize the revolutionary spirit which overcomes everything in life which is outmoded and carries life forward.

The mood of works of art and literature is also greatly influenced by the characters of the heroes, and the nature of the conflicts and plots.

The character of the hero sets the mood directly throughout a literary work. The thoughts and feelings of the people who create a situation are the basic factor in defining the emotions portrayed. The emotions and sentiments expressed in the lives people create and lead depend on whether their ideological and emotional state is sound and pure, or backward and rotten. Hence, the characters' ideological and emotional state, and particularly the state of the hero, are the major factor in setting the mood.

A clear understanding of the distinctive qualities of the conflicts and plots is necessary for a correct understanding of the mood. Conflicts define the mood of a work in the sphere of people's social relationships, whereas the plot defines it through the mode of its description of life.

If a writer does not place thorough reliance in life in the working-out of his plot and the resolution of conflicts, he may fall back into formalism and replace the mood with a mere show of form or make the mood itself uncertain.

The mood of a literary work must be harmonious throughout. The lives of the people who are described have definite purposes and orientations. For instance, the development of a person into a revolutionary in the course of practical struggle, is based on living a revolutionary life, permeated with noble thoughts and feelings such as faithfulness to the revolution, an indomitable fighting spirit, optimism and confidence in the future. This is the reason why the mood should be harmonious throughout, on the basis of the principal characteristics of real life.

A writer has to work out a systematic plot capable of representing the fundamental qualities of life before he can harmonize his work by means of emotional colour, and develop the story in a clear and interesting way.

In maintaining the mood of his work he must concentrate on the major factor and subordinate everything else to it in a harmonious fashion. If he begins by painting the hero's life in bright and cheerful emotional tones, he must maintain the colouring carefully and subordinate the different tints radiating from the lives of the other characters to maintaining the prominence of the basic line. Of course, he should never simplify the images of his work or make them monotonous as a result of pre-occupation with the character traits of any individual. Laying exclusive emphasis on the revolutionary aspect of a revolutionary's life purportedly in order to stress the basic feature in the description, will make it impossible to depict the various features of life in an appropriate fashion. Maintaining the consistency of mood does not mean maintaining emphasis on just one feature of the character. Consistency of mood can only be attained through the creation of an original emotional coloration of the images by forcefully carrying forward the characters' basic features and the main current of life's development, while at the same time harmoniously combining various important aspects of the characters' lives.

Maintaining the continuity of mood also requires that particular attention be paid to the emotions and feelings which are revealed in the relationships between the hero and the other characters. Even in legitimate drama, the negative characters are often presented in a comical way because of their inherent nature. But the mood itself must never be broken by putting undue emphasis on the emotional tones of individual characterizations which contrast with the mood of the work.

A reckless bias towards the line of any one character, because of its particular brilliance, with resultant emphasis on the complexion of the secondary line, will interrupt the flow of the work's mood, by overlaying the main emotional colour which has to run throughout the work. Since mood is related to a definite artistic convention, it must grow clearer as the story develops.

The mood of a work must conform correctly with the characteristics of its genre and also be attuned to the requirements of the period and the tastes of the people.

Many works of legitimate drama and light comedy are produced to reflect the situation in socialist society. If any of these works has no individuality of mood and distinction in its genre, it will be unable to win the audience. It would be ridiculous for serious dramatic films to attempt to provoke laughter without any reason or include a large number of the thrilling scenes usually found in detective films, just for the sake of adding interest to the story. It would be dull and boring if a comedy film supposed to provoke continuous laughter at the inconsistencies in human ideas and feelings, and the disparity between thought and action, intention and result, were to mention nothing but serious themes.

Mood cannot stand on its own, independent of the basic requirements, for instance, of a legitimate drama or a comedy. In both cases, the mood must have a specific emotional colouring which contributes to the fulfilment of the requirements of the genre.

In order to produce works of excellent ideological and artistic quality creative artists must pay particular attention to maintaining the mood, and also to exploring and perfecting it in accordance with the characteristics of real life and in harmony with the sentiments and tastes of our people.

The mood of works of art and literature is not completely fixed; it constantly changes and develops by acquiring new historical features.

Take the legitimate drama, one of the basic genres. It has acquired a series of characteristics in the process of representing the situation in our country today, when socialist construction is developing in depth and the revolutionization of the people and their assimilation to the working class is being accelerated. Our legitimate plays deal mainly with the working masses, the masters of the times, and provide extensive depictions of historic events of great socio-political importance. Moreover, in the works of this genre dealing with the struggle to overcome the survivals of outmoded ideas which still linger in people's minds, it is the internal seriousness of dramatic conflicts which is represented, rather than their external intensity.

Writers must describe our people's noble struggle for the revolution and construction in a clear new mood conforming to the requirements of the new era and the aesthetic tastes of the people, and thus steadily raise the level of art and literature to match the level of the developing revolution.

Nature may create scentless flowers, but every artistic product of man's aesthetic aspirations must always emit distinctive emotional fragrance.

ORIGINALITY IS THE ESSENCE OF CREATION

Creative work must always be original. Only when each artistic work demonstrates originality in describing the infinitely diverse and complex situation of life can it exert the unique and enhanced emotional influence of art on people's education.

A simple repetition, devoid of creative originality, of what has already been said by other writers, is incapable of cultivating in the minds of the people the ability to think independently, perceive the complex and diverse situation correctly and work to transform society, it cannot inspire them with creative enthusiasm. Art and literature must be original; this is a natural requirement of their mission to nurture the independent and creative spirit in people's minds and lead the way as they fulfil their role as masters of the revolution.

Art is only interesting when it is original. Nothing is more dull than a book which contains nothing new and has no individual features. Art cannot be forced upon people. It must attract people instead of seeking out an audience. An audience will gain nothing from a production if it is forced to watch.

Art must always be varied and original.

Art, which reflects real life, must vary just as men and their lives do; since every thing and every event in the world has an individual and real existence, art which describes it must also have a real and specific character.

The writers and artists who understand and describe life are all individuals. Because they have different ideas and feelings, different experiences of life and art, creative artists must display their own individuality in the observation, analysis, evaluation and description of life. If writers with different creative personalities produce similar works, it means that they have failed to see life with their own eyes and describe it in their own way.

A hundred writers should produce a hundred works which are all individual and different in content and form. If everyone wrote in exactly the same way, without any creative individuality, we would not need a hundred writers to produce a hundred works.

We do not need stereotyped works; we need a diversity of works with diverse features.

Artists can only make a real contribution to the period and the life of the people by creating original works. Our famous artists were all ardent patriots and staunch fighters, who dedicated their incomparable creative abilities to devoted service to their country and people.

Creative originality enables artists to make an independent contribution to the development of art and literature. A writer must always hew out an original creative path, discovering something new every time he writes. The history of art progresses through the artists' ceaseless creative quest. Only by creating original images can a writer forward the development of art and literature and make a valuable contribution to the treasure-house of human culture.

Creativity is by nature original and not repetitive. Originality is the essence of creation.

The creation of original images requires a keen eye for the important new issues which arise in the people's lives and their struggles, and the ability to resolve them in a particular way. If a writer takes a schematic approach to life and attempts to portray it according to a preconceived pattern, he will be unable to discover important new subjects in life, or to create typical images, even if he does discover them. A formal approach or a rigid pattern means the death of art.

The originality of an image depends on its creator. If a writer ceases to take a fresh view of life and fails to discover what is new and important in it, he will be unable to create a world made up of original images, no matter how often he is advised and urged to select original seeds, to represent the theme in an original manner, to describe the characters in a fresh way, and so on. No one can take the writer's place in creation.

Creative originality is only attainable when the writer's own creative individuality is clear. Only those who can see life with their own eyes and describe it well by applying their own distinctive artistic talent and skill, are capable of producing original images.

A writer's originality finds expression first of all in his ability to perceive the facts in an original manner. Every writer has his own way of seeing the facts, of feeling and understanding them, of portraying them. Even when different writers deal with the same fact or event, the results are different, because they all observe, judge and describe the varied and complex processes of life in their own way.

A writer's outlook on the world is the basic determining factor of his creative individuality. His ideological point of view provides the basis of his understanding of facts, his discovery of the meaning of new subjects and his creation of images.

A writer's creative experiences, artistic tastes and preferences also have a major influence on his creative work. Writers who are used to describing life in the form of legitimate drama, dealing with serious problems and analysing them seriously and acutely, usually choose to describe life from that angle and in those hues. Writers who are used to providing clear-cut solutions to social problems in a humorous fashion most often produce works in this style. They are not to be blamed for this.

What must be guarded against here is the bad practice of decrying the importance of a writer's outlook on the world by simply attributing his creative individuality to formal aspects of his work. An artist's creative individuality only demonstrates its true worth when it serves to strengthen the revolutionary character of our art and literature and provides a highly original and artistic representation of the ideological content of his work. The bourgeois critics' malign slander that socialist art is "not varied" because of the single world outlook which underlies it, is, in fact, only a sophistry intended to emasculate the powerful ideological effect of artistic works by deliberately ignoring the significant role played by world outlook in the manifestation of the artists' individuality.

A writer's originality in creative work is also expressed in the manner of his artistic thinking as he explores the world and discovers what is new. Some writers delve deep into the heart of everyday life to discover in this way what new and beautiful developments are taking place, while others seek and discover these developments for the most part in stirring lives involving fierce struggles. It is impossible to say which approach is better, as long as they both provide a vivid portrayal of the essential features of the facts; the angle from which they view life or the motive of interest is not important. Writers must make use of all the available artistic possibilities, probing into ever more diverse aspects of life at various moments, in order to draw on its diversity and richness to create truly profound pictures.

Describing new things requires no less originality from a writer than discovering them and he needs a high degree of skill for a successful portrayal. A writer therefore has to demonstrate original skill in resolving artistic problems throughout the whole process.

The general principles of creative work do not define for writers the specific methods by which to display their originality. The more originality a writer shows in applying the general principles of the creative method of socialist realism to specific lives, the higher will be his level of creativity and the more fully will his creative individuality blossom.

Creative individuality must be expressed firstly in the selection of seeds and their specific artistic representation.

A writer who has chosen his seed must create an image with definite features, conforming to the seed's requirements. If the theme and characters are hackneyed, although the seed is fresh, this means that natural logic has already been distorted. Since the theme cannot possibly be determined in isolation from the seed, a disagreement between seed and theme indicates that the latter has not been derived from the former but introduced from some other source, or perhaps that it is the writer's own idea.

At a certain time, our creative artists attempted to produce two films in succession, both dealing with the dignity of work in socialist society. We pointed out that a film which had a barber as the heroine had already dealt with this problem on the basis of the seed that in socialist society no job serving the welfare of the people is mean or lowly, and that there was no need to take up this question again, whether the film was to deal with a cobbler or a park-keeper. We also added that the proposed film, which had a park-keeper as its hero, would be able to present a new theme if its orientation were changed to the development of a valuable new seed, demonstrating that love of a single tree is love of the country, and if the character of the hero were described accordingly.

However hard a writer might try it is impossible for him to work out a theme in a fresh manner, unless he discovers a new seed. The original working-out of a theme requires its correct definition, based exclusively on the nature of the seed, and its development in a way which expresses a definite artistic and political meaning.

Originality only finds its genuine expression through both aspects of the process—definition and depiction. All the definitions and descriptions in an artistic work must be novel, original and individual. In this way every piece can be rendered original and distinctive in its seed, ideas and characters and in the lives it portrays

Originality in the creation of images acquires its truly distinctive features in the process of generalization and individualization, and finds its ultimate expression in the skill and techniques of description. A writer must not depart from the principle of creating typical images, but he must be free to vary the use of his techniques. This enables the writer to employ his imagination freely on the basis of real life.

The creation of original images also requires the effective use of the various means, techniques and skills of description, without making them banal. An original representation of the idea of the work is only ensured by their use in an original way. Even if a new seed has been discovered, a writer is not able to develop it into an original idea unless he is able to present it as a new and original image.

There are no special means and technique of description exclusively reserved for particular writers. These techniques are general and common; they constitute the common armoury of all writers The important point is the use which is made of them. Thus the same means of depiction, used by different writers, result in different styles, expressed through the specific features of their attitudes to life and its artistic interpretation and representation.

A writer must have a good command of the means and techniques of description in order to make free and full use of them as he requires, and develop his own style in using them. A man who is inexperienced or awkward in the use of a saw or a plane, can only imitate others by watching how they use them. The same applies to a creative writer. Imitation will result in formal writing and the following of patterns, and needless to say, no originality can be displayed by a writer who is committed to an established pattern.

A writer must not stubbornly persist in bad habits on the excuse that he is preserving his originality. He must indeed preserve his creative originality, but that is not an end in itself; it is directed to the creation of numerous diverse and original works for the education of the people. A writer's originality must therefore always accord with the masses' aesthetic aspiration to the beautiful and the noble, and must always be acceptable to the people. If a writer develops purely personal tastes or bad habits, not only will he debase the cultural level of his work, but he will exert a bad influence on people.

The artist's individuality determines the distinctive character of the image and augments the artistic force of his works. This individuality can only be justified on the basis of his artistic achievements, and there can be no expression of individuality divorced from clear artistic images. Individuality in creative work must therefore be thoroughly subordinated to resolving the questions raised in works in a way which enhances their ideological and artistic quality.

Writers must not establish a pattern and restrict themselves to that stereotype. Individuality must be expressed in originality which must, in turn, further increase and enhance individuality.

Man is by nature individualistic. But the individuality of an artist is a creative individuality, expressed through his artistic work rather than a personal individuality. A writer reveals his ideological opinions and attitudes, his artistic views and cultural standards, his feelings and emotions in the course of his creative work. The combination of these elements is precisely the expression of his creative individuality through his work.

Not all artists are endowed with creative individuality. It is only possessed by creative artists who have acquired a high level of political understanding and highly-developed artistic qualities. These are the major elements which distinguish excellent artists. Artists must therefore endeavour to raise their level of creative individuality through unremitting effort and enthusiastic enquiry. Those who seek to test their talents and try their fortune in art, simply because they consider it to be fascinating work, will never become fine artists.

Individuality for individuality's sake, the so-called "individuality" which seeks popularity for the sake of money and fame, has nothing in common with the creative individuality which produces genuine art. By advocating individuality for individuality's sake modern bourgeois art cripples large numbers of artists condemning them to spend their days as slaves to money.

The creative individuality of writers and artists can only flower fully in a socialist society, which has finally been freed from the restriction of individuality by repressive power and the encroachment upon human rights by money, and which provides all the necessary preconditions for according genuine respect to artists' individuality and giving free rein to creative originality.

DIRECTING FOR THE CINEMA

"Like the leading article of the Party paper, the cinema should have mass appeal and should keep ahead of new developments, thus playing a mobilizing role in each stage of the revolutionary struggle."

KIM IL SUNG

THE DIRECTOR IS THE COMMANDER OF THE CREATIVE GROUP

If cinematic art is to be developed to meet the requirements of the Juche age, a fundamental change is required in methods of film-making. From the time of cinema art's first emergence to the present, changes in customs and social institutions have resulted in many changes and advances in artistic and technical matters, but the vestiges of the old system and its methods have not yet been overcome in creative work. There still remain significant remnants of capitalist and dogmatic ideas particularly in the system and the methods of direction, which constitutes the nucleus of film-making Unless the old pattern is broken completely and a new system and new methods of creative work are established in direction, the tasks facing the cinema in its new stage of development will prove impossible to accomplish.

The task set before the cinema today is one of contributing to people's development into true communists and assisting in the revolutionizing and remodelling of the whole of society on the working-class pattern. The successful accomplishment of this historic task requires, above all, a revolutionary transformation of the practice of directing, which is the guiding and controlling activity of film-making.

To revolutionize directing means to completely eradicate from it all capitalist elements and all remaining dogmatism and to establish a new Juche-inspired system and methods of directing.

In establishing the new system and methods of directing it is particularly important to define the duties of the director clearly and continually enhance his role, in keeping with the intrinsic nature of socialist society and the character of revolutionary cinema.

The director is the commander of the creative group. He should carry overall responsibility for creative work, organization of production and ideological education and he should guide all the members of the creative team in the making of films.

The director's role in the socialist system of film-making is fundamentally different from that of the "director" in capitalist society. In the capitalist system of film-making the "director" carries that title, but in fact the right of supervision and control over film production is entirely in the hands of the tycoons of the film-making industry who have the money, whereas the directors are nothing but their agents.

In capitalist society the director is shackled by the reactionary governmental policy of commercializing the cinema and by the capitalists' money, so that he is a mere worker who obeys the will of the film-making industrialists whether he likes it or not. In socialist society, by contrast, the director is an independent and creative artist who is responsible for the quality of the cinema to the Party and the people. Therefore, in the socialist system of film-making, the director is not a mere worker who makes films but the commander, the chief who assumes full responsibility for everything, ranging from the film itself to the political and ideological life of those who take part in film-making.

The distinctive features of directing require that the director should be the commander of the creative group. In the cinema, which is a group form of art, directing is the art of harmonizing the creative efforts of all the artists to produce an integral representation of the theme.

Just as victory in battle depends on the commander's leadership ability, the fate of a film depends on the director's skill in the art of guidance. All the director's efforts to make a good film will prove unavailing unless he has the ability to direct the creative team in a coordinated way towards the realization of his creative plan. The film is conceived and completed by the director, but it cannot be created without the collective efforts and wisdom of the creative team. Success in film-making therefore depends on how well the director works with all the artists, technicians and production and supply personnel in the creative group.

If the director is to unify the ideology and purpose of the creative group and produce an excellent film of high ideological and artistic value, he must free himself once and for all from the shackles of the old domineering, bureaucratic system and methods of direction. Under this system the policy is one of director first and the relationship established within the creative group is that between a boss and his gang of workers: arbitrary decisions are made and creative workers are ordered about and commanded to produce results. If the director resorts to bureaucratic methods and suppresses or ignores the creative team, their ideological unity and cohesion of purpose—the very basis of collective creation—will be destroyed, and he will be deprived of the potential to create films and find himself bound hand and foot. Not only do the old system and methods of directing not conform to the intrinsic nature of our socialist system, in which the basis of social relations is the unity and cohesion of the popular masses, they also conflict with the collective nature of film-making and the intrinsic nature of directing itself.

In film-directing, the most important thing is to work well with the artists, technicians and production and supply personnel, who are directly involved in the process of film-making. This is the essential requirement of the system of directing inspired by the principle of Juche. This is our system of directing, under which the director becomes the commander of the creative group and pushes forward the creative work as a whole in a coordinated fashion, giving precedence to political work and laying major emphasis on working with the people who make films. This system embodies the fundamental features of the socialist system and the basic principle of the concept of Juche that man is the master of everything and his decisions govern everything. This system, therefore, is in full conformity with the collective nature of film-making and the distinctive features of directing.

Since a film is made through the joint efforts and shared wisdom of many people, every participant in the production process should play his role and fulfil his responsibilities like the master he is, and in order to achieve its joint creative assignments the collective should become firmly united in its ideology and will. This fundamental requirement deriving from the distinctive features of film-making can never be met by the old system of directing; it can only be properly met by the system which attaches fundamental importance to working with people, to working with the creative team.

Under the new system of directing, film-making becomes the work of the director himself as well as the joint work of the entire creative group, and both director and creative team assume the responsibility for the creative work. Therefore everybody is firmly committed to the work on a voluntary basis. Also, while the films are being made the director assists and guides all the members of the collective, and the creative staff learn from one another in the course of their work. Full scope is given to the expression of communist ethics in creative work and the revolutionary way of life. Thus everybody is knit closely together by a collectivist spirit and all pool their creative efforts in the attainment of the common objectives.

Under the new system of directing, the director is responsible not only for the creative work of the team but also for their political and ideological life. Therefore, he conducts regular political work and ideological education in close combination with their creative activities and therefore in the process of creative work they undergo revolutionary transformation and are assimilated to the working class.

In short, the system of directing based on working with people is not only in harmony with the intrinsic nature of film-making and directing, it also enables the director to extricate himself from the grip of domineering and bureaucratic tendencies and decisively improve his ability to guide creative work; it also enables him to eradicate any tendency towards the deviation of art for art's sake, which accords exclusive precedence to the act of artistic creation, and to advance significantly the creative value of his work and the revolutionary development of the collective.

The strength of the new system lies in the fact that it guarantees the firm unity and cohesion of the creative group on the basis of the concept of Juche, allowing free play to the awareness and creativity of all its members, and the depth at which the director guides the creative work and the life of the group results in an uninterrupted flow of innovation.

Under the new system the director should lay special emphasis on the artistic guidance of the creative workers.

The basic duty of the creative group is to create revolutionary films of high ideological and artistic value, which are effective contribution in equipping the people with the entire armoury of the Party's monolithic ideology and imbuing the whole of society with the great concept of Juche. Whether this duty is fulfilled in a timely and correct manner depends on the way the director works with the members of the creative team.

The creative workers are the central figures, the immediate executors of the revolutionary tasks devolving on their group. The director's plan is realized through the activity of these workers and every task relating to the creation of artistic images, which arises in the course of the work, is also carried out by them. The director should, therefore, work well with the creative workers and constantly strive to fulfil his role as their guide as best he can. The creative group will then be able to carry out the revolutionary tasks facing it successfully.

The first thing the director has to do with his creative team is to achieve a consensus of opinion concerning the production they are going to deal with. This is the initial guarantee of the success of their creative work, and the first element of the director's job. If each creative worker retains his own separate views on the production, the director will be unable to coordinate them in achieving the creation of a unified work of art and their creative activities will be thrown into turmoil from the outset.

The director must carefully analyse the general characteristics of the content and form of the production in hand, so that the creative workers are all able to understand it correctly and come to accept it.

The director should not be over-egotistical in his analysis and judgement of a production. Every artist has his own creative individuality and each may have different views of a production. If the director fails to take account of this, and clings to his own views, while ignoring the opinions of other creative workers, the establishment of a firm concensus on any production will be hindered.

The interpretation of a production should be clearly understood and assented to by everybody concerned; when the work has been accepted by everyone as their own, it will be carried out effectively.

The director must always clearly state his own opinions on a production and create an atmosphere of free discussion in which many different constructive opinions may be voiced. He must be sincere in his acceptance of the views of the creative workers. Once agreement has been reached in discussion, the director must act on it promptly, firmly basing the production on it and never deviating from it, no matter what happens. If the director vacillates, so will the whole collective, and if that happens, the production will fail.

When every member of the creative group has correctly grasped the basis of the production, the director must begin working with them individually.

Artistic guidance offered to individual creative workers must always be specific. If the director gives only general outline guidance, it will not be of any significant help to them, or inspire them with the confidence required to achieve his aims.

The director should take into account the distinctive features and requirements of a production in giving the creative workers their assignments in its realization and the ways and means of carrying them out. He should consult with them on any problems which they may encounter in the course of their work, so that his guidance may be appropriate to their situation.

Take, for example, the guidance of acting. An analysis should be made of the roles and relative positions of the characters to be represented by actors and actresses throughout the film, and also of their personalities. The direction of the acting should be founded on this basis, and the particular tasks of characterization and the methods of acting for each situation at every stage of the drama should be specifically taught. When the director's guidance is precise, then his plan will harmonize with the plan of the creative team and their work will proceed smoothly.

The most important aspect of the director's work in guiding the team's interpretation of a work is to assist them in developing a clear understanding of the seed of a production and representing it skilfully.

The ideological kernel of a production is the seed which the director and all the other creative workers must bring into flower through their collective wisdom and joint efforts. The seed is not only the basis of the artistic images to be created by individual creative workers, it is also the foundation on which they base all their cooperative efforts to produce a single cinematic art work. When all the elements of artistic interpretation are derived from a single seed, they become the components of a unified cinematic image, because they all share a common foundation, although the images created by different artists differ according to their different personalities. Therefore the director should take extreme care to avoid any member of the creative team losing his grasp of the seed or introducing into the production anything which is irrelevant to it.

Another aspect of the director's work which requires particular attention is to ensure effective creative interaction between the individual artists and to guide their teamwork correctly.

A comprehensive artistic representation of a theme cannot, by its very nature, be created effectively through the talents and efforts of individual artists. When every artist establishes a close working relationship with the others and contributes effectively to the work of the team, the various elements which go to make up the comprehensive artistic representation will harmonize well with each other.

The director should always be at the centre of the creative endeavour, providing a close link between the activities of the individual members of the creative team, and taking care to avoid any possible friction between them and any tendencies towards fragmentation into smaller groups.

The director must guide the artists in such a way that they will manifest a high degree of independence and initiative in the course of their creative work. Allowing free play to their independence and initiative is the most important means of heightening their sense of responsibility, of stimulating their creative energy and imagination. Successful creative collaboration between the director and the creative workers and amongst the workers themselves can only be achieved when each individual plays his own appointed part properly.

The director must be strict yet enlightened in his guidance of the creative workers. For their part, the creative workers have to accept and understand each of the director's plans and realise them in a creative manner. In offering his guidance, the director should therefore work on the principle of getting the creative workers in charge of particular aspects of the production to assume full responsibility for their own creative work. This is effective artistic guidance.

Original ideas created by the members of the film-making team should contribute to the perfection of the overall harmony of the comprehensive interpretation of the theme, while also serving to bring individual characterizations to life. The director must be talented enough to raise the level of artistic interpretation in all areas and allow the artistic originality to contribute to the overall harmony of the whole film. This is creation in the true sense of the word.

While encouraging the creative workers to express their originality, the director should not allow the harmony of the overall interpretation to be destroyed, nor should he have to suppress their originality in order to guarantee the harmony of the work.

As the commander of the creative group, the director should also work well with the production and supply personnel.

The director must take responsibility for the production of the film and must ensure that the work proceeds in a coordinated manner.

Film-making is a complex and extensive task in which progress is impossible without the support of flawlessly organized production work. The processes of creation and production are inseparably linked in film-making. If production is not well organized, then the smooth running of the whole process of creation and production is disrupted. Only when production is well organized is it possible to create an excellent film in a short period of time and with the minimum of manpower, funds and materials.

The proper organization of production is essential to the success of film-making. It coordinates and plans the movements of the creative group so that the various units in all areas are properly integrated and observe strict order and discipline, and it also provides for the rational use of materials and equipment by controlling finances and supplies. This is an important task which the director must control in a responsible manner.

The director should not deal with production workers, technicians and supply personnel in an administrative and technical manner, simply because the organization of production is administrative and technical in content. Administrative and technical methods of guidance are in conflict with the intrinsic nature of the Juche-inspired system of directing, they prevent production workers, technicians and supply personnel from becoming actively involved in the process of film-making. In his guidance of production organization the director should be sincere in working with the people involved.

One of the major responsibilities of the new type of director is that of ideological educator of the creative group. The director should assume responsibility for their political and ideological life and should constantly intensify their political and ideological education, in order to encourage them in the conscientious performance of their mission as revolutionary artists.

The creative team's unity of ideology and purpose is fundamental to the successful completion of a film. Even if the director has the talent and skill to fuse together the divergent artistic interpretations organically, this is not sufficient to ensure the production of a harmonious film. No production of high ideological and artistic value can evolve out of a creative group which is lacking in ideological unity, which has not established discipline and order.

The creative team's unity of ideology and purpose is not only essential for maintaining the consistency of a film as a whole, it is also vitally important in waging a campaign to speed up production, establishing a revolutionary spirit of creation and accelerating the revolutionary transformation of all personnel, and their assimilation to the working-class.

The ideological education of the creative team should be based on education in the Party's monolithic ideology. This work should always precede creative work and should be conducted energetically throughout the course of the campaign for genuinely creative work.

Ideological education by the director is intended to equip the creative team with a comprehensive understanding of the Party's lines and policies, so that better revolutionary films may be made more rapidly. When ideological education is combined with creative work in this way, tremendous vitality can be released and artists can be stimulated to overcome the challenges of creative work.

The director must maintain his grip on ideological education throughout the course of the team's creative work, and he must give absolute priority to political work at each stage of the creative process The new system of directing is only effective when the director gives absolute priority to political work in everything. The system becomes meaningless if the director neglects political work and continues to work in the old bureaucratic style.

Giving priority to political work and the constant raising of the creative staff's political awareness, so that they participate willingly in the work of film-making, is a practical application in this area of creative work of the fundamental requirements of our Party's traditional revolutionary method. The director should adhere closely to this revolutionary method of creative work. Whatever kind of work he produces, the director must thoroughly explain its ideological content and artistic features to all the creative personnel, and inform them fully of the production's purpose and significance, in order to stimulate them to greater revolutionary zeal in their creative work.

The director should take control of the work of the creative team and energetically conduct political work prior to all other work. Only then can he perform his role as artistic leader, production organizer and ideological educator in a satisfactory manner, and become the distinguished commander of the creative group.

IN CREATIVE WORK ONE MUST AIM HIGH

The director must have confidence in himself, he must set high aims and work boldly.

The director's self-confidence derives from his strong artistic opinions, and is based on his profound understanding and independent interpretation of life and the arts. His self-confidence also emanates from an elevated political awareness of his responsibility for the process of film-making and a strong conviction that through his artistic activities he serves the cause of the revolution.

If he is to succeed in his creative work, the director must bring strong personal opinions and a bold approach to his task. If the director, the commander of the creative group, has no strong opinions of his own, the group loses confidence in the production and cannot work well. A director who has strong opinions of his own, who has a lively imagination and works boldly, will be successful, but a director who is overcautious will never produce anything worthwhile.

To say that the director should set his sights high in his creative work means that he should set himself the objective of solving certain new and significant problems in the re-educating of the people and the development of society.

The director must base his approach in the great concept of Juche and work from his own understanding and opinions concerning life and the arts. Then he will always be able to set himself new and higher tasks in the creation of artistic images and be able to achieve them.

Self-confidence is based on knowledge. If a person is ignorant, and yet insists on his own point of view, he is merely being stubborn. The director gains confidence when he has fully mastered the concept of Juche and possesses extensive knowledge of life and the arts.

If the director has set himself a high standard in creative work and wishes to attain it, he must put forward an original idea at the initial, conceptual stage of his work.

The director's conception is the blueprint of the film which is to be made, his creative plan for the coordinated guidance of his whole team in the creation of a consistent interpretation of the theme. Just as the military commander in charge of an army must have a clearly defined operational plan, so must the director, as the commander of the film-making group. The fate of a film largely depends on the working-out of this plan.

The director's conception should be distinctive and original. Just as a new plan is required if a new house is to be built, so the director must have an original conception if he is to create an original film. No original work of cinematic art can be expected from a director who has no opinions of his own, who copies other people's ideas and conceives every production in a stereotyped manner. The essence of artistic creativity lies in the ability to find new subjects and explore the presentation of fresh images in a distinctive manner.

The director must introduce new subjects in his own distinctive manner.

Every effective artistic image is achieved through the creative individuality of the artist, and in literature and the arts life can only be depicted in this way. When making a film the director must adhere scrupulously to the script but not blindly, word for word, producing an unintellegent copy. A director who has no ideas of his own, beyond those expressed in the script, cannot create any works which are his own. Such a director cannot even create a correct copy of a literary work.

In order to adapt the presentation of the theme set out in the script to the characteristic requirements of film art, the director must possess a high level of creative energy and passionate enthusiasm. When the director launches into his quest with zeal and spirit, he is assured of finding a new image. He can only create something new, something of his own, when he consistently maintains a high level of creative enthusiasm, throughout the process which begins with the interpretation of life and literature and ends in the creation of realized characters.

A bold new creative idea can only come to fruition if it is based on real life. However talented a director may be, he cannot conceive a new and audacious cinematic work if he lacks a thorough knowledge of the Party's policies and a rich experience of life.

The director can produce nothing new if he sits in his study, mechanically attempting to produce a script from a literary work which was created by a writer who entered into the situations of real life and lived amongst the people. If after reading the literary work the director does not conduct a serious study of the conditions of real life and just wastes his time in his study, hoping that the writer will be able to create a perfect cinematic realization of the theme, he will encounter many problems in his subsequent work.

The director must base his creative work on his experience and understanding of life. He should store away in his mind his experience of every meaningful occurrences, of every dimension, from trifling details to stirring historic events. When he has accumulated an experience of life and is so consumed with passion that he simply has to describe it, his creative work will flow smoothly and become pleasant and rewarding.

If a writer has spent time together with the heroic workers of a steel plant and written a work based on their noble and creative work, then the director should also seek to experience their way of life.

Needless to say, the director cannot follow precisely the same sequence of creative work as the writer. He must form his own opinions and accumulate his own experience, taking careful note of each vivid image of the human beings who are building a new life. Only in this way will the director achieve a good understanding of the lives of the men described in the script and be able to find accurate and appropriate means of representing them and so establish his own independent creative viewpoint.

The correct analysis and understanding of the seed of the literary work is fundamental to the process by which the director establishes a fresh and distinctive plan of work.

In the creative process the seed not only constitutes the driving force which propels the director's creative work forward, it is also the practical foundation which determines the scope and orientation of his activity.

How to work out the plan and write the script, how to realize its portrayal on the screen, how to manage the creative work of individual artists—these are all problems which have to be solved by the director in accordance with the requirements of the seed. He cannot conceive any plan of creative work without considering the seed. Only when his understanding of the seed of the work is profound and secure can he draw up a bold plan of action and embark on the creation of a full-scale interpretation.

It is not easy to arrive at a correct understanding of the seed of a work and define its ideological and artistic value and significance accurately. However talented and well-versed in literature a director may be, simply reading a work through a few times will not allow him to fully understand its content or develop individual characterizations. He has to study the writer's works closely and systematically in order to develop an accurate understanding of his creative individuality. Only then, can he correctly understand the artistic images in the work. He must study the way of life depicted in the script and then carefully consider their interpretation. Only then, can he clearly understand the writer's intention and attitude.

When analysing a work an able director does not draw hasty conclusions, he is not impressed by a few outstanding points and overcome by the urge to improvize. Even if certain individual scenes are quite impressive, an able director will be concerned if the work as a whole appears vague and unconvincing. He is not delighted by the appeal and impact of individual scenes, but by the fact that the seed which the writers have planted with such devotion is clearly expressed and provides a vital impulse for creative work. The force of the passion he experiences when nurturing an excellent seed fuels his activity.

The director must treasure the seed of a work as his own artistic discovery and support it enthusiastically, concentrating all his efforts on encouraging its unique growth and bringing it to full flower.

The seed of the work is not abstract; it lives in the lives of the hero and the other characters. The unity of the elements of representation derived from the seed is always achieved through the portrayal of the characters surrounding the hero. Therefore, the director must correctly understand the individual features of the characters represented in the literary work and clearly define the tasks to be solved by them in their actions. In particular, he must set the hero firmly in the centre of the drama and closely arrange the actions of all the other characters around the hero's line of action.

A character's personality is the result of specific circumstances. In visualizing the living characters of his production the director should accurately determine the basic facts and events underlying these circumstances which have an archetypal significance and carefully select the appropriate details. However interesting events and details may be in themselves, if they are not representative and obstruct the realization of the characters as living individuals they must be boldly discarded.

At the stage of initial conception the director must also establish the genre and mood of the film correctly. If the director fails to perceive them in the structure of the seed, he will not be able to find the appropriate genre for the content or determine accurately the appropriate emotional tonality for the production.

When the characters have become clear in his conception, and the circumstances of their lives are clearly envisaged, the director should go on to visualize their relationships to various events through which conflicts are established and the plot develops, taking a clear view of the overall composition of the film. At the stage of conception, when the content of the production is defined and the narrative line is determined, the genre and mood of the film must be established in greater detail.

When the composition of the film has been finalized and the means and techniques of interpretation have been selected on the basis of the requirements of the seed, the director should be able to see the individual scenes and the overall flow of the film in his mind. If the film is to be original and distinctive the director's plan must express a new human problem and portray new people and their new life.

To develop a mature plan the director requires a lively, creative imagination. When he has imagination, he can set high standards and attain his goal.

In order to create original artistic images the director must have a diverse, rich and bold imagination. If he is making a film from a literary work, the director must have the imagination to adapt it to the cinema, the creative imagination to produce something original based on real life. Imagination is crucial in the adaptation of literary works for the screen, but if one relies on imagination alone, it will prove impossible to modify the script to enrich its expression of the theme. If in the process of developing his creative imagination the director discovers aspects of life which the writer has failed to depict, the presentation of the theme will be enriched.

Creative imagination must always be based on real life. The director cannot depict life truthfully if he produces an absurd work which is divorced from life, or if he is engrossed in inventing spectacular scenes which are devoid of all intrinsic significance.

A debate once took place on the problem of filming the story of an ancient general who had repulsed foreign invaders. One director said that he would produce a wonderful portrayal of that heroic national resistance if only he was given 500 horses. Acclaiming the director's imagination as rich and bold, some people even envied him. But is this really rich and bold artistic imagination? What would happen if one started making films, excited by the idea of a spectacular panorama in which 500 horses charge like a hurricane over a wide expanse of fields and thunderous cheers are heard above a forest of glittering spears?

A film director who does not see the essential content of life and considers that only the genre and scale of the work are important cannot be successful. Before imagining the 500 horses, the director should have pictured the gallant people who rose up against foreign aggressors and should have planned a vivid depiction of their heroic struggle.

There should be no hasty improvisations in the process of artistic creation. Improvisation leads to error. In creative work it is impossible to ignore the momentary impact of a strong emotion and the image which springs from it, but careful and deliberate consideration is necessary before including it as a link in the chain of development of the overall conception. Improvisation is especially taboo for the director who commands the creative group. If he is carried away by emotional impulses and starts introducing random changes in questions of creative work which have already been agreed by the group, that work will be thrown into irretrievable confusion and the production will be marred.

The idea of the work which has matured at the stage of conception should be specifically stated in the director's script.

The director must not hastily attempt to write down the script as soon as his conception has begun to mature. However hard he may have worked on the conception, he must subject it to careful review. He must carefully examine whether the seed has been precisely planted, whether the character portrayals are distinctive, whether real life is truthfully reflected, whether the fabric of the story is woven in a cinematic manner, and whether the sequence of scenes is smooth and holds the viewer's attention. In brief, he must check thoroughly to make sure that the cinematic realization of the work achieved at the stage of conception has been clearly defined.

The director can only transcribe the conception into his script when his perception of it is clear, both logically and emotionally. The director's script is the blueprint of the film, in which the cinematic depiction formed at the stage of conception is realized in words. It is the director's initial creation.

In preparing this script it is better to combine the efforts and wisdom of many creative workers, such as cameramen, art designers, composers and assistant directors, than to leave it to the director's unaided efforts. However distinguished a director may be, he cannot match the combined efforts and wisdom of the collective. Since this script is to be transformed into a film by the teamwork of all the creative workers, the combination of their efforts and wisdom from the very beginning has many advantages. Only when the film depicted in the director's script comes to life as a single, unified image in the minds of all the creative workers, can the intentions of the director be reflected accurately on the screen.

The director must be confident of his abilities and perform the work of artistic creation boldly and thoroughly, moving from the study of life and the literary work to the conception, from the conception to the script, and from the script to shooting. Only in this way can he be assured of attaining a high artistic level.

THE DIRECTOR SHOULD CLEARLY DEFINE EMOTIONS

Seeing a film once is different from seeing it a second time There are some films one would like to see again, and others one would not. A certain film may awaken fresh interest, and excite greater passion and warmth each time one sees it. This sort of film may be called sincere art.

If a film is to move the audience through an effective interpretation of the theme, the dramatic content must be well organized, and the outline of the emotional content is fundamental to this dramatic organization.

In the past, emphasis was placed only on the plot since its organization was regarded as the basis of dramatic organization. Therefore, there was a widespread formalistic tendency to subordinate real life to drama for its own sake, catering for the lowbrows by the use of incidents, instead of providing insight into human ideas and feelings by means of their correct depiction.

The organization of the plot is always intended to lay the foundation of life which links together the relationships of the characters and conditions their behaviour. Their lines of action should be determined in accordance with this organization, and the sequence of feelings manifested through their actions should be revealed in such a way as to express the ideas that lie behind their emotions. Only in this way can the interpretation of a work be made effective.

The delineation of emotions is a means of conveying the essence of a character, by unfolding its emotional world naturally through a logical sequence of tension and relaxation, buildup and climax.

Intrinsic human nature requires the effective delineation of emotional content to be the central task of depiction in the arts. Ideas and emotions are both aspects of man's inner life. Without emotions, therefore, it is impossible to express the substance of a character's innermost thoughts and depict human nature accurately. The unity of ideas and emotions is an essential feature of artistic representation. In the arts, an idea divorced from emotions is an abstraction which can only produce a sterile conception. Only an idea which has been revealed through the flow of emotions can tug at people's heartstrings and make a deep impression on them.

When the emotions are carefully delineated, every person appearing on the screen comes to life and gives the impression of being real. When the audience see people who are true-to-life on the screen, they forget that they are watching a film and are drawn into the story which is being presented. They internalize the ideas and emotions of the characters and assimilate the idea presented in the production as their own. Only an idea which has won their approval through experience will be implanted deep in their minds: only an idea which has been absorbed from vividly depicted scenes will create a profound impression and remain engraved in their memories. This is why we say that the more clearly the emotions are delineated, the more profound will be the audience's response to them.

The clear delineation of emotions contributes fundamentally to the enhancement of a film's characterizations. The way in which emotions are described can determine the kind of impression a film makes and the artistic quality of its depiction of life.

The delineation of the emotions in work of art should be realized in accordance both with the personalities of the characters and general logic.

The major stimulus to people's emotional response is life itself.

Human emotions emerge from life, find expression in life and affect life. Various feelings, such as joy and sorrow, which are experienced by every person, result from the relationship between the person and the situation. Human emotions cannot exist outside of real life. Accordingly, the delineation of the emotions in drama is only clear and accurate when it accords with the logic of life.

Emotions are based in reality itself, but they only mature as a person reacts to it. The fact that reality is the basis of emotions and that emotions are a particular mode of reflection of life does not mean that every aspect of life rouses the emotions. Moreover, the same object inspires diverse emotions in different people and each person is moved to a different extent. Therefore, emotions can only be perceived as genuine when they are structured in accordance with the logic of the human character and of life itself.

If the delineation of emotions is to accord with the logic of life and of human character, the first requirement is to penetrate people's inmost thoughts and feelings and understand correctly what arouses and colours their emotions.

If the director embarks on a descriptive work having made only a superficial study of the characters who appear in the literary original, he is liable to overlook a whole range of specific, diverse and subtle human feelings.

The stimuli and the shades of emotion experienced differ according to the personality of the characters and the situations they find themselves in. Moreover, their diverse emotions are not only unfolded in the process of life's change and development; they are also interwoven in various ways even within a single situation; if the emotional state of the characters is not thoroughly elaborated, it is impossible to gain a precise understanding of the nuances of emotional development.

In the film "The Flower Girl", when Ggot Bun is on the point of dying, she is overjoyed to meet her brother whom she has only ever dreamt of seeing again. However, her heart is torn at the thought of her mother, who has died without seeing the brother again. Ggot Bun's joy is mixed with grief; her emotions indicate a mental state beyond the power of words to describe, as she is gripped by a feeling of reproach for her brother who has returned too late and an overwhelming longing for her dead mother. At the same time Ggot Bun's emotions are fused with her hatred for the cruel world which treats her so harshly that she sheds bitter tears.

According to the particular situation in which the character finds himself and his own experience, diverse shades of feeling are interwoven and one shade replaces another within the space of a single moment. In real life, it is not uncommon for joy to change to sorrow and sorrow to hatred in this way.

Thus various emotional shades emerge and mix, one replacing another according to the specific situations in which a man finds himself, and his experience. As time passes, emotions may change; the rousing is replaced by the sentimental and the joyful by the sad. This means that in order to delineate emotions precisely the director must be able to recognize the various emotional changes brought about by changes in life and in the characters and to discern the shifting shades accurately.

The director must be sensitive enough to understand any emotional change and distinguish the delicate shades correctly. He must explore every emotion in depth. Therefore, he must have the sensitivity to feel delicate and varied shades of emotion and the ability to explore every single emotion fully, overlooking nothing.

To delineate emotions in a realistic way it is important to build up emotions in accordance with the characters' personalities and the logic of life and in this way bring them to a climax.

The strength of the emotions must be built up and there has to be a motive for their coming to a head. In the final analysis even improvisation may be used, on the basis of appropriate personal experience. A natural effect is achieved in drama when the emotions of the characters are carefully built up and then brought to a head by a specific motive. Emotions which come to a head without any buildup or motive are either unnatural or false.

The force of the characters' emotions should build up as the drama develops and the motive for the emotions to be expressed has to be supplied at precisely the right moment. If the buildup is excessively prolonged, the emotional current is weakened and the film becomes boring.

Tension in the development of emotions is always related to a crucial moment which determines the character's action. The feelings must be continually built up until the decisive moment for action is reached and they can be brought to a head. Only in this way is it possible to generate powerful dramatic tension and emotional excitement. If the emotions which have been building up do not come to a head at the right moment, they will fail to make any impression on the audience, because they will lack credibility.

If the scene is hastily changed following the emotional climax, merely to allow for the introduction of the next scene, the emotion will be dissipated and the flow of the film will be interrupted and deadened. In drama, the emotional climax must linger in the imagination. This effectively prolongs the emotional arousal of the audience and gives them a sense of security. It is the emotions, not the actions, which make a lasting impact. In a film an emotional pause is introduced following a specific incident in order to produce a stronger and more lasting effect on the audience.

This lasting emotional impact forces the audience to reflect seriously, keeping the image of the film fresh in their minds for a long time. The director should skilfully create an emotional ambience by the use of various descriptive methods and then guide it on to the expression of the next emotion so that the audience try to anticipate the next scene.

An appropriate precondition drawn from real life is essential in preparing the escalation of emotions. In the presence of such a pre-condition, an emotion emerges naturally. A merely logical connection of incidents does not bring about the buildup of emotions. When the flow of emotions formed in the change and development of life is consistently maintained, an emotion can develop and accumulate strength gradually moving towards a climax.

The moment of emotional climax should not be defined merely for the sake of creating the maximum of tension or amusement, with the main emphasis being placed on the events. It must be determined so as to give the most emphatic expression to the unfolding of the drama and ensure its ideological depth.

The delineation of emotions is not merely intended to create tension in the audience or amuse them, but to amplify the ideological and emotional impact of a film. The delineation of emotions is meaningless if it makes no ideological impression on the audience. Emotional scenes in a film have to be subordinated to the profound emotional expression of the idea of the production.

In the arts the process of emergence of a new emotion must be very clearly portrayed and closely combined with the process through which a revolutionary view of the world is created and developed. In the process of establishing their revolutionary view of the world, people not only form a correct impression of the nature of life and the will to struggle, they also enrich and enlarge their emotional experience.

The director should effectively demonstrate in precise detail how a person's revolutionary awareness and emotions are formed and developed and how they relate to each other.

The film "Sea of Blood" clearly portrays the radical changes which occur in the mother's ideological awareness and emotional state as life changes and develops. A number of emotions are interwoven until the mother, having lost her husband, arrives at the village of Pyoljae with her children. Her strongest emotions are grief over the death of her husband and anxiety for the future of her fatherless children. But when she encounters the old man in the village, and learns about the General's Star over Mt. Paekdu, there is a change in her state of ideological awareness, which brings about an alteration in her emotional state. The mother, who had been engrossed in her grief, now begins to place her hopes in the advent of a new world, and having become friends with an underground guerrilla fighter, she is fired with enthusiasm for revolutionary ideology and enters an entirely new emotional state.

The fluctuations of the emotions should be depicted accurately as ideological awareness changes and develops. In this way it is possible to construct a sequence of emotions in keeping with the characters and the logic of life and to express in effective emotional terms the process by which people's revolutionary world outlook is created.

In direction for the cinema, while the diverse emotional shades engendering different feelings in different persons, according to the context of their lives, must be maintained, secondary lines of emotional development must always be subordinated to the main theme. Needless to say, this main theme is the hero's line of emotional development, which plays the dominant role in expounding the theme and idea of the work.

There are many different emotional shades in the life of any individual. In relationships between different people, each with a different personality, the emotional entanglement produces an even wider range. The more complicated the scene, the more closely the main emotional line should be adhered to, and the greater attention should be given to an unequivocal depiction of the process of its development. This makes it possible to achieve a satisfactory unity of emotions and harmony of interpretation.

One cannot and must not explore the emotions of all the characters to the same extent on the grounds that their emotional world should also be described in depth. If one attempts to do so, it becomes impossible to maintain anyone's emotional line adequately, and the relationship between the main line and secondary ones becomes blurred, so that the impact of the theme of the story is deadened and the harmonious sequence of the emotions is disrupted.

In any scene the audience can only orient itself securely to the main theme of the drama when attention is focussed on the main character's emotional line and emphasis is placed on arousing the central emotion, into which the emotional lines of the other characters are channelled in a natural manner.

If the emotions are to be delineated in depth, they must be controlled by the character's unfolding destiny.

People undergo their most profound experiences when their destiny is at stake, or is being decided and in consequence, their emotional state becomes extremely sensitive. In revolutionary films, in particular, the destiny of the heroes is linked with the future of the revolution, the country and the people, which makes their experience and the emotions which it arouses all the more critical and sensitive. The significance of an incident and its drama are highlighted when it is linked with the destiny of the characters. The development of the plot constitutes the realistic basis of the dramatic structure, and the foundation of the delineation of emotional content, but it only acquires truth and significance when it is absolutely subordinated to the elaboration of the character's destiny.

It is essential, therefore, to explore in detail the incidents which change the destiny of the characters, and minutely depict their emotional state at every moment. In this way the emotional flow is intensified.

In a film emotions should be portrayed in such a way that they capture the hearts of the audience from the very first scene.

If the first scene is awkward, the initial dramatic development of the film will fail to involve the audience, and the emotional structure of the entire drama will be slackened. The dramatic relations of the characters are not fully revealed in the first scene, nor is the story of their lives fully developed. Therefore, the main problem can only be suggested when the emotions have been defined, and the interests of the characters have been made absolutely clear.

Dramatic entanglements formed at the beginning of the story lead inevitably to conflict in the main scenes, and the ideas and emotions of the characters find sharp expression in this conflict. Therefore, in the main scenes of the drama's development the delineation of emotions should be based on the relationship between the two main conflicting forces. The struggle between the two forces as they each try to realize their respective aspirations generates the dramatic tension and relaxation, which stimulate the audience's interest and anticipation as they move towards the climax.

It is important to depict the emotions skilfully in the main scenes, particularly at the climax, when all the characters reveal their true nature and act decisively, in a determined and focussed manner. The climax finally reveals what the real objectives and aspirations of the two forces have always been, the road which life should follow, and how it has been developing so far. The climax is therefore the most important scene both in terms of its ideological significance and the intensity of its dramatic tension. The climax should deal only with the main conflict and main event and their effect on the main characters: the emotions should be depicted in a way which fully explains the main idea of the drama.

In the final scene the conflict is resolved, the idea of the film is fully explained and a clear answer is given to the main problem which has been raised. So, the screen should be filled with the emotions aroused in the hero by his triumph. This is the only way to present the idea of the production really succinctly, through the victory of a single emotion, the emotion which confirms the victory of the good.

In depicting the emotions of the characters the director must bring their inner world to life by making full use of every element and means of interpretation to focus attention on their emotional development.

People are deeply moved only when the emotional development of a film proceeds smoothly, harmoniously combining the various elements of the work in accordance with the characters' emotional development.

THE QUALITY OF ACTING DEPENDS ON THE DIRECTOR

In any job of work the first thing to do is to identify the main knot in the whole string and make a special effort to untie it, thereby making it easier to unravel the other knots and carry the whole job forward successfully. This applies equally to the creative work of the film director.

Having completed his literary discussion with the writer, the director has many other tasks to go through with the cameramen, art designers, composers, actors and the various other members of the creative team. However, the director cannot possibly perform all this work simultaneously, still less is he able to do it without some order of priority. He must first grasp the main knot and concentrate his efforts on untying it in order to speed up his creative work as a whole. This is the only way he can succeed.

Work with the actors is the central element of the director's creative activities.

The actor is the real creator of a human character: he stands at the centre of the cinematic interpretation. It is only through the actor that the director is able to portray the human character set out in the script as a live character on the screen. It is the actor who creates the true portrayal of a character which moves the audience.

As he directs the creative work of all the artists towards the single task of a unified portrayal the director lays great emphasis on the efforts of the actors. Control of the actors' creative work is the director's only means of stimulating the general process of creative endeavour and raising the level of the cinematic representation of the theme. Experienced directors therefore always give priority to choosing the actors and concentrate on guiding their acting.

The starting point in work with the actors is the selection of those amongst them who are suited to the personalities of the characters. Even if the character depicted in the script is clearly defined, and the actor has good acting ability, and the director gives him meticulous guidance, a successful portrayal can hardly be expected if the actor who has been chosen is not suited to the character.

It is true that actors should be prepared to portray any character at any time, but since each of them has his or her own creative individuality, they may be well-suited to one character but not to another. The more similar the actor is to the character he is playing, the faster and more easily is their unity achieved. If there is no similarity, no amount of effort and enthusiasm will suffice to perform the part successfully.

However, it does not require a great deal of effort to find a "suitable actor". The actor who fits a part 100 per cent is one in a hundred or in a thousand, or even more. In the final analysis, a director who pins his hopes on finding a "suitable actor" is taking a gamble in his creative work. And no director who relies on luck in creative work has ever achieved real success.

Choosing an actor suited to a part means finding one who has the ideological and artistic qualities and the physical characteristics required to play the part. The director must not, therefore, shape a character to suit the actor, but select an actor to fit the part.

In portraying a character, the actor always starts from within himself, but the selection of the actor by the director should always be based on the character. This is a realistic way to bring the personality of the character to life and enhance the ideological and artistic quality of a production.

In order to select an actor, the director must have a profound understanding of every aspect of the character's personality. He must examine the actors against this personality and not against external appearance. An actor may physically resemble the character he is to play, but if he is spiritually and morally inferior to the character, then he is inadequate for the part. An actor may not look exactly right for the part, but if he has the ideological and artistic ability to portray the character's spiritual and moral qualities, there is little cause for concern. Makeup can help to alter the appearance of the actor to match the character.

In selecting an actor, one must pay close attention to every aspect of his personality and also accurately assess his political and ideological life and his level of artistry. Since his political and ideological preparedness and his artistry are reflected in his daily life and creative activities, the director should study all of the actor's creative work and subject the social, political, cultural and moral aspects of his life to close and regular examination.

In his assessment of an actor, the director must not be enthralled by a couple of skills he may possess and overlook more important aspects of his personality. The actor must be ideologically well prepared before he can acquire high-level skills. The director should therefore acquaint himself closely with the actor's artistic qualities on the basis of a profound understanding of his ideological preparedness. Through this overall study of the actor's creative work and the social, political, cultural and moral aspects of his life, the director can get to know all of his qualities—his ideological preparedness, his views on life and the arts, his creative individuality, and his merits and failings as an actor.

When the director has learnt everything about every aspect of an actor's personality through studying his daily life and creative work, he is able to picture the face of the right actor while he is studying the personality of a character in the script, and he can decide how to work creatively with him.

In the process of selection, the director should not merely consider a few well-known actors. He should consider many others as well, and he should pay particular attention to new actors. This is essential if he is to make the best possible choice, create fresh and distinctive characterizations and extend his experience in the guidance of acting.

The director must be particularly careful not simply to use actors who have been trained by others, but should be bold in placing his faith in new actors and training them himself. One of the director's basic duties is to discover and train a large number of new actors.

The selection of suitable actors is only the beginning of the director's work with them. Even when he has chosen a good actor, he is bound to fail if that actor cannot represent the personality of the character truthfully. The director should choose good actors, but he must work all the harder to guide them in their creative work.

The portrayal of a person on the screen begins and ends with the actor, but acting itself largely depends upon the guidance of the director. However talented and experienced he is, an actor can scarcely be successful if the director does not give him proper guidance in his acting. On the other hand, even new actors may achieve good results if they are given meticulous guidance.

It is the director alone who guides the actors and judges whether they are portraying their parts correctly. Just as a man looks into the mirror when he is making himself presentable, the actor can accurately gauge how well he is acting and can improve his skills by consulting the director.

The actor creates his portrayal of a person independently; but in a film he cannot complete the task without the director. In the theatre the quality of the player's acting is always reflected in the immediate response of the audience, but in films, the player's acting can only be perfected through the efforts of the director. The director therefore has to offer the actor meticulous guidance from the start of shooting throughout all the subsequent stages, until his best possible performance has been captured on film.

Above all, the director must provide the actor with the stimulus he needs to create the character. The actor needs practical motivation, which will push him on and lead him to higher creative achievement. The road he has to travel with the character he is portraying is not a smooth one. The action in each scene is a link in the character's long course of life, it reflects his present life as well as his past, and offers an insight into his future. The actor must be powerfully motivated if he is to identify with the character and attain the creative goal of his portrayal.

The actor must seek powerful motivation to play his part in a full understanding of the seed of the production and a profound exploration of the life of the character. Whatever role the actor may be playing, the goal of his acting and the specific purpose of the action can only be made clear and convincing if he has completely understood the seed of the production and the life of his character.

Since the seed which exists in the characters' lives is only revealed through their action, the director must teach the actors to understand both the seed of the production and the personality of the characters, and make perfectly clear to them the parts their characters play in unfolding the potentialities of the seed. Although the production's seed is the ideological kernel of life, he must not try to convince the actors of its correctness on the theoretical level. Just as the director himself has become convinced through his own experience and ideological response, so must the actors be made to understand the seed and grant it emotional credence as a seed of real life.

The director must lead the actors to an understanding and acceptance of the content of the production and then ensure that they are perfectly in harmony with the characters, and capable of giving a natural performance.

If the actor does not completely accept the ideas and emotions of the character as his own, he may possibly imitate the words and the actions, but he cannot create a real person who is true to life. This living person can only be created when the actor is completely at one with his character, that is, only when he lives and behaves as the character would do.

The most important factor in the integration of actor and character in the performance is the actor's profound and detailed understanding of the character. His real experience of life is also important in enabling him to speak and act and live like the person he is to portray.

The director must guide all the actors as they enter into the world of the production and develop a precise understanding of the personalities of their characters, and he should ensure that they are genuinely responsive to the characters' ideas and emotions and accept them as their own, that they impart life to the characters' personalities through their own unique individuality. The director must also ensure that the actors believe in the characters' lives as their own and behave naturally as the characters would do.

This response to the characters' lives and belief in them are only evident when actors enter the state of feeling as the characters would. The director should therefore know how to lead actors into this state naturally through the experience of the characters. He must not, under any circumstances, attempt to force them into feeling as the characters would. In persuading the actors to enter the characters' world of their own accord, the director has to make them believe in the situation and the atmosphere. Then the actors can make themselves part of the action taking place on the screen and speak and act like the people they are playing.

If the actor and the character are to be fused into an integrated characterization, it is important to maintain the consistency of the player's acting throughout the film. He may act very well in certain scenes, but if his acting is not consistent, then the character he is creating will, in the final analysis, fail to come to life as a person motivated by his own ideas and convictions and will become a capricious, unstable personality.

In contrast with the stage actor, who takes part in each scene in sequence according to the plot, the film actor has to act in fragments which are frequently out of sequence because of the complexities of film-making. Under these circumstances, it is not easy for the film actor to ensure the consistency and integrity of his acting. This can only be achieved in the cinema when the acting in each scene is effectively guided by the director, who plans the general orientation of the characterizations, the tasks to be achieved in each scene, and the actors' overall goals.

Acting must be guided in an enlightened manner, using a method which continually develops the independence and creativity of the actor in order to enable him to portray characters independently. This method is based on the idea that the actor himself—and no one else—is master of the art of character portrayal.

This method is only effective when exacting demands are made on the actor, while he is patiently assisted to identify the essential issues.

Although the actor has to be taught and assisted to progress, the director must not meddle in matters which the actor should manage by himself or try to teach him more than necessary. If the director tries to teach the actor everything, it will bind him hand and foot, and the actor's independence and creativity will be suppressed as a result. The method described here does not allow the director either to interfere unnecessarily in the acting, or to leave everything to the actor, without imposing strong demands on him.

The essence of directing is guiding the actors' performance. If the director is to do this properly, he should set the actors high objectives and guide them in solving the problems of portrayal correctly.

It is important for a director who is teaching an actor to develop in him a high degree of political awareness of his responsibility as creative artist. The director has to guide the actor in such a way as to enhance his awareness, at all stages of creative activity, of the responsibility and initiative he must display in fulfilling the mission assigned to him by the Party and the revolution.

The enlightened method of guiding acting achieves its best results when it is applied on the express basis of specific instances drawn from real life.

The actor's creative work in understanding and portraying the personality of his character is a process of exploring the character's life and giving expression to the various features of his personality. The director cannot, therefore, stimulate the actor's ideas and emotions solely by logical explanation, which cannot lead him to a natural portrayal of the character. In the guidance of acting, the director should always explain life through the expression of feeling and attitude. This immediately allows the actor to picture the life of the character and depict it on the screen as it is, to express the character's life accurately in his acting.

In order to produce a good film a director must work well with the actors from the time of their selection, and throughout his guidance of their acting.

EXACTING STANDARDS SHOULD BE SET IN FILMING AND ART DESIGN

A film's images must look good on the screen. The cinema is a visual art, and when the images are attractive to look at, they can instantly draw people into the world of the film so that they remember the idea of the production and the vivid images created on the screen for a long time afterwards.

If the visual construction of images in a film is not good, the production will fail to come to life however well the actors may perform and however fine the songs and music may be. The actor's characterization is only seen on the screen, and so is the work of the artists. If it is all to be successful the presentation on the screen must be well organized.

It is impossible to correct anything once it has been captured on film. A theatrical production can be constantly polished even in the course of the actual performance. In the cinema, however, it is impossible to delete or correct anything which has already been filmed. Re-shooting a scene because of its poor visual construction is a waste of film, manpower and time, and sows confusion in the complicated process of film-making.

When making a film, the director must make a special effort from the outset to create visual images of the highest quality. He must draw up an accurate plan, before he works out the details with the cameraman and the art director.

In a film, the images appearing on the screen are specifically created by the cameraman and the art director.

The visual quality of the film depends primarily on how well the director works with the art director. Defects in art design cannot be rectified during shooting. Work with the art director is the first step in realizing the director's conception as a work of cinematic art. The screen interpretation conceived and noted down by the director finds its first visual expression in his work with the art director.

Before starting work with the art director, the director must make sure that he can meet all the requirements of the script and see what needs to be added to the written interpretation. When the art director's individual creative contribution has been assessed and his work is clearly pictured in the director's imagination, then consideration must be given to the relationship between the script and the design and the relationship between the design and other forms of dramatic expression. Every scene in the film has to be examined in the context of the other forms of dramatic expression such as acting, framing of shots and music, before it is possible to decide correctly whether the art director is able to provide an accurate visual expression of the work of cinematic art.

In his initial discussions with the art director, the director should convey the literary content by expressing it in vivid images, rather than by showing him a plan which has already been prepared. When the art director has submitted a draft plan they should exchange views and come to an agreement on the conception of the work, which makes it possible to finalise the screen interpretation without any hitches. Active guidance offered to the art director in this process, in order to draw out his creative individuality, is extremely important in giving the screen interpretation a distinctive life of its own.

The director must render the art director every possible assistance in bringing his conception to maturity and maintaining the vitality of his individual creativity. He must also ensure that the art design's interpretation of the conception harmonizes with the other interpretations.

The art director's enthusiasm and talent must be fused with the energies of all the other creative artists, but their unification with the efforts of the group of actors is particularly important for the achievement of good results.

As the actor stands at the very centre of the creative process in cinematic art, the director should see to it that the art director respects the actors' intentions and takes account of them in his own creative work. The actors should thus be brought to regard the faces of characters drawn by the art director, and their costumes, as their own, and, furthermore, they should familiarize themselves with the sets, the props and even the decorative elements used in various scenes and live in the specific world that they make up. In this way the character portrayed by the actor can be united with the character depicted in the art design.

In his work with the art director, the director must ensure that the artist is not distracted by anything which is not strictly connected with the screenplay's interpretation of the director's conception. If the art director strives for effect simply in order to please himself, the actor will be constrained in his acting and the general atmosphere will be disrupted. The art design must be in keeping with the characters' personalities, the environment and general atmosphere, thus supporting the acting and enhancing the overall harmony of the film's portrayal of events.

The fundamental problem in the joint work of director and art director is the accurate depiction of the period concerned and the general character of the people portrayed.

In one film about the life of a female shop assistant, the heroine was made to change her clothes a number of times for no particular reason, and in another film about life during the Fatherland Liberation War, the barracks of the US imperialist troops of aggression and the south Korean puppet army were shown as being too luxurious. These may seem to be trifles, but they are distortions of the truth, which undermine the realism of the production and, furthermore, have an adverse effect on people's education.

The director must consider whether each design produced by the art director accurately reflects the period and the situation, correctly reveals the social and class essence of human nature, and establishes a truthful visual harmony between the character and his environment; he should also guide the art director's creative work in the right direction by making ever greater demands on his designs.

In his work with the art director, the director should also take into account the technical requirements of the film. However excellent it may be, a visual design cannot be filmed if it does not meet these technical requirements adequately. Once the art director has clearly defined the main line of the film's visual interpretation, the technical requirements must be decided upon without delay. This procedure will improve the quality of the design, while at the same time satisfying the technical requirements.

In the creation of the film's visual images, the director is primarily assisted by the cameraman, as well as the art director.

The cameraman is the creator of images, the one who assesses actor's characterization and the art design to be projected onto the screen with a cinematic eye and finally captures them on film.

The director's work with the cameraman is a major process, completing the creation of the work of screen art. For a film to be successful the framing of the visual image must be well done.

The film as visualized by the director is transferred to the screen by the cameraman. Even if there is a fine script and the acting is flawless, the whole project will fail if the film is not shot well. It may be said that skill can introduce certain improvements in the stages which follow filming, but nothing can be done about scenes which have been missed or badly shot.

The director must work closely with the cameraman from the time when he prepares his script, selects his actors and inspects the locations for shooting. In the course of this work the director must help the cameraman to appreciate the idea of the film and conceive an appropriate and original screen interpretation, embodying both parties' conceptions. The cameraman can only reflect the director's intentions in the shooting script when he has come to appreciate the idea of the production and assimilated and digested the literary narrative and directorial conception.

The joint work of the director and the cameraman should be at its most intense in the drawing and shooting of scenes. The director's conception and the cameraman's fuse in a specific depiction of life in the scene drawings. The perfect union of the director's and cameraman's conceptions is achieved in a scene, which can be regarded as the joint creation of the two artists.

At the filming stage the director must guide the cameraman to define and highlight the most important features, so that the camera's interpretation vividly expresses the ideological content of the production. Filming which fails to do this is merely pleasing to the eye. It is the director's talent which ensures the expression of excellent ideological content through the images on the screen.

This pictorial expression of the ideological content of the work requires a focus on the essential content of the image, instead of a simple search for visually effective shots. The ideological content of the production is to be found in the way the characters are played, and it is expressed through their actions. It is therefore essential in filming to achieve an accurate screen portrayal of the characters and their lives, in particular, of the hero and his life. A scene which does not contain a full picture of life cannot express a profound idea.

The director must make sure that the scenes contain only the essentials; the effective depiction of the hero and his life must be the determining factor in deciding all matters related to shooting, such as where the camera is to be placed and how the object is to be viewed, from which angle and from what distance.

Cinema's ability to make unfettered use of time and space allows it to depict life in rich and varied ways. But it is not easy to fill the limited space of the screen with a rich and complex image showing only the essentials. The director should ensure that while focusing attention on the portrayal of the character, the cameraman views him in different ways from different angles and that the camera moves in order to reveal his actions in detail.

The camera should also depict life from different angles. Both the background and the events involving the main characters in the foreground must be shown. The background complements and emphasizes the foreground, while widening the scope of the image on the screen and maintaining its spatial depth. The director must be particularly careful to use free movements of the camera to show life in a varied fashion from different viewpoints, even within a single scene.

In order to enhance the pictorial quality of the scene the director should guide the cameraman to an expressive and correct depiction of the scene's content. When the scene is well structured visually, the ideological content can be effectively portrayed.

Perspective and harmony are important in enhancing the visual quality of a scene. Everyone appreciates the harmony of form and perspective which constitute the beauty of an object.

In order to achieve the artistic visual effect which he requires, the director should get the cameraman to maintain the scene's perspective by the skilful application of various means of depiction, and should see to it that the art director and the cameraman create a harmonious screen interpretation through good teamwork. The harmony of a cinematic image can only be achieved through the complete fusion of the art designs and the camera shots.

From the very start of the process until the film is shot, the director should assist the cameraman and the art director in the creation of a fine piece of cinematic art by effectively ensuring their creative collaboration.

THE BEST POSSIBLE USE SHOULD BE MADE OF MUSIC AND SOUND

Sound is part of people's experience of any situation, and music is part of life. Sound and music are heard wherever nature works and man lives.

A film which has no music and sound is deprived of vibrant life and, if there is no vibrant life, there can be no true representation of the theme.

In a film which gives an accurate picture of the way in which people see and hear things, music and sound are important ways of depicting, more clearly and precisely, man's inmost thoughts and feelings, his way of life. They also add an emotional dimension to the ideological content. Music and sounds which are appropriate to the situation and express profound meaning make a tremendous contribution to the ideological and artistic value of a film.

The director has to work well with the composer and the sound technicians and engineers to ensure that the simplest melody, song or sound contributes to a clear picture of life and inspires profound emotions in those who hear it.

The first condition for music to fulfil its potential in a film is for the composer to produce a good piece; but the director should also have a good knowledge of music and be able to use it appropriately in the film. If he knows a great deal about music he is able at the planning stage to consider what music should be used in each scene, he may have a good idea of its content and form and even the ways in which it will be used. Furthermore, he can take the initiative in working with the composer, if he has a definite plan for the structure of the musical score.

In working with the composer, the director must ensure that the composer has a correct understanding of the production and that he responds enthusiastically to the ideological content. If this is the case, the composer is able to enter into the world of the film and draw from it a creative stimulus, on the basis of which he can create a musical score appropriate to each scene. The director must therefore be enthusiastic in guiding his work on the production.

The director must check that the composer's musical conception accurately reflects the requirements of the production, and that it conforms with his own intentions regarding the score. He must reach agreement with the composer on every question, such as the theme, the nature of the melody, the structure of the music and how it should be used. He can thus fulfil his plan for the direction of the film precisely.

It is extremely important for the director to be conscientious in listening to and assessing the music. If he neglects this assessment he may encounter difficulties at the dubbing stage.

Once he has listened to the music, the director must clearly explain to the composer the good and bad points in its relationship with the film as a whole, particularly the relationship between the music and individual scenes and he must collaborate with him in the search for means of correcting any faults, and bring the musical score into closer accord with the requirements of each scene. However excellent the music may be, it is useless for the cinema if it is not appropriately matched to each scene. It is impossible to correct or replace scenes just because good music is available. In the cinema, the music must be appropriately matched to each scene, if it is to enhance the effect of the film as a work of art.

In ensuring that the music used is appropriate to each scene, the director should pay particular attention above all to securing perfect harmony between the narrative flow of the film and the music. When the flow of music is properly matched with the flow of the drama, the story line can be depicted to proper emotional effect while the music retains its vital freshness.

In editing the music to conform with each scene, it should not be made to rise to a crescendo or go quiet according to the superficially observed features of life, nor should it be used mechanically, merely to illustrate the story line. It hardly needs to be said that music should be used to intensify an atmosphere, but even given this fact, it should be subordinate to the vivid depiction of the hero's emotions.

For example one cannot always use stirring music in order to sing of life at a busy construction site. The construction site at which dynamic labour efforts are made, may be the spot where the hero meditates over the kindly care of the Party that has provided him with such a fine life. The music which flows from his heart may be lyrical. Or the hero may be stirred by a powerful emotion while surrounded by a quiet atmosphere. The music which expresses his heightened feelings can also be exciting. The director must have a total grasp of the scene's focus of artistic interpretation and use music which matches the hero's inner experience, thus adding depth and clarity to the depiction of the situation.

In the cinema it is important for the music to remain consistent even while it is appropriate to each scene. If the music is interrupted too often, the film's content will not be expressed clearly in a consistent flow of emotion, the moods will lack consistency and, in the long run, the musical score will become clumsy.

The director must guide the composer in such a way that he will direct the music from the beginning to the end of the film in the way the scenes require; at the same time, he must use his skill in solving any problems which might arise between the musical artists and other creative sectors.

When music follows the story line of the film it can overlap an actor's words or blend with the sound effects. In these cases, preference must be given to whichever element is intended to play the dominant role in clarifying the ideological content of the scenes, and every subsidiary element must be made to support it. If an attempt is made to sustain two kinds of sound on an equal basis, the harmony of the sound is destroyed and the expression of the main artistic statement of the scene suffers accordingly.

The different means of depiction used in expressing the ideological content of the scenes do not function together in the same way in every scene. In one scene the music will be more important than the words and in another the sound effects will predominate. It is therefore essential to select carefully the means of expression which match each scene and, if one sound element is more important than the others, then they must be subordinated to it.

One method of using music throughout the film is to use songs continually and to repeat good songs to suit the situation.

When using songs which are appropriate to the scenes, the director must ensure that they fit naturally into the flow from one scene to another. The more often a good song, in particular, is repeated in a manner appropriate to the situation in a number of scenes, the richer is its emotional contribution to the content of the film and the longer it can be sustained.

Although it is good to use music continually, it cannot be employed without good reason. When music is heard where it is not appropriate, it is annoying and the scene becomes awkward. Music must only be used when the correct preconditions have been created. Only then can both the scenes and the music be effective, and the audience can hear the music with a sense of security.

The reason for the use of music should be provided by both the content and the form. If music is to be used naturally in any scene, there must be a motive for the concurrent development of the event; the thoughts and feelings of the character should be built up and a realistic emotional atmosphere should be created. Moreover images should be properly harmonized within scenes and the visual depth and scope of the frame should also be appropriate.

While making use of a variety of music and songs, in keeping with each scene, the director must ensure that the musical elements of all the scenes are harmonized in a consistent manner. If music and songs are used disjointedly, the overall harmony of the musical score is destroyed. Complete musical harmony throughout the film can only be achieved when the theme music and theme songs in the film are complemented by other music and songs, but precedence is given to the theme music and songs.

The director must pay particular attention to the proper use of sound, in addition to music and songs.

In the cinema sound can replace words and actions in subtly revealing the characters' ideas and emotions and changes in their psychological state; it can also be used to describe the surroundings and the atmosphere of life in a lively and emotional manner. Sound can also be used to amplify the story line and link one shot with another. In conjunction with other expressive elements it can be used in the portrayal of emotions and it can act on the creation of the general flow of the film. The specific reasons for the use of sound and the way it will be used to enhance the film's quality are determined by the director's intentions.

If he is to create realistic and expressive sound effects, the director must have a comprehensive knowledge of sound. He must know a wide range of sounds which can be used in the depiction of life and he must understand the meaning of all these sounds and the emotions they evoke.

The thrilling whistle of an electric locomotive pulling into a station with a load of thousands of tons is not just a whistle to most people. They think of it as the triumphant announcement of an accident-free journey, an ardent summons to new and energetic efforts in their work. To those who love work, the sounds constantly associated with worthwhile work are not simply the sounds of machines. This is why the sounds of creative labour are often compared with a great symphony.

People also become emotional when they hear the beautiful sounds of nature. On hearing the song of the skylark, the harbinger of spring, they think about ploughing, and on hearing the hooting of an owl in the dead of night, they become melancholy.

Many sounds rouse people's emotions because of their connection with life. A director who knows the meaning of various sounds which are connected with real life, can use sound effectively and he can use any sound to reflect the feelings of our people.

The director must know how to use, in keeping with each scene, the sounds with which he is familiar and which he remembers from his own life. When properly matched to the scene, sounds express the inmost thoughts and feelings of the characters. They can also create a typical depiction of their surroundings and bring the scene to life, by expressing it in greater detail, in a variety of ways.

Of the various sounds which may be heard in a scene, the director must give greatest prominence to the main sound, the one which is most suited to expressing the situation, and use it to portray the character's inmost thoughts and feelings and specify the surroundings and the atmosphere. In this way it is possible to achieve a perfect harmony of pictures and sound and exploit the descriptive potential of sounds to the full.

If they are to be used in a manner suitable to the scenes, natural sounds must be artistically transformed. Not all the sounds one hears are artistic, and they do not all need to be used in the film exactly as they really are. If the director approaches the question of sound with the idea that lightning brings thunder and that when a train moves nothing can be heard but the sound of the wheels, his use of sound in the film will be neither artistic nor meaningful. In the cinema sound must always be expressive.

The director must give an artistic gloss to sound, according to the requirements of the scene and what he wishes to convey, by altering such elements of natural sound as its volume and tone. However, the individual character of each sound must be retained. If this is not done, the distinctive qualities of the sound will be lost. Therefore, all the elements of a natural sound should be transformed in order to meet the requirements of each scene, but the individual character of the sound must be retained.

In order to use sound in a manner suited to each scene, the best possible use must be made of methods of expression which correspond to the features of sound in real life. In films the volume of sound may be increased or exaggerated intentionally, or only one sound may be used, while all the other sounds which might be heard in the scene are muted, or sound may be totally suppressed in another scene. The question is how well the director exploits the expressive potential of various sounds in keeping with the content of the scenes and the sounds' natural qualities.

Since expressive sound in the cinema is directly created by the sound technicians and engineers, the director must work closely with them. However, he must not become obsessed with the technical aspects of the use of sound. The creation of cinematic sound is effected through complex technical processes, but technical matters are not the concern of the director.

Sound is art. The director must always pay attention to artistic matters such as the direction of sound projection, the relationship of sound to each scene, the choice of sounds and their artistic use.

Only a director who is well-versed in the secrets of expressing an artistic conception by means of music and sound and is capable of working closely with the artists engaged in this sphere, can use the correct sounds, those with the distinctive qualities which harmonize with each scene.

THE SECRET OF DIRECTING LIES IN EDITING

A film usually consists of hundreds of shots containing fragments of life. Editing plays an important role in the creation of a work of cinematic art by linking all these shots together.

Editing is a means of linking the shots together so that the drama flows in accordance with the logic of real life, and an integrated cinematic interpretation of the theme is created. Through editing the director can select and emphasize only those aspects of the complexities of life that are essential, or he can combine general and specific depictions of life. Through editing the director can also develop a consistent plot, by combining the characters' actions and the events contained in the shots to perfect the composition and secure the total harmony of the work. The secret of editing is to create shifts of emotional emphasis, and yet produce a single, unified flow of images throughout the film.

Editing is an effective creative tool for the director because of the varied yet central role it plays in developing the interpretation of a theme. Even when shots have an identical plot, editing can either develop the flow of the story line logically and naturally, or disrupt it so much that the thread of the story can only be followed with great difficulty. Only a director who knows how to exploit to the full the abundant expressive possibilities that editing provides is able to move people with a clear and convincing depiction of life.

Throughout the whole course of making the film, the director must constantly consider the work from the point of view of editing and must always seek, by exploring new possibilities, to enhance the role played by editing in interpreting the theme.

From the very moment of a film's conception, the director should be thinking how to make the fullest use of the artistic possibilities of editing.

Some people regard editing as a creative process that takes place after filming is over. They are mistaken. There is far more to editing than just cutting.

Editing is a form of imagistic thinking that is specific to the work of the film director and also a method for rendering an artistic conception accessible to the public. The ability to consider matters from the point of view of editing enables the director to approach the overall situation analytically in accordance with the particular features of any film and to construct each shot and combine the separate ones together in a flexible manner to produce an integrated sequence. Without due emphasis on editing no director can possibly adapt literature for the screen or properly sustain the expressive elements that are peculiar to the cinema.

Editing is conducted in accordance with the director's conception of the film. The editorial continuity that was defined in this conception is established in the script and realized during filming. Therefore, the editing after filming is concluded should be based on the editorial interpretation that was determined when the literary work was studied and the basic concept was developed.

At the stage of conception the director should already be interested in the arrangement and connection of the shots in each scene even while he is concentrating his efforts on solving the larger problems, such as how to include only the essential elements of life in each shot, how to develop the story line logically and clearly, and how to guide the flow of the film's images along the same lines as the plot.

The director should pay great attention to editing even during the filming. Whilst the filming is going on he should already be defining the speed and rhythm of the flow of shots which are laid out in the director's script, and he should also provide the conditions for the switch from one shot to the next, taking into account the fact that they must be connected in some way. The director should particularly bear in mind the editing that must be done within individual scenes by means of directing the movement of the camera, because this must be determined during the filming itself.

Since the editorial interpretation of a film is finally defined and completed after filming is over, the director should closely examine every shot and structure the shots that are essential to the film into an orderly sequence. The director is an artist behind the scenes, but his artistic and ideological opinions, personality and talent are displayed on the screen. The director should therefore exercise great caution in selecting only those shots that are essential, taking the attitude that he is responsible to our times and the people for each shot that he uses.

The most important thing in editing a film is to sequence and link the shots logically. When the process of editing conforms with the natural progression of life, the action of the film will flow in a realistic and lively fashion.

The director can edit the flow of scenes in a logical manner by correctly depicting the cause and effect of each event as it develops, and its absolute necessity, while at the same time accurately portraying the actions of the characters involved. Determining the length and the scope of every shot, creating the conditions for linking them together and switching from one to the other, selecting the colour and shade of each shot, and deciding the various movements of the camera and their speed— all these must be subordinated to the expression of the characters' personalities and the depiction of real life.

It is especially important in editing to link shots precisely according to the requirements of logic. If the shots are to be perfectly geared to each other, they should be connected according to the principle of cause and effect. The first shot should be made the cause which produces the second and the second shot should be the result of the first and at the same time the cause of the third.

However, the logical connection of the shots which embody the links of cause and effect in the characters' actions and the events is not always sequential. In the cinema it is not unusual for a shot to follow another one to which it is not directly related, whereas the effect of an action or an event in the first shot may be shown later. Of course, the link of cause and effect in the character's action and the event does not disappear just because the shots which show the cause and effect are not themselves directly linked.

Even in real life, an effect sometimes does not appear immediately after an action or event has taken place. At times, actions and events develop rapidly and at times different episodes which are not directly related become interwoven. In the cinema, which exploits the possibility of free play with time and space, the line of a character's action or an event may be developed along a number of paths, which may cross each other or run parallel, or even turn back in retrospection.

If the director thinks only of the logical connections between shots and simply links in sequence the shots which are the cause and effect of specific actions and events, he will be unable to depict the complicated and diverse nature of life in a lively and interesting way, and in consequence, the action of the film will seem dry and flat.

In editing a film, the linking of shots according to the principle of cause and effect should be managed through various forms and methods, derived from real life and the requirements of the film. The forms and methods that are used should certainly be based in logic, but nonetheless shots should not follow one after another without any interruption in the sequence, simply showing the character's actions and the events without revealing the logic underlying their development and their effect.

Connection according to the principle of cause and effect is an important principle in editing; but when it is used mechanically and a rigid pattern is set, the depiction of life proves to be dry and uninteresting. On the other hand, if this connection is ignored and a diversity of connections is maintained, editing becomes formalistic, it rejects the law of real life. Only when the principles of cause and effect and of diversity are combined in the linking of shots can the film portray the inevitable development of life in a natural fashion.

The director's views should be clearly revealed in his editing. An artistic image is created by the union of objectivity and subjectivity. Realism is a method of depicting life objectively, and yet it opposes the tendency to approach life coldly, and demands that the writer take a positive attitude to life.

The director must carefully explore the world of his drama and not approach the lives of his characters with the attitude of an onlooker, arranging or linking the shots mechanically. He should be fired with creative passion, and feel genuine warmth for the characters and their lives, and then inject his own emotional rhythm into the sequencing and linking of the shots.

In his editing the director should express the ideas and emotions of the characters through skilful use of methods such as symbolism, the association of ideas, and illusion.

If he is too particular about the sequential logic of actions and events in editing, he will be unable to devise different editorial methods to achieve an emotionally powerful and profound depiction of the inmost thoughts of the characters, and consequently, the flow of the film's action will be sterile and stiff. The inserted shot which is used in the cinema to express a symbolic meaning is not related directly to the character or the event, but it is still an essential element in the emotional depiction of the character's mental state or the emphatic statement of the ideological content of the drama.

Supplementary shots used to depict the innermost world of the characters more clearly and delicately should accord with their ideological and emotional state and their moods and yet be clear and simple. Those which can only be understood and enjoyed by the director, but not understood by the audience, are not only entirely meaningless, they also hinder the clear expression of the characters' thoughts and emotions and disrupt the emotional flow of the film.

The director should make quite sure that the supplementary shots used are easy to understand and reveal the characters' thoughts and emotions in an appropriate manner. As for the inserted shots, they should not be employed for filling in gaps in the development of the story. The flow of a film is disrupted when the director makes inappropriate use of supplementary shots which are not suitable to the emotional depiction of the characters' inmost world and are ambiguous in meaning.

In film editing the importance of the director's subjective views should be emphasized, but not over-emphasized. If logic and film grammar are ignored in editing, and only the director's subjective views are highlighted, the film will become superficial. This superficiality in editing means that shots are not linked together as logic and film grammar require, but are patched together entirely on the basis of the director's subjective views, and only certain abstract impressions tend to receive emphasis. Film editing is directly influenced by the director's experience and intentions, but they should be derived directly from life itself.

Through skilful editing the director should draw the audience into the artistic world of the film, leading them to accept the life depicted on the screen as real and respond to it with warmth. The creative strength of editing is that it allows you to capture the hearts of the whole audience, each member of which is an individual with his own particular tastes in art.

If the attention of the audience is to be focused entirely on the story unfolding on the screen, the flow of the film's action should be well-knit and dynamic, and at the same time the characters' diverse emotions should develop harmoniously, so that the sequence of shots moves along energetically.

It will obviously not do to continue piling up dramatic tension simply to make the flow of the film dynamic. If the audience is subjected to too much tension, they will be unable to fully understand the content of the production and, of course, they will grow tired. On the other hand, if the sequence of shots progresses sluggishly, the audience will become bored and their minds will wander. In the final analysis, both extremes hinder the effort to involve the audience in the world of the film and convince them of the truth of its content.

In the realm of the arts caution is imperative in handling any matter that affects people's ideas and feelings. The director must not force the audience to cry because the hero cries, nor should he be so insolent as to expect them to watch a tedious performance to the end. The director should know how to use his creative ability and his talent to pluck at the heartstrings of the audience. Whatever situation he is dealing with, he should never forget the audience.

In the art of making revolutionary films, the ideological relations between the director and the audience should be sound and pure, and a noble moral attitude of respect and trust should be established between them.

THE ASSISTANT DIRECTOR IS A CREATIVE WORKER

It is important in cinematic art to define clearly the position and duties of the assistant director and to enhance his creative role. This is not simply a matter of an administrative job, it is a matter of somebody who is actually engaged in film-making. So unless the correct solution is found to this problem, it is impossible to direct the creative group in a satisfactory manner.

At one time the role of the assistant director was hotly disputed in the world of cinema. In fact, the role of the assistant director was not clearly defined in the past; as a result, at a meeting to review a particular film, one assistant director went so far as to raise the question, "Is the assistant director a creative worker, too?"

The debate concerning the role of the assistant director resulted from the fact that a scientific system of film-making had not yet been established and the position, duties and role of the assistant director had not yet been accurately defined.

No other sphere of creative work involves activity on such a large scale or possesses such complex content as film-making. Film-making is not undertaken by one person as is the case in the writing of a novel or a poem; it is carried out through teamwork involving many artists, and the process is extremely complex. The creative work of the director covers a particularly wide range. However able he may be, it is clearly beyond his power to undertake such a huge number of creative tasks without the help of the other members of the creative team. Hence, the assistant director is necessary to support and assist the director in his creative work.

The post of assistant director was originally established under the capitalist system of film-making. But under this system the "assistant director" is not a creative worker. Like all other artists, the "assistant director" is tied to the purse-strings of the tycoons of the film industry. Moreover, he is not allowed to express any views of his own in the course of the creative work; he is just a kind of "servant" who blindly carries out the instructions of the "director", and even has to attend him in his private life. He is in the position of a humble lackey who liaises between the "director" and other people and curries favour with them. In short, his position is that of a servant, shackled to both the film-making industrialists and the "director".

The problem of the role of the assistant director had already been raised under the capitalist system of film-making, but it could not be solved correctly in capitalist society, where money rules everything. Even in socialist society, while the remnants of capitalism still survived in the sphere of film-making and a socialist system of film-making had not yet been completely established, the problem of the assistant director's role and position still awaited a correct solution.

Because of the old viewpoint left over from the capitalist system of film-making the assistant director was regarded as a person who attends on the director and carries the actors' costumes and properties.

It is also wrong to regard the assistant director as a person who has failed to become a director or as a trainee director. To regard him as an apprentice, learning the ropes, and to assume that his position is an intermediary one while he trains to become a director, is tantamount to not regarding him as a creative worker.

Under the socialist system of film-making, the assistant director carries out the duties of a true assistant director in all areas. Like other members of the creative team, the assistant director is entrusted with the important duty of film-making and has a particular sphere of creative activity assigned to him.

The assistant director should himself organize and help to realize the endeavours of the creative group in the creation of films, he should guide the acting and also be responsible for the actors' costumes and properties.

The creative group may include a number of assistant directors, and among these the first assistant director should undertake the role of chief of staff, directly organizing and implementing the work of making the film.

In order to produce a film, the organizational and financial basis of the artistic and creative work should be laid first, so that the production is provided with the necessary material and technical support. The most important point here is the organizational work underlying the artistic and creative work. This is complex and responsible work involving planning the activities of the creative group and scheduling their teamwork in detail. It should therefore not be undertaken by different people alternately or at random. The efficiency of the activity of film-making is significantly increased when a specialized post carries responsibility for organizing the work of artistic creation.

This organizational work should be carried out by the first assistant director who, in company with the director, is well acquainted with all matters concerning the creative group and is able to control, organize and set them to work in a coordinated manner. Since the director is the commander of the group, it is reasonable for the first assistant director to perform the role of chief of staff. Thus, on the basis of the requirements of cinematic art, we have defined the first assistant director as chief of staff of the creative group.

The first assistant director, or chief of staff, should control the organization of the artistic work in the creation of a film, also ensuring that it is well organized from an administrative point and providing adequate material and technical conditions as appropriate and necessary. On the basis of the conditions for creative work provided by the chief of staff, the director, the commander of the creative group, can reach correct decisions and successfully command in the battles of creative endeavour.

The creative group can only work in an orderly manner and produce an excellent film in the minimum of time, using the minimum of manpower, funds and materials, if the first assistant director arranges things correctly and carries out the organizational work preceding artistic creation efficiently.

The first assistant director should always be well acquainted with the abilities and degree of preparedness of all the members of the creative group and able to make precise judgements in any situation, so that he moves the work forward on his own initiative. If the chief of staff wavers, does not have his own opinions and makes no active contribution to the work, he will be unable to guarantee that the work required will be done in the different units of the creative group or by their individual members, and, what is more, he will waste time, in answering calls from here and there to attend to petty matters. The assistant director is chief of staff and he should have his own opinions and be bold in organizing and seeing through the creative work just like the director himself.

The assistant director is an independent creative worker. His main duty as such is to offer dependable support to the director in his creative work, and assist him in producing a good film in accordance with the requirements of the times and the aspirations of the people.

Although he is an independent creative worker, the assistant director must not carry out creative work on impulse, and deviate from the director's creative conception. He should always work towards the correct embodiment of the director's creative plan. Only in this way does he function as a creative worker who provides substantial assistance to the director.

One of the main duties of the assistant director is to work closely with the actors.

Certain assistant directors once attempted to make films even though they were unable to offer proper guidance for the work of the actors. However well educated in literature and well-versed in the various means of cinematic production a person may be, if he does not know how to conduct creative work with actors, he is not qualified to be a director.

Work with the actors is the basis of directing. Just as the director's work is inconceivable unless he works with the actors, the assistant director's work on the interpretation of the conception, to assist the director in his creative work, is inconceivable unless he also works with them. If the assistant director is to provide adequate support to the director and assist him effectively in his creative activities, he should work closely with the actors.

The director invests immense effort in guiding the acting of the leading actors, whilst remaining aware of the work of all the actors. The assistant director should guide those actors assigned minor and extra roles, while still being involved in the individual guidance of all the actors. In the cinema, acting is guided to completion by the joint efforts of the director and the assistant director.

The assistant director's work with the actors should not be confined to the period during which the film is made, but should be continued without interruption in their routine training as actors. The assistant director should live together with the actors and give them responsible and regular guidance in the course of their training. For the assistant director, routine creative work with the actors is a process of accumulating experience, in order to guide the acting well during actual film-making, and of improving his own qualifications as an independent artist.

On the basis of his profound understanding of the actors' political and ideological preparedness and their abilities, the assistant director should map out a long-term plan for raising the standard of their acting and give them scientific guidance in their work. In parallel with this, he should also develop a deeper understanding of the principles and methods of work with actors and steadily improve his own abilities to guide the work of acting.

The assistant director should also know all about the actors' costumes and hand props.

Since his main task is to work with the actors, the assistant director should be familiar with their costumes and hand props, which are important tools for the actors in playing their parts. Obviously, the assistant director's primary concern in guiding an actor should be the actor's experience of the character's life and his characterization, particularly the way in which he expresses this in words and action. However, if the actor's portrayal is to be realistic, he should make good use of costumes and hand props and the assistant director should take an interest in these even while concentrating his efforts on dealing with the major tasks in the guidance of acting.

The assistant director should have a clear understanding of the historical period dealt with by the film and the class position, tastes and interests of the persons represented by each piece of costume and hand prop, and he should guide the actors to use them appropriately in their roles.

The assistant director should be as knowledgeable about costumes and hand props as a folklorist. Then he will be able to give substantial guidance to the actor in his creative work and help him to portray a real human being in the film.

When a production is made to reflect the life of olden times, new actors may not be very sure what sort of footwear they have to put on and what sort of clothes they have to wear in order to play their parts. In these cases, the art director may study the matter and come up with a solution, but only if the assistant director who guides the acting is familiar with the life and customs of the age represented in the production, will he be able to pick out period costume and hand props suited to the personalities of the characters, and thus dress the actors properly.

Since he has to be knowledgeable about costume and hand props, the assistant director should combine a full understanding of the script and the director's script with special knowledge of history and folklore, and he should also have a profound knowledge of the fine arts. Only then will he be able to develop his own independent opinions as a creative worker and assist the director in his creative work as he should.

A true assistant director finds fulfilment in his noble creative work of loyally assisting the director in his artistic endeavours to create an excellent work of cinematic art.

ACTOR AND CHARACTER

"Actors, too, should explore reality. Otherwise, they cannot accurately represent new characters in line with how people are changing and developing."

KIM IL SUNG

THE ACTOR IS THE FACE OF THE FILM

In the cinema the actor is the character's direct, autonomous creator. Without the actor, it is impossible to create the film character and, therefore, to make films at all.

Even if the script describes a person of excellent character who has led a good and noble life, it is the actor's interpretation in the screen which determines whether the character comes to life or not. A fine actor adds considerably to the quality of a production with his ideas and emotions, his experience of life, his creative imagination and talent. A creative actor brings to full flower what the writer has only half-done and perfects the presentation of the theme by focusing on things he has overlooked.

An actor's characterization is more vivid than a depiction in words or a sketch or a portrait and incomparably more substantial than a character depicted in the rhythms and melodies of music. No art can depict a man so vividly and breathe such palpable life into him as the art of acting.

In the cinema the harmony of the overall interpretation is also built around the realistic characters created by the actors. In cinematic art harmonious unity can only be achieved provided the diverse representational elements of the film are united around the character. The efforts of all the artists, including the director, ultimately bear fruit in the actor's screen portrayal of the character.

The actor is not only a creative artist who portrays a particular character, but also the guide who directly links the screen and the audience and leads the audience into the world of the film. Although many artists participate in the making of a film, only the actor can create a character and provide the link between the screen and the audience. Other artists can offer strong support to the actor's role but they can never actually take his place on the screen. Therefore, the actor has to act well if a film is to exert a strong influence on people.

People cannot immediately become familiar with the name of a character on the screen, but if they are told that the part is played by a certain well-known actor, then they find it easy to identify the character. And, after a time, they forget the various details of a production and find it hard to recall the name of the hero or even the actual title of the film; but when they are reminded that such-and-such an actor played the hero, they instantly recall the film quite vividly. This is the distinctive feature and the power of the art of acting.

The actor is an artist who contributes, through his portrayal of a character, to deepening people's understanding of life and the situation and to re-educating them in a revolutionary manner.

The actor's portrayal of character is fundamental to both the informative and educational roles of cinematic art. On the screen the actor vividly portrays an actual person with a genuine human character and, moreover, in this portrayal he demonstrates logical process by which life develops. People in the audience are thus made aware of the essential nature of life and the principles of its development by means of the actor's character portrayal.

The real objective of cinematic art is not merely to enhance people's awareness of the world, but to develop them as communist revolutionaries and thereby accelerate the pace of the revolution and construction. This objective is what is achieved precisely by means of the actor's character portrayal.

Only by giving a realist portrayal of a person in his acting can the actor effectively fulfil the noble mission assigned to him by our revolutionary times. Creating human characters, which is fundamental to cinematic art, is the essence of the art of acting. That is why the actor is called the face of the film. An actor cannot be called a genuine artist if he cannot create an archetypal man who represents and speaks for the interests and ideas of the masses.

The realism of acting is derived from the actor's outlook on the world. On the basis of this outlook the actor understands a production and shares the personality and experiences the life of a character he is to depict and embodies them in an accurate portrayal. Every character portrayal in the cinema is directly affected by the actor's world outlook. Just as every representational work of art is a depiction of life shaped by the artist's viewpoint, a character in a film is a depiction conceived out of the actor's own view of the world.

The actor always creates a human character according to his own level of political and ideological maturity and artistic talent. In depicting the character of a Chollima rider an actor should be true to the spirit of the Chollima age and embody it as well as his artistic attainment allows.

It is beyond the powers of a human being to express anything beyond the bounds of his knowledge and understanding. This also applies to the actor; he can only create excellent characters when he approaches each one with complete ideological and artistic understanding. When the actor knows ten elements of truth, he should express three or four. If he only knows three or four but tries to express ten, he is like someone drawing a puppy when he intended to draw a tiger. Therefore the actor requires a firm outlook on the world and a high level of artistry in order to portray a person realistically.

Before portraying a character, not only should the actor establish a correct outlook on the world, he should also gain direct experience of the life of that person.

This experience is the key to the actor's portrayal. When representing another person, an actor has to live and act with the ideas and emotions of that person. He cannot portray him honestly unless he has gained this experience and so can accept and assimilate his ideas and emotions.

The more the actor knows about a person and the more he deepens his own experience of the person's life, the more realistically he can bring the character to life. The actor needs this experience in order to respond warmly to the person's ideas and emotions, to regard him as his own self and speak and behave just like him. Experience which he cannot bring to life in his portrayal is entirely worthless. Only experience which contributes directly to the realistic representation of a human character is vital and meaningful experience.

In attempting to experience the life of another person, the actor should assimilate all of his inmost thoughts and feelings. But major emphasis should be given to assimilating the ideas which form the nucleus of his personality. Unless an actor assimilates a character's ideas, he cannot penetrate the heart of the character's personality, nor can he gain an accurate understanding of his other distinctive features. The actor should direct his attention in the main towards assimilating the character's ideas. Only then can he develop a comprehensive portrayal of the character and define his most essential features in bold relief.

To develop a profound and comprehensive understanding of a character, the actor should first study the script and use it as the basis for experiencing the life from which he has to draw his characterization. The actor should get to know the character from studying the script, and then go on to delve deeper into his life. This will make it easy for him to enter into the character's world. The actor should deliberately and consistently work towards a full experience of the character's life, and thereby ensure his own fusion with the character. If he starts practising his part without having experienced the person's life, he is first making a pattern and then trying to fit the content into it. This will not produce an honest portrayal.

An actor who has assimilated a character's ideas and emotions should be able to express the character's inmost world with his own words, deeds and expression. Only the complete unity of the actor's inner experience and its embodiment can produce a vivid human portrayal. In addition to being photogenic, therefore, the actor should also be well prepared spiritually, physically and technically.

The characteristically photogenic face is a typical Korean face, in which a noble spirit and balanced features form a perfect harmony with a fine personality. A face which some may call beautiful, but which is not supported by a noble idea, will not make any impression on people, and a face which is imperfectly formed cannot contribute to the beauty of the film.

A man's true beauty is not in his physical appearance but in his noble ideological and moral trait. However good-looking and well-dressed he may be, a man who is not spiritually and morally pure can never be called a beautiful person.

Since actors have the noble duty of appearing before people in order to educate them, they should be beautiful both ideologically and physically, although of course the same could be said of anyone. An actor who is not ideologically sound and whose features are not beautiful cannot present a noble portrayal of anyone.

Good-looking new actors often attract the audience's attention. The audience will even make generous allowances for the first one or two films of a new actor who is still immature. But an actor who has no substance to him, though he is good-looking, will not be welcomed by the audience.

The actor's physical appearance is not the basic requirement for him to portray characters. The nobility and beauty of the actor's ideological awareness is what is important. If an actor becomes conceited simply because he has gained popularity through one or two films and begins to neglect his ideological education and acting training, his face will soon disappear from the screen.

It is wrong to believe that positive characters should only be played by good-looking actors and negative characters by actors who are not good-looking. An actor who is ideologically and artistically mature is able to act the part of either the positive character or the negative character. A truly excellent actor can play any part. Generally speaking, the positive roles are not given to actors who have often portrayed class enemies, because of the impression they might make on the minds of the audience, not because they were born "villainous actors" or are incapable of depicting positive characters.

The actor's face on the screen changes from one film to the next because he himself matures, not because he plays a different role in each film, under different filming conditions.

The actor's screen face should be constantly improving. If an actor considers his good looks to be a gift of destiny and does not make any efforts to develop his ideological understanding and improve his acting, he will be weeded out before long. As the saying goes even jade has to be polished to make it shine, and the better an actor looks, the harder he should work on his ideological development and acting training, in order constantly to improve his screen face.

The days are long gone when exclusive preference was given to the faces of a few stars.

A film which merely aims to make a profit by showing off the stars' faces, cannot be real art. The capitalist cinema, which promotes a few "popular stars" to curry favour with the audience, is, in essence, a reactionary art form which reduces the stars to puppets and the film to a commodity. There cannot be a genuine creative spirit, and the beautiful flower of art cannot bloom where actors sell their faces and even their souls.

The actor's face is a means of the actor's creative work. His face should therefore be seen to accord with the character's, and not vice versa. The actor should not simply appear with his own usual expression unaltered on the grounds that this is going to make him look natural. What makes the actor an artist is not the stereotyped repetition of the same type of face, but his creative ability to represent a wide range of diverse individuals. The characters the people truly love are, without exception, the true-to-life individuals portrayed in an original manner by actors with their faces.

An actor who portrays a revolutionary should work and struggle like a revolutionary in his own life. For a revolutionary actor, creative work and life are fused into one. Actors should establish the constant habit of creating and living, of living and creating at the same time, and spend all their lives in uninterrupted inquiry and creative endeavour.

Only an actor who strives for creative achievement and involves every aspect of his life in the process of serious learning can become a real artist and earn the love of the people.

ACTING SHOULD BE MORE INNOVATIVE

All actors, without exception, would like to create many different realistic characterizations, which will make an unforgettable impression on people and become closely associated with them for the rest of their life. But not all of them are able to realize this ambition. One actor may portray numerous characters in the course of a long artistic career, but fail to create any memorable characterizations, which people cherish among their memories, whereas another actor may portray only a few characters in a short artistic career, and yet succeed in this so brilliantly that he carves out a place for himself and his characters in the history of cinema-acting. An actor's artistic reputation does not depend on the number of characters he has represented, but on the marvellous portrayals he has created of new characters.

To be a truly creative artist, the actor must portray a new personality each time he acts a new part. Only if he is capable of a fine interpretation of any character whatsoever, an actor with a hundred faces and a hundred names, is a genuine artist who can render worthy service to the revolution. If he portrays a number of different characters, but they all appear similar, he cannot be called a true creative artist, he is an artist in name only.

An actor requires the ability to depict characters accurately in order to portray their uniquely different personalities. Only when the actor portrays all his characters by bringing their individualities to life, can he show a true picture of life and really truthful and distinctive features of human beings

To create an original portrayal, the actor should trust in his own convictions when approaching his character as depicted in literature.

In a novel or a drawing, the verbal or visual portrayal of a person is the final portrayal. But the characters in a script or a play are recreated by the actors. In this process, the actor should not mechanically copy the character from another source. He will be unable to portray the person vividly if he adopts a passive approach to the character as depicted in literature and copies it mechanically, without creative passion and excitement emanating from his own convictions.

On the other hand, if the actor creates his portrayal arbitrarily, by gathering together various features unrelated to the character as depicted in literature, he will fail to portray the character correctly because his subjective desires are too prominent. It is true, of course, that the actor should have creative imagination. But if this imagination deviates from the literary source it is worse than useless, it is positively harmful. The actor should actively employ his creative individuality in the accurate portrayal of the character, always basing his work on the literary text.

When assigned a part, an actor should prepare thoroughly for his creative work by studying the literary text closely. He should analyse the character's personality from various viewpoints relating it to his knowledge of real life, and think carefully to determine precisely which of the character's distinctive features should be emphasized, how he should speak and act, how he should do his makeup and which costumes and hand props he should use. If he launches into his portrayal without this preparatory work, he will tend to squeeze himself into the character's personality or accommodate the character's personality to his own.

An actor who has strong ideas of his own when he works on a characterization is able to create fresh interpretations by creating a harmonious balance between his creative individuality and the character's personality.

The actor should maintain his independent viewpoint, not only in his study of the literary source, but also in his work with the director. If he relinquishes his independence and relies entirely on the director, reacting passively to the latter's directions, he will never create a vivid portrayal of a character.

The actor should have his own clear-cut views on creative work and participate conscientiously in teamwork with the director and all the other members of the creative group, in order to ensure the overall harmony of the film as a work of art and the quality of his own individual creative work.

The actor's creative individuality is specifically expressed in his portrayal of the character. The individuality of the actor only becomes meaningful when it contributes to the depiction of the unique personality of the character. In the finest screen characterizations the creative individuality of the actor is delicately and harmoniously moulded into the personality of the character.

An actor who cannot understand the character by starting from within himself, is incapable of distinctly expressing either his own individuality or the character's; an actor who is unable to adapt his acting to suit the character cannot express either the character's individuality or his own. A vivid screen portrayal of a true-to-life character is always based on the natural fusion of the individualities of both.

Acting based on the actor's individual qualities should be consistently distinctive throughout the portrayal of the character. Since individuality is not just related to one or two individual characteristics, the actor must not attempt to demonstrate a minor special skill or insignificant talent in one or two of his scenes. If his unique style of acting is confined to just a scene or two, it cannot be real acting based on genuine individuality.

Like the director, the actor should set himself a high standard whenever he portrays a character and should be able to express his creative individuality as an actor distinctly and consistently. If he concentrates on just a scene or two or only elaborates the minor points, he is either treating his acting as nothing more than a means of earning money, lacking self-confidence. Undermining the general standard of a characterization by emphasizing one particular point, and destroying the general harmony of an interpretation by overplaying in one scene, runs counter to the ethics of creative activity. Our actors should reject the old pattern, designed solely to win popularity, by which a certain point in a scene is elaborated to display one's own individual abilities to one's best advantage.

Only an actor who is not tied to any fixed pattern can create a unique character portrayal. In acting a set pattern is a deviation, which results from an incorrect understanding of the creative nature of the art, and this is due in turn to a basically mistaken attitude to creative work. Acting based on individuality is not achieved by emphasizing particular techniques or defining a special showy "style". Distinctive acting is the fruit of the creative passion with which the actor is fired and of his high sense of responsibility, which derives from profound knowledge of life and a correct understanding of the aims of acting.

In acting a set pattern is not an expression of individuality, but a bad habit that distorts the portrayal, a remnant of the old system of acting, which creates only artificial appeal Set patterns also arise as a result of technical professionalism in the art of acting, or from the lazy approach of gaining creative results without taking any trouble, by relying on experience and not actively cultivating one's artistic talent. Set patterns may also derive from bad habits formed in the actors' private lives and introduced into their acting.

A new character should always be depicted on a blank background, just like a picture drawn on white paper. The actor should not measure a new character against an outworn pattern or conventional ideas, but understand him for what he is and devote all his energy and talent to creating a unique interpretation.

Having identified the new features in the character's personality, the actor should introduce them skilfully throughout the process of portrayal, and so create an original performance.

Portraying of a new character means actually creating a new character. An actor inevitably acts the parts of various types of people living at different times. Yesterday he portrayed a worker, but today he may be a peasant or he may represent a student, even though previously he was a Party worker. The actor should therefore be prepared to play anybody at any time. Type-casting means that an actor's creative individuality is ignored and, in the long run, that he is crippled as an artist.

The actor should be able to act in a new way every time he portrays a new character. In this way he can maintain his creative individuality. His creative individuality should not merely be expressed as the characteristic which distinguishes him from another actor, it should also define the unique performance which allows him to represent one character in a different way from another. Individuality which is not manifested in a unique creative interpretation cannot be regarded as creative individuality in the full sense of the term.

In order to portray a person accurately, the actor must have a good understanding of life.

Without understanding how people live, he cannot picture reality correctly nor can he give full expression to the ideas, emotions and personalities of today's new people.

An actor who is ignorant of life cannot see into a character's inmost thoughts, and by concentrating on his outward appearance or his way of speaking and walking, he misses the essential features of the character's personality, and so fails to create a convincing portrayal.

A person's ideology, the kernel of his inmost world, is the essential factor that defines his personality. Even one and the same idea is expressed differently, to different degrees, and through different actions in different people. The manner of expression indicates the distinctive features of a character. The ideology of a man is formed and develops on the basis of his class origin, financial position, social and historical background and environment. Therefore, each man's ideology is different and a hundred people have a hundred different personalities. The actor should minutely observe a person's spiritual characteristics as his life changes and develops. In this way he will be able to develop a good understanding of his ideology and portray it vividly.

The actor should clearly identify the new features of a character's personality and seek a new method of portrayal with which to depict them distinctly.

He must not try to represent the worker of today with the acting method and techniques he used yesterday in portraying the worker of the past. Even though his makeup varies and he makes extensive and conspicuous use of costumes and hand props, if he uses only one acting method and technique in representing all his characters he will be restricted to a stereotyped manner of talking, gesturing and walking and, in the final analysis, will only be able to portray one type of character. Makeup, costumes and hand props also play an important role in a characterization, but no one should try to solve acting problems by using an odd moustache or a fantastic hat or a strange pair of spectacles.

To develop a new method of acting for each new character the actor must acquire a profound understanding of the character's personality by examing minutely how it was expressed in the course of his life, and then search for suitable methods and techniques of interpretation.

As a creative artist the actor should set his artistic sights high whenever he portrays a character, and make every possible effort to attain this high level in a distinctive and characteristic manner. In this way he will be able to create admirable portrayals of a hundred characters with a hundred personalities.

BEFORE ACTING HE SHOULD UNDERSTAND LIFE

It can be argued that in the cinema the actor is the creative artist who holds the key to the honest depiction of a person and his life. Through realistic acting that portrays a character directly he helps create a film that is true-to-life.

Realistic acting means that the actor speaks and acts as if it were real life. The actor should not "act" before the camera but behave as he would in real life.

A true to life screen characterization can only be portrayed when the actor and the character are united as one. When the actor and the character form a single unity in the portrayal, the actor can become the character and the character can become a living human being through the actor. This unity cannot be achieved simply by the actor looking like the character, making himself up, donning the character's clothes and acting in his name. The actor cannot create a true-to-life portrayal by simply making himself up skilfully to look like the character outwardly. Unless the ideas and actions of the actor and the character are moulded into one, it is impossible to portray a man as he would be in life.

In order to achieve this union of himself and the character, the actor should acquire the experience of the character's life by exploring his world in depth and carefully analysing his personality.

Analysing and understanding the character's personality is fundamentally important to the actor's creation of characterization. His ability to solve all the problems that arise as he gets to know the character better and plays his role will depend on how well he performs this analysis. Unless an actor develops a profound understanding of a character's personality, an actor cannot respond genuinely to his ideas and emotions, nor can he summon up the enthusiasm to create a portrayal that is truly fresh.

The actor should study the personality and the life of his character, not only in the chronological perspective of past, present and future, but also from the point of view of his relations with the other characters.

The most important thing in understanding a character is an absolutely clear idea of his ideology, the essence of his personality, and the changes and developments it undergoes. The ideology formed in the course of a person's life can only be vividly portrayed when it has been understood in detail through studying his daily life. In analysing a character's personality, the actor should not confine himself to idle words and the understanding of what is written on sheets of paper. If the understanding of the character's ideology which underlies his acting is merely an abstract concept, he will be unable to create a conscientious and realistic portrayal. The actor should analyse the ideology of the character in the context of his life. This will enable him to gain a precise understanding of the character's socio-class background and the personality traits resulting from it. The more seriously the actor explores the life of the character and the more deeply he experiences it, the better he can understand the character's personality and the more realistically he can act before the camera.

The actor must always rely strictly on real life even in case when he has to invent or use illusion in understanding the character. Realistic invention and illusion which are conducive to creation can only emerge from life itself. The more the actor understands life, the more his imagination develops; and the wider the scope of his imagination, the more life he can breathe into the character he is portraying.

When studying real life, the actor should set himself the realistic goal of analysing only those things that are essential. Then he can identify what is meaningful.

In the past actors used to apply the method of preparing a character's "autobiography" in order to analyse his life systematically. This is still a good method. Since a person's present life is a continuation of his past, it is possible to understand his present life in real depth and portray his personality fully and vividly, only when his past life is well understood. In this case, too, the relevant aspects of his life should be gathered together to support a profound and multifaceted understanding of the character within the framework of his life as depicted in the production. The "autobiography" must not be created for its own sake.

An actor was once assigned a minor part as a Japanese policeman. To fulfil his boast that he would make a profound and comprehensive analysis of his character, he prepared a long and complicated "autobiography", even going to the extent of fabricating unnecessary aspects of his life, which were entirely unrelated to the character's life as depicted in the literature. This approach is no help whatsoever in studying a character and gathering experience of his personality.

"Autobiographical work" is not an essential exercise, it is not necessary for all roles. It is pure dogmatism to assert that the actor must prepare the detailed "autobiography" of a character in order to assimilate that character's ideas and emotions and depict him as an individual.

For the actor, the process of studying a character is one of coming to understand him, an initial process of preparation which creates a basis of shared experience. The actor should first understand the character and then concentrate on experiencing his life.

This process can be called the transfusion of the actor into the character he is to portray. The actor must experience the character's life before he can play his role. In this process of experiencing the life of the character, the actor establishes a real relationship with him, on the basis of which they come to form an indivisible whole.

The important question in defining the actor's experience as the character is which particular aspects should be embodied and how and from what viewpoint.

The actor cannot understand the character's personality and really experience his life without taking into account his own class position nor can he assimilate the character's ideas and emotions without taking his own into account. In order to act the part realistically the actor must make the process of acquiring his experience as the character a process of understanding the essential and representative traits of his personality and life, a process of accepting the character's ideas and emotions as his own, so as to achieve an organic unity with the character.

Quite a number of characters in our films are based on archetypal people. Actors therefore frequently visit the places where archetypes live. In such cases, they should strive to experience the archetypes' life in depth and breadth and not try to copy their faces and physical appearance. In fact, whatever character an actor is portraying, he should not try to copy the archetype's physical appearance. Attempting to do so will shackle his creative spirit and prevent him from highlighting the essential points of the character's personality in an artistic fashion and creating a characterization which is true to life.

When the actor is really prepared to accept the character's ideas and feelings, he has no difficulty in experiencing him and producing realistic results. In order to understand, accept and truly experience the ideas and emotions of the working class and the other labouring masses an actor requires a warm love for his class and people and a passionate devotion to the revolution. An actor who does not love the working class cannot understand its revolutionary spirit, and an actor who does not love his people cannot assimilate their ideas and emotions. A well developed class consciousness and a high degree of revolutionary ardour allow the actor to lay a broader and firmer foundation for truthful experience of the ideas and emotions of his character.

This foundation is equally decisive for an actor who is playing a villain. No revolutionary actor has ever actually been a Japanese policeman, landowner or capitalist, nor could he become such a person. But the actor must portray him, and he can do so faithfully.

To effectively embody the hateful enemy the actor requires an ardent love of his class and people and a burning hostility towards the enemy. He must have an intense, deeply-rooted hatred for the enemy in order to achieve a genuinely profound insight into their reactionary nature, a keen understanding of their anti-popular ideas and emotions and the foul behaviour springing from it, so that he can embody it vividly and express his fierce hatred. If the actor does not feel a strong hatred for the enemy, he will not be able to understand their essentially anti-popular nature and the vileness of their actions. If he cannot gaze straight into the enemy's eyes with a feeling of burning hatred, he will not feel their brutality in his bones, and will forget their crimes. Thus, even in portraying the class enemy, the actor's level of ideological awareness is decisive and, moreover, the depth and faithfulness of the actor's experience of the character are determined by his own outlook on the world.

In order to create a perfect portrayal of the character's personality, the actor should delve deep into his life and experience it for himself.

A person's ideas, emotions and psychology are demonstrated in his life through his actions. Since human life is a purposeful struggle to transform nature and reform society, it is impossible to understand human beings without seeing life, and if someone is ignorant of life, he is in no position to talk about human being.

The actor's tendency to minimize or idealize the representation of his character results from an attempt to act without having gained real experience of the character's life. If he does not know about the character's life, the actor cannot understand either the character's ideological background or the person himself. No talent, no matter how great, is capable of experiencing a character's life purely on the basis of logical analysis. If the actor does not know about life, there is nothing for him to do but invent it. If he does not strive for an understanding of the man and his life, and is only concerned with fabricating them at his desk, his acting inevitably becomes false.

An actor who is ignorant of life will become capricious and it does not take long for a capricious person to be weeded out. Faithfulness to the experience of the character's life and vivid acting do not automatically result from many years' experience of acting or from the actor's clever use of his face. If the actor attempts to manage the situation by drawing on a single scene from everyday life which he once saw and remembered or on a single experience, he will inevitably be weeded out.

An actor whose ample political knowledge and rich experience of life are supported by fine artistic qualities and experience, never grows old. If an actor continues to improve his political knowledge, and perfect his artistic attainments through the profound study of life's many different aspects, he is able to assimilate any new part assigned to him.

The actor should closely examine every occurrence with a mind to the lofty goal of creating genuine art, and in seeking experience of local situations, he should be zealous in his deliberate efforts to spot events that will interest people.

The actor's creative endeavours should fill 24 hours of his day. He should not separate creative work from his private life in either time or place. He should foster the habit of using every minute and creating as he lives, in the revolutionary spirit of living through struggle and struggling even as he lives.

An actor who goes off to gather realistic experience when he has been assigned a creative task and only starts studying a production when rehearsals have already begun, cannot be called an artist of the revolutionary age. Gathering realistic experience must not be regarded as a burden imposed on an actor. This experience only acquires meaning when it becomes of prime importance in his life. Even when he is not working on an assignment, an actor should always be gathering experience of reality, so that he can assimilate the revolutionary ardour and creative spirit of the people of our age, and can feel the very warmth of their breath. Then he can play the role of any person with skill and conviction.

Experience of life can be gathered anywhere, any time. Everywhere the actor can find life which he should observe, experience, and study closely. In the first place, it is important for him to actually go and live in a busy iron works or a cooperative farm. At the same time, the actor's home life should be exemplary, he should participate conscientiously in the business of his neighbourhood unit, attend parents' meetings at school and stand duty at his workplace. All these are essential elements of the process by which the actor accumulates experience of life.

The actor must also develop his ability to observe, study, analyse and assess the phenomena of life anywhere, any time. He must foster the habit of close observation in order to familiarize himself with the life of the people he meets on his way to and from his office, for example the bus drivers and the guards at the front gate of his workplace.

In his study of life the actor should employ various methods, to supplement direct, realistic experience, gained by entering into real situations, mixing with people and striving to understand their ideas and emotions clearly so as to master them as his own.

Even though an actor may have a vague idea of what the exploitative society is like, he will have no personal experience of exploitation and oppression and will not have been personally involved in carrying out the revolution. This applies particularly to young actors who have grown up in socialist society. It is therefore no easy task to create a faithful depiction of life in prerevolutionary times. In order to make good this gap in their experience, actors need to read many excellent literary works, especially revolutionary novels, and conduct their lives like revolutionaries. Visiting revolutionary museums and revolutionary sites, and studying historical documents can provide actors with invaluable insights into life.

An actor must have the ability to assimilate experience. Experience of life is a major asset for gaining a realistic and vivid understanding of a character, but it is not sufficient in itself to achieve the complete unity of the character and the actor. Not only should the actor study life in depth, he should also be able to assimilate his experience.

If an actor is not capable of vividly internalizing his character's precise feelings, his ideas are likely to produce a stiff interpretation which cannot support a lifelike portrayal. On the other hand, if he becomes engrossed in exploring his character's psychological world, forgetting the purpose of the portrayal and the goal of acting, the class line is likely to appear ambiguous in his work.

The actor should be well-versed in acting techniques which allow him to understand and assimilate in detail the diverse and subtle changes of the character's ideas and emotions in relation to a particular situation or event, so that the moment he goes on camera, he is quite naturally drawn deep into the world of the character's life.

An actor who cannot genuinely enter into a character's state of feeling is not yet an actor. He must enter into this state in order to believe in the character as his own self and to act naturally, as though the scene were reality.

A genuine smile and a false smile result from different causes and, moreover, they express the character's personality differently. The audience's perceptions of these smiles, and their response to them, are quite different. If an actor can smile or cry on request he is merely capricious. The actor cries when he is supposed to cry, not only because he understands the logic of why the character does so, but because he experiences his ideas and emotions with all his heart.

The actor may have a theoretical understanding of how to act before the camera, but if he has not yet entered into the state of feeling as the character would, his mental and physical responses will be slow; he will find it hard to move his limbs appropriately, word will get stuck in his throat, he will be unable to look into his co-actor's eyes and will simply stare at his forehead.

The ability to act and live on the screen and on the stage requires the actor to enter into this state of feeling as the character which is achieved through his realistic experience of the character's life. This is the only way of ensuring the realism of a performance.

However, the honesty of the portrayal is not guaranteed simply because the actor can feel as the character would. Even if he has achieved this state of feeling, he will not be able to portray the character honestly unless he can develop a natural manner of acting from it. The character can only be portrayed as he really is when the actor's experience of his life and his state of feeling are expressed through realistic acting.

Realistic acting requires, firstly, a full understanding of the distinctive features of film acting, and, secondly, the ability to distinguish the precise nuances and shades of acting required by the mood of the film.

Acting in a film is in essence the same as acting on the stage. However, the various different features of cinematic art and stage art do result in several related differences in the manner of acting. In some cases, an actor's style is suited to the theatre but not to the cinema. Both actors who are accustomed to the dramatic exaggeration required by the restricted conditions of theatrical performance and experienced professional film actors must be clear in their understanding of the distinctive features of film, and act in accordance with them. The acting of the film actor is characterized by great realism and vividness.

In order to depict the character's personality faithfully and vividly the actor needs to understand the precise nuances of performance required by the mood of a particular film and the distinctive features of cinematic art.

The actor should not be hasty in deciding how to shade his acting, or base his decision on preconceived ideas. He should strive to grasp the specific mood of a production, so that he can determine the nuances of performance which conform most closely to the character's personality, and can establish his own character's proper relationship to the others.

Acting in legitimate drama, comedy and tragedy requires different emphases of performance. Even within the legitimate drama, the different lives and personalities of the characters mean that some plays are rich in lyrical elements and others in elements of light comedy. It is thus quite impossible for an actor to maintain the same emphases and nuances of performance in all of his parts.

In the legitimate drama, if the actor does not make a proper study of the play's distinctive features and contents himself with a superficial understanding of its general conception, he may portray a lively and optimistic character as frivolous, and a dependable and respectable character as morose. An acting manner which does not fit the mood of a production distorts the character's personality, provoking laughter and even destroying the honesty of the production.

The case is similar with comedy. The laughter in a comedy must not be the actor's; it must always be the laughter of the character or laughter derived from the plot. If the actor uses a ridiculously exaggerated manner of acting, laughing first and forcing the audience to respond, they will find it very difficult to laugh and if they do, it will be the laughter of embarrassment. The actor can only make people laugh or cry naturally when life is depicted honestly in the performance.

In art an outburst of laughter should be evoked through the development of a necessary situation. Laughter which lacks this essential precondition of a basis in real life, transforms a character into a loafer, thus undermining the realism of the character and his life.

If acting according to the mood of a cinematic production is to remain true-to-life throughout, the shades of all the actors' performances should be fused into a single pattern. The unity of this overall pattern of nuance in the acting of a production cannot be guaranteed by the efforts of the small number of actors who play the main parts. The emphases in the characterization of the hero should first be determined in detail, and then the precise nuances of all the characters around him should be harmonized with these emphases, so that the interpretation throughout the production will remain true-to-life. The acting of the whole collective must be in natural harmony for an individual performance to stand out clearly and for the overall performance to maintain its essential character. If an actor fails to take account of the pattern of the overall performance and attempts to give prominence to his own role without establishing any genuine relationships with the other characters, or if he attempts to dominate them and focus all attention on himself, he will win, not popularity, but shame.

Only an actor who explores reality in depth and attempts to acquire a rich experience of life can act realistically and vividly enough to create a new character which will make a profound impression on the audience.

THERE SHOULD BE NO AFFECTATION IN SPEECH OR ACTION

The actor is a creative artist who portrays a human character through the basic means of words and actions. He does have other means at his disposal, such as makeup, costume and hand props, but they can only depict a character's inner world indirectly. Words and actions reveal the character's inner world directly and fully: they are the means by which contact between characters is established and relationships are built between them.

Speech expresses a person's ideas and emotions most clearly and in the greatest detail. Movements such as facial expression, gesture and gait, also reveal these ideas and emotions, but they can only create a rich and precise depiction of a person's inner world when they are combined with the spoken word. Without speech it is difficult to fully express a person's ideas, emotions and psychology.

However, even though the role of the spoken word in portraying a character's personality is so important, it would be a mistake to believe that actions merely support speech. Action is an expression of ideas just as the spoken word is. Even speaking requires acting. There is, therefore, no need to debate whether speech or action is more important in the art of acting.

In a person's life, words and deeds form a single unity; sometimes the word reinforces the deed, and sometimes vice versa. The spoken word expresses a person's ideas and emotions directly and precisely and it can be communicated to another person, but when it is combined with gestures, it becomes much more expressive. Actions, on the other hand, can express some ideas, but they can do so much more completely when combined with words. In some cases, actions speak louder than words.

This relationship between the words and actions which express a person's ideas and emotions in his daily life should be reproduced in the art of acting, which creates human characters through the depiction of their lives.

Above all else, the actor should be particularly careful in his verbal portrayal of a character.

The actor should speak in a natural and realistic way which matches the character's personality and the particular situation. The same words may be used to different effect, depending on the character and the situation and they will be heard differently depending on the manner and technique of speech. The actor should therefore endeavour to speak in a manner which suits the character and the situation, and should never play with words by raising and lowering his intonation.

To be able to speak in keeping with the character and the situation, the actor needs to develop a profound understanding of the character's life and personality and to be quite serious in his efforts to experience them. This is the starting point in the creation of a verbal portrayal suited to the character and the situation.

Having first come to understand the character's life and personality and experienced them, the actor should develop his verbal portrayal by using his own voice to express the character's distinctive manner of speaking. The actor should not ignore the character's unique manner of speaking and allow his own voice to emerge, contrary to the requirements of the situation in the character's life. On the other hand, he should not try to express himself in an assumed voice and completely suppress his own. Either of these two deviations disrupts the depictive unity of the actor and his role, and distorts the life and personality of the character. When the actor is able to blend his own voice with the character's, and speak in a manner suited to the character's personality and his particular situation in life, he has mastered the technique of fine verbal portrayal.

The actor must be able to speak in an unaffected manner. If he puts on airs or tries to force a certain style of speech, his words will become awkward and the character's personality will seem preposterous. If he puts on airs in his speech, he is apt to do the same in his gestures and, if he forces a certain style of speech, his movements will also become forced, and eventually the character's entire personality will be falsified. Words can only depict a character's personality faithfully when they are as plain and unaffected as they would be in daily life.

A truthful verbal portrayal can only be created by an actor who has freed himself from the old pattern of acting and speaks as naturally as in his daily life.

The actor's speech should also be precise and subtle. This requires him to be highly sensitive to the ideological and emotional state of his character, and clearly understand his individual manner of expressing himself. The actor needs a refined mastery of the art of speech in order to deal with any dialogue skilfully.

This mastery of the art of speech is an important artistic quality which the actor must acquire. The actor is an artist of words, just as the writer is. The writer is a master who uses words to construct sentences which accurately express a person's psychological state at any given moment and in any given circumstance, whereas the actor is a master who expresses the true meaning of these sentences through subtle and precise oral interpretation. This is the only difference between them. If an actor has a poor grasp of the art of speech and the roles which he can be assigned are restricted or if he has to correct his words after recording or even have another actor record in his stead, he is actually crippled as an actor. The actor should therefore spare no effort or time in developing and training his technique and his ability to portray a character's speech precisely and subtly.

If his oral interpretation of the part is to be good, the actor must be well-versed in the many excellent expressive means of our native language and be able to make good use of them. Only if he has a thorough grasp of these means can he create an admirable expression of his role in his words, and portray the character accurately, in a manner which accords with the taste and sentiment of the masses.

In particular, actors should possess a good knowledge of the beautiful and noble cultured Korean language of our own times and make good use of it in their acting.

The exemplary use of this cultured language in the cinema is extremely important in educating people in socialist patriotism and communist morality, and it contributes significantly to raising their level of general culture and establishing a sound way of life in society. By creating oral interpretation of a high ideological and cultural standard, actors should also contribute actively to educating people in our language.

The actor should use actions as accurately as he uses words.

A person's actions are always typical of his character. Even when people have common ideas and objectives, their specific actions differ according to their level of ideological consciousness and general culture. People act differently even in the same situation, and even when they do act in a similar fashion no person ever repeats an action in exactly the same manner. Every action results from a definite cause and occasion, and each time its expression is characterized by new features.

Since the art of film depicts life through the behaviour of actual people, the acting should be truly representative of people's ideas and emotions, and should dramatically depict the achievement of their aspirations and objectives amid the struggle between the old and the new.

In distinction from the actions of real life, acting is a form of action undertaken by the actor on the basis of his previous understanding and anticipation In real life, too, people act with definite ideas and purposes already in mind, but they do not know as clearly as the actor does what the results of these actions will be. However, the actor is being unfaithful to reality if he reveals his character's actions beforehand because he has prior knowledge of each action and is anticipating it. At the appropriate moment the actor should introduce each action in an unaffected manner and act naturally, as if he is encountering a genuinely fresh event or situation.

The actor should discover the unique action which his character will take in a particular situation or on a particular occasion and apply it in a spontaneous manner. In order to portray the actions of a real person in a manner true to reality the actor must discover the action a character would really take in a given situation, the action which conforms with that person's ideas, emotions and aspirations. If he uses ambiguous actions which each member of the audience may interpret differently his acting can no longer be called truthful. When his acting is flawless, the actor convinces the audience.

The actor should therefore take a careful and responsible attitude to every word he utters and every gesture he makes.

SUCCESS IN ACTING MUST BE ASSURED BY PERSISTENT EFFORT

In order to act realistically, in front of the camera the actor should live like the actual person he is portraying. To do this he has to acquire specialized knowledge of his own craft and a high degree of artistic skill, and he must be sure that he knows everything that his character has done.

A writer or painter needs to get to know a person and his life before he depicts him, and then to be able to portray him in words or sketches or paint, and that is enough. However, the actor not only needs to be familiar with the person and his life, he also needs to be able to act. A writer who is going to depict a football player imagines himself in his position and vividly expresses his thoughts and his actions when he is playing with the ball, and that is enough. The actor, however, has to actually become the football player himself and run, sweating, across the pitch to kick the ball.

In order to serve the Party and the revolution faithfully, actors must have both a rich knowledge of life and a high degree of artistic ability. The actor is an artist who serves the Party and the revolution by creating outstanding new characters for different films. It is therefore absolutely essential for him to acquire an adequate knowledge of life and the artistic ability necessary to fulfil his mission and discharge his responsibilities satisfactorily.

Knowledge of life and artistic ability are the essential conditions for an actor to become a genuinely creative artist, and the fundamental criteria for assessing his quality as an artist. If he lacks a broad knowledge of life and a high degree of artistic ability, there is nothing to distinguish him from people who work in other spheres of activity in our society.

Furthermore, the actor's knowledge of life and his artistic ability are the prerequisites of the creation of characterizations. Without them, he is unable to create any artistic portrayal.

The actor's ideological and artistic maturity is directly reflected in his portrayal of a character. He plays his role at his own ideological and artistic level, and he cannot expect to achieve a great success if his own level of preparedness is inadequate.

Success in acting must be assured by persistent efforts. Through uninterrupted study and training, the actor must become an expert in his own specialized field, so that he always achieves great success in every role he plays. An actor will never be successful if he relies only on his innate ability and hopes for a stroke of luck when he is acting, instead of making an effort to study and train.

An actor should always be fully prepared ideologically, mentally, technically and physically. If he has theoretical knowledge, but is unable to apply it in practice, or does not know how to express his intentions, he is not a genuine film actor.

If an actor has a rich knowledge of life and is able to apply it in his acting, if he is prepared to create a perfectly-rounded portrayal of his character, then he is a master of the art of portrayal, who has perfected the mental and technical skills required in his acting, and is capable of undertaking any role in the performance.

The actor should not rely on luck or expect miracles from trick shots or the "magic" of editing. If he is driving a car or riding a horse, for example, he must master the techniques involved. Otherwise, he cannot act realistically on an imitation car or horse. Let us suppose a car is running along a straight and smooth road. If the actor turns the steering wheel this way and that, thinking that the vehicle cannot move unless he does so, he is simply producing a clumsy imitation of life.

The days are long gone when actors used "tricks" to conceal the defect in their acting. The diversification and enrichment of film techniques in the modern cinema industry actually require the actor to create a better portrayal. The reality of socialist society, in which all people are being prepared as the new type of communists, who have all developed along diverse paths and are all equipped with a wealth of knowledge, a highly-developed morality and a strong physique, requires the actor to become versatile and to possess a wealth of knowledge and techniques.

The actor should not confine his thinking within narrow limits, he should be constantly expanding the scope of his observation and study, and striving militantly to achieve creative success. Then his creative work will indeed be successful.

The actor should, in the first place, be fully prepared politically and ideologically.

Man's ideological consciousness is the force that motivates and determines his social behaviour, and the results of his social behaviour depend not only on the content of his ideological consciousness, but also on its level.

Actors who are engaged in creative work, should be thoroughly trained politically and ideologically so that they can understand the real nature of life and achieve good results by setting realistic goals for their creative activities and conscientiously and energetically endeavouring to attain them. The knowledge and ability of an actor who is unprepared politically and ideologically is merely knowledge and ability for its own sake; it is of no use whatsoever in creating art for the people, art for the revolution.

Actors should pursue their political study and skills training intensively, in order to raise their ideological level and steadily improve their artistic ability, so that they will not be tempted to envy or imitate others when acting. An actor who has a high level of political self-awareness and a strong sense of responsibility as a film worker will always make conscientious and persistent efforts to improve his artistic ability.

Actors should study and train both collectively and individually according to a long-term plan. Skills training is an excellent educational method that combines artistic theory and acting practice, and is most effective in consolidating and refining an actor's skills and other qualifications.

All actors, whether new or experienced, should work hard at all times and in all places to improve their artistic skills through steady training. Only through constant and effective study and training can they achieve an outstanding level of ability and develop their talents fully.

In principle, skills training should cover a wide range in order to improve any weak areas in the actor's work. It is good for an actor who has only played the role of the positive characters to portray negative characters and for one who has only represented negative characters to play positive characters. If an actor always represents characters with similar personalities, he is liable to become "crippled", and unable to develop his acting ability in a harmonious manner. If an actor who has portrayed many villainous characters has to represent heroic characters, he will be able to look back on the characters he has played in the past in the light of the opposite role he is now playing, and in the future will be better able to create further portrayals of villainous characters.

All actors must undergo skills training which is directed to raising the level of their artistic ability. Experienced and competent actors should train themselves in order to attain a higher goal, and new actors should make every effort to attain the same level as the creative collective.

There is no doubt that if an individual actor's ability is raised so as to reinforce the creative strength of the collective, the ideological and artistic level of the films being made will also be raised. Therefore, skills sessions should not be run as if they were competitions or be attended only by the most competent actors. Every actor should train himself thoroughly and strive to improve his artistic ability in order to be able to contribute to improving the quality of the creative collective. This contribution is the main benefit of skills training.

Skills training should enhance an actor's artistic ability and also strengthen the acting collective's unity of ideology and will and firmly establish the communist mode of creative work.

All the actors should arm themselves with a full grasp of the concept of Juche and apply it so as to strengthen their unity of ideology and purpose. They should all help each other to advance and improve their level of political and ideological awareness, as well as their artistic and technical skills.

The cinema is not an art which can be successful if only a few actors are performing well. If ten actors appear in a production, all of them must be prepared to work as one man and all must act at an equally high level. Then a good film will be produced.

In film-making the success of one actor is the success of the collective and the success of the collective brings honour to all the actors. The communist ethic of creative work requires the whole collective to support and help new actors or actors whose standard is low, so that all of them may work at the highest possible level and produce a splendid film. If training and creative work are conducted on the basis of this communist ethic, the unity of ideology and will of the group of actors will be consolidated and a militant and revolutionary atmosphere, an atmosphere of inquiry and creative energy, will prevail throughout the collective.

Good results in skills training depend upon the choice of training tasks suited to the level of each actor's preparedness and the provision of numerous, various and interesting training activities.

The actors' skills training will be improved if it is based on top-quality scripts. A production already filmed may be used as well as the one which is being prepared for filming. Playing out on stage the major scenes of a production ready for filming as part of the actors' training can help to deepen their understanding of the film's content and assist them in the successful performance of their creative assignments, from the analysis of characters to the process of creating specific experience and its depiction.

It is also a good idea in skills training not to use only scripts, but to choose a one-act play or other short dramatic works, a novel or a poem, which have a profound psychological structure and express diverse shades of emotion. Dramatic works are particularly suitable and effective for intensive skills training, because in the course of a stage production it is possible both to improve the actors' ability to analyse a work and raise the standard of their acting. Furthermore, the frequent reading of novels and recitation of poetry is highly conducive to enriching the actors' emotional range and refining their art of speech.

Actors should undergo varied training, including singing and playing on musical instruments, in order to develop a deep understanding of the world of music and improve their artistic sensitivity. In singing practice it is a good idea to use various forms such as solos, vocal ensembles and choruses, and, in some cases, even to don the appropriate dress and sing with professionals. The actors will then be able to understand the content of the songs and the specific qualities of the singer and his environment as fully as the singers do, and immerse themselves naturally in the world of the songs. By repeatedly training in this way, they will develop the ability to perform with ease even in musical scenes and build up their repertoire of expressive techniques.

An important means of improving every actor's standard of acting is regular training under simulated theatrical conditions. This regular training will remove difficulties in acting technique and conversation and will eliminate persistent bad habits.

However, actors should not confine themselves to training under simulated conditions, but also, having gained some experience of acting on the stage, try to perform before a live audience. Performing dramatic pieces and presenting the songs and dances which they have rehearsed at a theatre, at a factory or other enterprise, is a good means of encouraging the masses to greater efforts for increased production. It also provides the actors with local experience and contributes to their skills training.

The actor's job is by no means an easy one. The satisfactory performance of the duties assigned to him by the Party and the revolution is a difficult, yet immensely worthwhile revolutionary task.

Film actors should thoroughly prepare themselves politically and ideologically, artistically and technically, culturally and morally, so that they can legitimately be regarded as the face of the film.

CAMERA AND IMAGE

"Only realistic works of literature and art which provide a vivid and profound portrayal of real life, can touch the hearts of people."

KIM IL SUNG

FILMING SHOULD BE REALISTIC

The art of filming deals with a world of infinite breadth and diversity. There is nothing in society and nature, in human life or the physical world, which cannot be captured by the camera.

Shooting a film for the cinema is the art of transferring onto the screen an animated, visual depiction of human life.

Every image on the screen is animated. However, shooting should not be confined simply to mechanically following moving objects and depicting the way in which they move. Shooting should not only reproduce the moving objects as they are, it should also depict inanimate objects as if they were moving; it should create cinematic movement by combining the movement of an object with that of the camera. This is the only way to create a specifically cinematic moving image and a rhythmical flow of imagery which will evoke a tapestry of emotions.

Although shooting a film is the art of creating moving images, the cameraman must not concern himself only with the outward movement of a character or the mechanical movement of an object. If he only attempts to produce the effect of movement and disregards the content of the scene, he will fall prey to formalism. Shooting should be concentrated on clarifying the theme and idea of the work through the movement of the images.

Shooting should show life in movement while presenting a vivid visual portrayal. The object projected onto the screen is concretely and accurately depicted because the camera vividly captures its form and colour. No matter how intricately and accurately man may copy life, his imitative ability cannot match the ability of the camera to copy. Shooting must make good use of this ability to create a concrete and animated portrayal of life.

The art of shooting depicts the form of objects in perspective, but a scene cannot be given perspective if objects are all shown on the same level. Since each scene depicts a different object, it should be deliberately arranged to suit the distinctive features of that object, and the position of the camera should be freely altered and the distances and angles adjusted in a varied fashion, so that the object is observed from various angles. This provides each of the objects with perspective and ensures the harmonious unity of the various objects which are pivoted around the main one. In this way a balanced screen composition is achieved with a depth and scope of image which give a true reflection of nature. When full use is made of these various possibilities in shooting, it becomes possible to show the object in perspective, which keeps it within the audience's field of vision in a realistic and natural way.

Although the cameraman has to ensure perspective on the screen, he should be interested in far more than just the graphic depiction of objects. Even if he creates wonderful pictures through skilful graphic depiction, they will be entirely void of meaning if the expression of the film's ideological content is not vividly sustained. In addition to providing perspective for the images, the camerawork must also give detailed expression to the film's profound meaning and the distinctive emotions which cannot be fully expressed in the words and actions of the character.

In his endeavours to depict life, the cameraman should always give particular emphasis to the main points. He should only film what is essential, depicting it from various angles, according to the demands of logic.

A film's potential for vividly portraying the essential nature of human life is realized mainly in the shooting. It can thus be said that the film's success depends on the camerawork. The attitude and the viewpoint from which the cameraman shoots the object, determine the ideological and artistic quality of the image.

An image which has been captured by the camera and projected onto the screen cannot be corrected, but only cast aside. A stage production can be revised and added to constantly in the course of repeated rehearsals and performances and it can be improved in any way the author wishes, but once a film has been transferred to the screen, it cannot be altered.

The cameraman should therefore explore the world of the work in depth, making a profound study of the personalities and lives of the characters and clearly defining his own attitude towards them. He must not start shooting until, working on the basis of his own independent opinions, he has carefully checked through the various complex problems of screen representation—whether the object which is to be projected onto the screen is authentic, vibrant and distinctive; where the main emphasis should be laid in the composition of the image; what exactly the lens should be focused on in order to capture the essential nature of the character and his life; what means should be used to create a vivid portrayal of the action and so on.

A character and his life have to be brought into focus in the camerawork if a faithful screen portrayal is to be created. Cinematic images are a reflection of human life. A faithful and adequate screen portrayal cannot be divorced from human life, and the cameraman can only create it when his interest is focused on the life of man, while still encompassing natural and other phenomena.

If a character is to be captured faithfully in the process of filming, his personality must be revealed through his actions. In whatever form the character may be portrayed, he is influenced by his environment and he reveals his thoughts and emotions in his reactions to it. The cameraman can therefore only cast accurate light on a character's inner world by faithfully reflecting the relationship between the character and his environment.

In portraying a character's environment, the cameraman may portray the natural surroundings and social manners and customs of the period, but he must not overemphasize them at the expense of the socio-historical environment which is the direct formative influence on people's personalities. The cameraman should concentrate for the most part on the social and historical environment, which is decisive in the creation of a realistic character, but he should support this environment with a depiction of the geographical surroundings and certain social manners and customs. Only in this way can he provide an accurate reflection of the life of a particular time.

Even in depicting nature, the cameraman should be sure to pick out a landscape or certain subjects which are related to human lives and can add relevant colour to the character. He must not bury man in nature or indulge an interest in nature and ignore man altogether. In art the beauty of nature only acquires meaning when it serves the meaningful depiction of human life.

The cameraman should portray life in a natural and realistic way.

When they view a street or watch a football match in a stadium, people want to be in a position where they have a clear, commanding view of everything going on. An object may or may not be entirely visible, in full detail, depending on where it is viewed from and how. These points should be applied to the depiction of action on the screen.

As people only see objects on the screen from the camera's point of view, the cameraman should always ensure that the audience are able to see the objects as naturally as if they were seeing them in real life. To do this he has to position the camera correctly and shoot carefully.

Every object has a focal point and every event has a crux. The cameraman should correctly identify life's centre of gravity and select a position from which it can be easily and distinctively portrayed.

The position of the camera, the way the object is viewed and the organization of movement should be determined by people's customary experience in their daily lives. Since the cinema is a visual art, the spectators will be drawn naturally into the world of the work if the images they see are what they are used to in life.

In order to depict life faithfully, the cameraman should portray concrete objects in a vivid manner. If he ignores reality and the real facts of life in his camerawork, claiming that he is attempting to reflect the essence of life, he will actually be unable to transfer life onto the screen faithfully and nobody will believe in the reality of the life depicted. A film can only appeal to the audience if it portrays life in vivid detail, just as it is in reality.

However, the qualities of concreteness and vividness are not automatically created simply by depicting life as it is. In order to create a living screen portrayal the cameraman must reveal aspects of life which clearly display its essential nature, he must add and subtract in such a way as to create a realistic image, he must discover novel methods of depicting life's essential aspects more effectively.

The camerawork of a film should portray everything clearly and concisely.

People can only examine an object closely when the cameraman has a clear understanding of the essence of the object and depicts it distinctly. The sequence of images in a film is continuous, so even meaningful objects lose their meaning if their essential significance is not depicted clearly.

By being concise and clear we mean highlighting the central focus of the image and laying particular emphasis on its most fundamental features, while clearly expressing the object's meaning.

In order to be concise and clear, it is also necessary to know exactly what people perceive; this means picturing large or small objects just as they are, gradually discerning complicated objects and uncovering hidden ones, just as people do in real life.

One can command a general view of a large, imposing building such as the Grand Theatre from a certain distance. A mural can be clearly viewed from a point at which the images of the people in it are distinct. If one stands too close to the mural or too far from it one cannot fully appreciate it. In similar fashion, objects and phenomena can only be clearly understood at suitable distances.

The cameraman should depict the diverse aspects of human life in an effective and interesting manner. However, he should not use his camera simply to create interest, and deviate from the depiction of the essential and authentic nature of the object. The cameraman should always focus on the essential aspects of life and depict them in an effective and attractive manner.

People will interpret and understand the essential nature of the same object in different ways, according to the attitude adopted by the cameraman.

In depicting people and their lives the cameraman should be strong in his determination to safeguard the interests of the masses, from the ideological viewpoint of the working class. The cameraman who speaks for the ideas and feelings of the people should film with passion; when the hero is celebrating victory over the enemy in battle, the cameraman should share his elation, hugging his camera in his joy, and when the hero is struggling in a difficult situation, he should help him through his ordeal.

An image into which the cameraman has not breathed his own life is incapable of involving the audience in the drama. The more strongly the passion of the cameraman is felt in the film's flow of images, the more deeply excited and affected the audience will be.

THE CHARACTERISTICS OF THE WIDE SCREEN SHOULD BE USED EFFECTIVELY

The wide-screen film is not merely a product of technological progress. It is the result of the artistic endeavour to present life in the film in a natural and vivid way, as it is in reality, and to expand our knowledge of it.

The expanded screen space of the wide-screen film offers abundant potential for a broader reflection of life and for depicting objects with greater definition of form and perspective, so that life is depicted the way people see it in reality. It is therefore important for wide-screen filming to address the problems arising from the relationship between the different types of screen and the content to be projected on them.

Some people attempt to exploit the advantages of the wide screen by presenting nothing but large images of objects and crowding a lot of things into a single frame. In doing this they are thinking of nothing but the scale and form of the screen and ignoring the requirements of the content to be presented on it.

The relationship between a film's content and form does not change in a wide-screen film simply because the scale and form are different. In a wide-screen film, too, scale and form are meaningless apart from the content of life, just as meaningful depiction is unthinkable without a profound idea on which to base it.

Whatever forms are used in art, the content must not be trimmed to fit within a frame. Life provides the content of art, and the content demands a suitable form. Content is expressed through the form and determines it, so the form of the work of art is always in effect the form of its content. When the form of a piece of work is regarded as good, it is because it matches the content, which has been expressed in an excellent and distinctive fashion, and not because the form itself has some appeal of its own apart from the content.

A literary work is not regarded as a masterpiece because of its scale, but because of its content; in camerawork, also, it is not the physical scale but the expression of content that should be broad. The artistic value of an image is not determined by the scale of the object depicted on the screen but by the scope, depth and reality of the portrayal of the life. A wide-screen image which only shows life on a grand scale is inferior to an ordinary screen image with substantial content.

The scale of life should not be mechanically enlarged just because a wide-screen film has the potential ability to depict life with more realistic scope and depth. No artistic form, however large, can reflect life by producing an exact reproduction of it. The larger the scale of a cinematic form, the more careful consideration is required as to how the wide-screen space is to be used.

The scale of the screen only acquires significance when it contains a broad depiction of life with clearly expressed ideological content. If an ordinary crowd scene is simply composed by bringing together lots of people, or if objects of a large scale are exclusively used in the shooting because the wide-screen film is itself large in scale, the film will be gorgeous in form but entirely lacking in substantial content. Sometimes the depiction of the film's content and of real life requires the filming of large objects but they should not be selected exclusively simply because the film is a wide-screen production.

The essential nature of life is revealed through the portrayal of a living person in specific circumstances. Film scenes should therefore always be concrete. If the cameraman has no precise grasp of the nature of human life and does not present it in depth, but concentrates only on showing the movement of huge crowds, the scenes become abstract and, in the final analysis, produce only a vague general impression. However large the crowd represented on the wide screen may be, if the individuality of the different people is not clearly expressed on the screen, if the details of life are not revealed and if the heroes are not portrayed as living human beings, the film cannot be regarded as successful.

The same principles apply to the selection of objects. When he views the dam of a hydroelectric power station, the cameraman should not concentrate initially on its magnificence, but try to appreciate the mass heroism of the working class and their creative exploits that are embodied in the dam and think of how he can present them in wide scope on the screen.

If the cameraman sees only the physical scale of an object and fails to capture an image of man, he loses his grasp on life, and his scenes become pictures devoid of content. He must not loosen his grasp on human life on the grounds that he has to see things on a grand scale, and he should not deviate from the creation of the portrayal of typical images in order to enhance the form of the scenes.

Before he directs his camera at a large object, the cameraman should consider how to compose the scene so as to make a small object appear large and to represent the whole object by concentrating on one aspect of it.

Artistic generalization is effective because it does not show a hundred facts with a hundred strokes, but because it creates a hundred facts with one stroke. Putting a hundred things on the screen in order to show a hundred things cannot be called cinematic portrayal. An able cameraman uses a single minute detail to depict a man and his life in their entirety, and at the same time he provides a clear characterization of an entire age.

A great idea can be depicted by something which expresses the essential nature of life, however tiny and commonplace it may be. There are "artists" who are incapable of even telling the story of a family or a single person, yet they brag that they are raising problems that are vital to the whole of humanity. In contrast, there are excellent artists who, in describing the destiny of a family or a person, expound the destiny of a nation and a class and clearly express the flow of history.

A cameraman should be able to use a small thing to portray a great thing and use a few things to depict many things. To do this, he has to explore the essential nature of life in depth and shoot scenes which depict its various aspects vividly. By depicting the various aspects of life's essential nature in depth, a cameraman can produce a scene which embodies an ideological kernel in rich content.

When shooting a scene, it is essential to give it substance by making it a profound and rich expression of life, while also ensuring that the scale and form of the scene suit the characteristics of wide-screen film and that the sequence of scenes flows in an appropriate manner.

It is impossible to effectively realize the potential of the wide-screen film if emphasis is laid only on the content, because it is basic to the scene, and scale and form are not adequately dealt with or the plot of the story is not developed in an effective manner. The camerawork should be adequate to the content and form of the scene. Then it will be possible to achieve a harmonious unity of content and form and combine ideological and artistic values in an appropriate fashion.

The wide screen is far superior to the ordinary film screen in providing a natural image which shows the size of a real object and its perspective in space. The wide-screen film is distinguished by its ability to depict life with great clarity in natural scope. If these merits of the wide-screen film are effectively exploited in the camerawork, impressive screen portrayals of life can be produced, but if the scope of the screen is improperly used, the quality of the portrayal will be diminished. If one thinks only of expansive scenes and marvellous compositions, one is apt to exaggerate the objects or embellish them.

The frequent enlargement of objects in special close-up scenes and the unnecessary enlargement of the characters' faces is a manifestation of formalism.

As a rule, in these scenes the facial expressions of the characters are emphasized, but it is a method which should only be applied once or twice in the course of a film, where it is necessary. A character's inner world is disclosed not only in his facial expressions but also through his general behaviour, and it is revealed most fully in his words. It is important to portray a character's facial expressions in depicting his inner world, but this is not in itself a solution to the fundamental problems. In daily life a person who attempts to express his ideas only through his facial expressions, instead of by words or actions, will be criticized for his affected manners. In the scenes of a film, this wrong emphasis will inevitably produce a similar negative impression on the audience.

The simple enlargement of objects and restriction of the general view is an outdated method which was developed in making ordinary film. It fails to express the essential significance of an object or improve the form of scenes. It is true that specially devised close-up scenes can be advantageous at times, in that they specially emphasize a particular object and portray it in accurate detail. However, they will fall flat if they are misused and there has been no build-up of events and emotions. If objects are only shot in close-up their image becomes imbalanced and the harmony of the scenes is disrupted. A scene that is not balanced or harmonious will lack form, and a scene without form cannot be considered truly cinematic.

The form and perspective of a scene in a wide-screen film are not entirely determined by its scale and composition. The true form and perspective of a scene can only emerge when the meaning of objects, in their natural state, is made quite clear and all the images are concentrated on throwing the essential features into bold relief and ensuring that they are harmoniously arranged and related in a single unity. There is no pure form or perspective that is divorced from the content of the scene.

When making a wide-screen film it is essential to arrange the sequence of scenes in conformity with the distinctive features of the wide screen.

The wide-screen film has great potential for facilitating the natural flow of emotions, but its scenes change less often and are more prolonged than in an ordinary film.

If the camerawork does not present a broad composition of the whole of life which is in keeping with the flow of emotion, but dissects the scenes into many pieces, skipping from one object to another, it is in conflict with the requirements of the wide screen and the tastes and sensibilities of our people.

In a wide-screen film, it is better to shoot long scenes which match the flow of life and to prolong the effective emotional content by means of efficient editing based on the unrestricted movement of the camera. Since the emotional flow is realized in the actions of the characters, the cameraman must not lose sight of their movements, but faithfully record them on film.

The cameraman should think of content before scale and determine the latter according to the scope of his depiction of life. He should portray life in depth and breadth by making the most of the advantages of the wide screen. The value and significance of a wide-screen film lie in the depth of the portrayal of life.

A SCREEN PORTRAYAL DEMANDS FIRST-CLASS FILMING TECHNIQUES

The cinema is an art which has emerged from the achievements of modern science and technology and which continues to develop on the same basis. Without the support of science and technology, the cinema cannot exist as an art. For a work of literature to be made into a film the artistic and the technical have to be combined. It is the art of filming which achieves this. Filming is a distinctive field of creative work which fuses the artistic with the technical. Technique should therefore never be ignored in filming.

Some cameramen claim that they are not technicians but artists, and refuse to learn the camera techniques which they ought to know. Such an attitude is entirely wrong. By no means should technique be ignored in filming, in view of the fact that the filming equipment and technique are subordinated to clarifying the idea of the production and affect the quality of its realization on the screen.

It is imperative to guard against both the tendency to make camera techniques absolute in the creation of a film and the tendency to ignore them altogether. Technicalism separates art from technique in filming and lays more emphasis on technique and skill than on content, thereby weakening the creative role of the cameraman and reducing camerawork to the mere solution of technical problems.

The policy of art-first and technicalism both hinder the proper development of the art of filming when they are manifested in the cinema industry. These two deviations must be avoided in order to develop the cinema to a high ideological, artistic and technical level, which requires an absolutely clear understanding of the importance of both art and technique in filming. In particular, the development of camera techniques and the acquisition of a thorough knowledge of them is immensely important in enhancing the quality of a portrayal and broadening its scope.

Camera and filming techniques involve problems of mechanical engineering, optics, chemistry, physics and electronics engineering, problems ranging from the skilful handling of the various cameras, to the disposition of the lighting for illuminating objects and the diverse methods of manipulation in accordance with the particular features of various films.

In order to produce a first-class portrayal a cameraman requires a perfect knowledge of these techniques. A cameraman whose technical knowledge is inadequate is unable to depict an object properly, nor can he create independently a distinctive screen portrayal of reality. A cameraman who has a good knowledge of film and camera techniques can contribute substantially to the general quality of a screen portrayal through his own independent creative efforts.

The use of lighting in filming provides clear evidence of the immense influence that film and camera techniques have on the quality of an artistic portrayal. The cameraman uses lighting not only to create a visual depiction of objects, but also to create depth and perspective, establish the emotional atmosphere of a scene and define its essential nature more clearly. The expression of changes in the characters' inner thoughts and psychological attitudes, the definition of the surroundings in a variety of colours, the softening of the tone of the visual images and the ultimate clarity of the scenes all depend on the technical disposition of the lighting.

A cameraman must possess a good knowledge of both art and technique in order to create first-class screen portrayals which are flawless in both their artistic and technical aspects. The cameraman should be not only a good artist, but also a good engineer.

The cameraman should be familiar with all the latest developments in filming techniques, and should possess a perfect knowledge of both simple and easy technical matters and difficult and complicated ones. He must possess a comprehensive knowledge of the science and techniques that underlie technicolour, the wide screen and special camerawork, which are of particularly great importance in the development of contemporary film art.

He must not simply think that since cameras and films are made by specialized technicians, it will be enough for him simply to know only about their structure and the way they work and that since lighting and electrical techniques are taken care of by experts, he may simply give them instructions. He requires a good knowledge of everything, in order to demand higher standards and guide the technical operations correctly to the realization of his creative plans.

On the basis of his understanding of both art and technique, the cameraman should bend his efforts towards developing film techniques that enhance the ideological and artistic value of the film. It is particularly important for him to be able to develop special shooting techniques and trick shots quickly. As science and technology have developed, the expressive power of film has grown very strong. The development of celluloids of different quality and of new optical instruments for creating special effects have increased the potential of film to define the form of scenes and created unlimited possibilities for screen images.

Special effects enable the writer or the director to indulge his creative fantasy freely and make it possible to transform any illusion which has real meaning into a vivid screen image. They also make it unnecessary to expose actors to danger during filming and enable them to act freely and in safety; they enhance the artistic value of a production and considerably shorten the duration of filming, while contributing to the economic use of manpower, materials and funds in the making of films.

Without developing special effects it is impossible to make good use of the rich descriptive potential of cinematic art or to raise this art to the new heights required by the changing times and the aspirations of the people.

In order to exploit to the full the potential of special effects in creative work, the cameraman must first thoroughly study the scenario and the director's script, then go on to apply the most advanced expertise in the area of special effects. If he clings to one or two conventional methods, he will find them inadequate to the requirements of a faithful and vivid reflection of life in its many complex and diverse aspects and unable to create the necessary artistic effects. Since there are various kinds of trick shots, for example, he should closely consider which will be most effective to suit the distinctive features of his objects. In creating the special effects for a film the cameraman should not simply apply the methods which have already been used in this field, he should seek new methods in order to create fresh possibilities and expand the potential scope of film-making.

A basic function of the creation of special effects is to ensure the faithfulness of the portrayal of reality. Special effects are film technique for the faithful reproduction of life: they should not be thought of as mere magic.

To convey a faithful portrayal of reality through the use of special effects, the cameraman must appropriately combine technical requirements with the principles of realistic depiction. If the need for this combination is ignored, the portrayal of life will become distorted, no matter how skilful the camerawork may be. For instance it is possible to achieve a deliberate effect in the movement of objects by intentionally increasing or slowing down the film speed, but if people are moving in the scene their actions will be distorted, and the film's credibility will be destroyed.

The cameraman must hold fast to the standpoint of Juche and base his efforts on successes already achieved, developing filming techniques adequate to the specific features and requirements of the development of the cinema in our country. The most important thing in this regard is to continually improve the techniques, developing them in our own distinctive way in order to satisfy the immediate and long-term requirements of this development. However, technique should not be regarded as valuable in itself. This is unsuitable and inapplicable to the revolutionary cinematic art of our country.

We should also certainly endeavour to develop filming techniques by relying on our own efforts and wisdom, our own raw materials and equipment. The comprehensive, swift and effective development of our filming techniques is quite possible on the revolutionary principle of self-reliance, which involves solving technical problems by our own efforts and in keeping with the specific situation in our country and relying on the strength of our own Juche-inspired industry.

If we attempt to rely exclusively on imports to obtain important technical equipment for filming, while continuing to produce films in large numbers, we will be unable to establish a stable film industry. We must therefore take a firm stand against conservative tendencies, the fear of technology and sycophancy in the film industry, and demonstrate the revolutionary spirit of self-reliance in solving the technical problems by our own efforts.

We must not rely on foreign filming techniques instead of trying to develop our own. On the other hand, we must not close our eyes to international trends in the development of cinematic technique or close the door against foreign achievements in this field. We should assimilate foreign experience critically and develop techniques to our own liking, applying our major efforts to the development of techniques on the basis of our own strength and our own wisdom.

The cameraman must employ first-class film techniques in order to create a cinematic portrayal of reality. He must apply these techniques in the support of noble ideological and artistic values, thereby ensuring that our cinematic art is first-rate not only ideologically and artistically, but also in its technical aspects.

SCREEN ART AND FINE ART

"Not only painting, but also fine arts for the cinema and the stage, industrial art, sculpture, embroidery, crafts, and so on, should continue to be developed on the basis of traditional Korean forms appropriate to the sentiment and aspirations of the builders of socialism."

KIM IL SUNG

OUR FILM ART SHOULD BE BASED ON KOREAN LIFE

Films which are easily understood and liked by people are made up of scenes which are as vivid as real life. These vivid scenes are brought to life by clear images which are produced with the help of both art and film technique. The impression produced by a character's face, the proper costumes and realistic street scenes are all created by film artists.

Film art design uses make-up, costumes, hand props, scenery and other elements to give distinctive expression to the personalities of the characters and the times and create a comprehensive depiction of a complex way of life. Film art design creates different portrayals according to the content of each film, but it should all reflect the personalities of the characters, the features of the period in which they live and the diverse aspects of life in that period. In this way the setting of a film and the characters' costumes and hand props assist people to understand the personalities of the characters and the material and cultural standards of life in a particular age. Cinematic art design represents the period and the life of the characters through portraying their own physical appearance and that of their surroundings. It employs various formal means to create the formal beauty of the scenes.

In the cinema art is an effective means of depiction which gives form to a person's overall appearance and the outward appearance of his life, but it must always be subordinated to the film's ideological content, artistic features and technical conditions. Aft which ignores a film's ideological, artistic and technical requirements is of no assistance in film-making, however pictorially superb it may be.

Fine art employed in the making of films should be national in form and socialist in content. Only then can its ideological quality be high enough to suit our people's tastes and sentiments. Only this kind of fine art work can conform to the nature of revolutionary cinematic art and make a positive contribution to the ideological and artistic qualities of a production.

Art in the cinema industry should be based on Korean life and make extensive use of our own outstanding national artistic traditions.

From olden times, our people have lived in a beautiful land of golden tapestry, have demonstrated resourcefulness and wisdom and an unusually highly developed aesthetic sense. Throughout their long history of five thousand years, our people have developed a brilliant national culture and created a variety of beautiful national forms of art. The beautiful national arts created by our people include the prominent example of traditional Korean painting.

Traditional Korean painting is an excellent artistic form particularly well suited to the sentiments of our people. Korean painting clearly embodies the distinctive features of our people, the national features that have been formed over the ages.

Korean painting is characterized by a simple, clear, distinct style and by soft, light yet clear colours. Even in a single line, it is capable of expressing a person's ideas and feelings and his diverse movements, with astonishing succinctness and richness. In its use of colour, it lays the main emphasis on the true colours of the object, and the harmonious unity of the tones of the whole picture. These features of Korean painting should be developed, not only in painting but also in all other fields of fine art, including film art.

The comprehensive nature of film art, which comprises various fields of fine art, ranging from make-up to montage, means that it requires a firm basis in Korean culture even more than any other realm of fine art. Film art should make extensive use of the excellent wealth of costume, architecture and industrial art that are peculiar to our country, as well as of Korean painting.

Our national costume is widely known throughout the world for its beauty and elegance. Korean clothes are unique in form, pattern and colour and possess great grace and simplicity.

Our people's national sentiments have found profound expression in the architecture that has been built to harmonize with the beautiful scenery of our country, in the elegant ornamental art which adds to its refinement, and in the industrial art which bears eloquent witness to the noble minds and artistic skill of our people.

Fine art in the cinema should make wide use of our national tradition in various forms of fine art, but it should not mechanically copy the old. The tendency to resurrect the old is a reactionary ideological trend to restore things of the past mechanically, which is contrary to the revolutionary stand of the working class and the aspirations and sentiments of the builders of socialism.

The creation of fine art for the cinema requires a close study of the artistic heritage bequeathed to us by our ancestors in order to distinguish between the progressive and the backward, the popular and the anti-popular, so that we may always critically assimilate all that is progressive and popular and audaciously modernize it to meet the requirements of the revolutionary age. Only then will it be possible to create artistic portrayals of reality that suit the nature and the mission of revolutionary cinematic art and to further develop our traditional national forms of fine art so that they conform with modern aesthetic tastes.

In order to develop cinematic fine art on a Korean basis we should not only modernize our national forms of fine art to meet the requirements of the present age, we should also engage in original creative work using our own equipment and materials. If we use foreign equipment and materials to draw, paint and make clothes, scenery and properties, we cannot claim to be developing the cinematic fine arts on a Korean basis, even though they remain Korean in form.

Among our national forms of fine art, Korean painting, in particular, is distinguished from foreign forms not only by its simple, clear and distinct style but also by its distinctive colouring. The colours used in Korean painting are typically clear, light and soft; they have been developed over a long historical period, and they are unique colours which are particularly congenial to the aesthetic tastes of our people. In the past paints have therefore been produced which match the palette of Korean painting. While maintaining the positive features of the paints which have developed along with Korean painting over the ages, we must also make and use paints which are suited to the new tastes of the people of our age. This is essential to ensuring that the principle of Juche is firmly established in all the creative activities of fine art, including art for the cinema.

We can, of course, obtain clear, soft and light colours that are congenial to our people's tastes and sentiments even by using foreign paints. Needles to say, however, their quality cannot match that of our own paints, which reflect our people's unique sense of colour. Only painting which uses our own colours is true Korean painting.

Not only paints but all other materials and equipment should be produced and used in our own way to conform with the distinctive features of our national fine art. This is particularly important in ensuring that the development of our fine arts is founded on the principle of Juche and that our own material and technical foundations continue to be developed.

We should not dismiss all foreign forms of fine art on the grounds that we have to develop ours on the basis of Korean life and culture. Alongside the traditional forms of our national art, there exist in our country today artistic forms which have emerged through cultural exchange with foreign countries. In addition to the forms of fine art that are peculiar to our country such as Korean painting, there are foreign forms, such as oil painting and woodcut printing. The existence side by side in a single country of artistic forms of different origins is an inevitable result of the development of human culture. The only question is what attitude should be adopted towards the two forms of art. We must, in all circumstances, give priority to the development of our traditional forms of national art, while critically assessing and assimilating those foreign forms of fine art which accord with our people's tastes and are worthy of adoption.

We should not make foreign forms of fine art absolute, and cease to regard Korean culture as our basis, simply because some particular feature of the use of fine art in the cinema might seem to require them. However, it would also be wrong not to accept things which are worthy of creative adoption, simply because they are foreign. It is necessary to establish the principle of Juche in the practice of cinematic fine art, too. It will then be possible to develop cinematic fine art by laying emphasis on Korean sources, while accepting oil painting and other foreign forms of fine art insofar as they suit our own needs.

If fine art in the cinema is to be national in form and socialist in content, it must create portrayals of reality which suit the socialist content of a production.

Since a revolutionary film should have a socialist content, cinematic fine art must also have this. The socialist content of a film is intended to destroy the old and create the new, to contribute to the overthrow of capitalist society, the building of a socialist society that is free from exploitation and oppression, the revolutionary transformation of the whole of society, and its assimilation to the working class.

Fine art work in a film should always reflect the content of life which is being dealt with in the production. Make-up, costumes and hand props have no meaning apart from the characters in the film, and the scenery and props have no meaning apart from the character's lives.

Fine art in the cinema should faithfully portray the various aspects of the characters and their lives as they are portrayed in the original literary work. The make-up, costumes and hand props which represent our working class and the other labouring masses should vividly express the beauty and nobility of their minds, and the fine art work of scenery should accurately reflect the revolutionary habits and way of life of the people of our age. In particular, the fine art work of cinematic scenery should reflect the realities of socialist society and clearly depict the socialist aspects of the buildings of our age, which are functional yet comfortable, beautiful yet durable.

Only when fine art in the cinema is based on Korean life and culture and has a socialist content can it develop into a revolutionary fine art orientated towards our people and suited to their feelings and thereby make a substantial contribution to the ideological and artistic quality of the film.

MAKE-UP IS A NOBLE ART

Both on the screen and on the stage the actor portrays the inner thoughts and feelings of the character as well as representing his outward appearance. We can only consider that he has depicted a living person when these two aspects of his portrayal are properly coordinated.

Make-up is an art which contributes to an actor's portrayal of a character by giving his features the form of the features of the character. It is the art of transforming the outward appearance of the actor into that of the character, by emphasizing certain elements and suppressing certain other unnecessary ones according to the character's distinctive personal features. Make-up is a noble art since it unifies the external appearances of the actor and the character and creates a new human image.

If the realized portrayal of a character is likened to a ripe fruit, make-up may be compared to the bloom and complexion of the fruit. Just as it is possible to anticipate the taste of a fruit from its appearance and its colour, the external appearance of a character can be of great help in understanding the mind of a character.

Inadequate make-up hinders the accurate portrayal of a character's personality even if his inner thoughts and feelings are admirably expressed through refined acting. If the face of the actor simply appears as it is, it will be impossible to identify the character's true appearance and therefore the character will be incapable of inspiring confidence and sympathy.

Make-up should faithfully conform to a character's personality while yet being based on the actor's own outward appearance. Make-up artists should have a thorough knowledge of the actor's natural features in order to be able to use them as the basis for the faithful representation of the character's appearance.

If make-up artists attempt to create a character portrayal by thinking only of the character's personality, and give no thought to the actor's essential features they cannot help the actor, and the make-up is reduced to a mere superficial display. On the other hand, if the actor's natural features are left untouched, the result will be the accommodation of the character to the actor, and the truth of the portrayal will suffer accordingly. Only make-up which conforms to both the actor's natural features and the character's features can be said to constitute a faithful portrayal.

Make-up should equip the actor to portray a person's character subtly and truthfully. It must therefore provide a distinctive external characterization of a person's inner thoughts and feelings. Although the outward appearance of a person does not fully reveal his mind, his outward appearance does indicate his position in society and traces of his past, so it should be depicted in conformity with his inner world.

Only when the character's outward appearance and inner world are unified can the actor penetrate deep into the character's life, clearly expressing his inner thoughts and feelings even through his external appearance. An actor whose outward appearance is in conflict with the character of his part can hardly be expected to enter the state of complete readiness for acting.

However, if exclusive emphasis is laid on the character's ideological characteristics, on the grounds that make-up should be based on his inner world it will prove impossible to avoid bias and repetitive depictions. A character's ideological consciousness is basic to his personality, but if it is exclusively stressed and the other diverse expressions of his individuality are ignored, a set pattern will emerge whereby positive characters are always made up to look attractive and negative characters to look unattractive.

A clear understanding of the character in its entirety must be formed before make-up can be composed correctly. Make-up artists should study and analyse in depth the various aspects of a character's personality and make every possible effort to reflect it in detail in the make-up. The characterization will prove sterile if the essential aspects of the character's personality are maintained at the expense of the subtle balance of his other individual features. Make-up artists are creative artists in that they give emphatic expression to the essential features of character's personality while skilfully harmonizing them with his other individual features.

Facial depiction is a fundamental aspect of make-up. An actor's facial make-up plays an important role in characterization. The actor's body movements also play an important role in acting, but they cannot match the subtlety of his facial expressions. A man's face subtly manifests not only ideas and emotions such as joy, sorrow, love and hatred, but also highly complex psychological changes. The eyes, in particular, reveal a man's inner thoughts most intensely and sensitively and even express the thoughts in the depths of his heart. The eyes can often meaningfully express even the most delicate feeling or intricate psychological state which cannot be fully expressed by words. For this reason a man's eyes have been called the mirror of his soul.

In a film the actor's face, and the eyes in particular, should be made up well, because a person's face can be captured by the camera in different scales in different scenes. In a scene which shows mainly the actor's face the background is merely a supportive element and the central element is the character's face. In this scene the face is clearly represented and the meanings of the ideas and emotions contained in its expressions are clearly revealed, and the character's personal features are conspicuously emphasized. Therefore, if the face is made up badly, the depiction of the character cannot be truthful and subtle, and the faithfulness of the entire characterization will be impaired.

Facial make-up should never exaggerate one particular aspect of a personality. If it is exaggerated, it will blur or distort the characterization. A tendency to exaggeration is frequently encountered, particularly in the make-up of negative characters. Some make-up artists make up a landlord's face in a pictorial fashion and so make it impossible to grasp the reactionary essence and inhuman nature of the hostile class correctly. It is necessary to closely examine the inner world even of a negative character and represent it accurately in his make-up.

We should guard against coarseness and crudity in facial make-up, as well as excessive exaggeration.

There was once a painting which showed a man looking up at a green pine tree, and everybody praised it to the skies. But a painter who saw it is reported to have said, "When a man raises his head, the nape of his neck is always creased. So there is a great blunder here."

It must be remembered that in facial make-up if any single spot is missed or handled coarsely, it will spoil the accuracy of the entire characterization. The make-up artist would be committing a "blunder" like the one in that "celebrated painting" if he were to apply a moustache, create a scar or draw in lines in a slipshod manner, because he regarded such jobs as simple and easy.

The make-up artist should not only be clever with his hands, he should also take a serious attitude to his creative work, so that even in drawing a simple line on a face, he carefully considers the features of the character and the overall harmony of his make-up.

It is extremely important to make the most of various methods of applying make-up to give appropriate form to the character's personality.

As a rule, a variety of people who have different class origins and different occupations, ages, tastes and hobbies appear in a film. They include historical figures who should be portrayed with absolute faithfulness, people who have lived a long life up to old age, and, in rare cases, characters of a foreign nationality. The actors who represent the various characters in the film each have different creative individualities and physical features. Since there are different characters and different actors, it is impossible to restrict oneself to one method of applying make-up. Make-up artists should be able to select methods of applying make-up which are suited to both the physical features of the actors and the personalities of the characters, and should continually strive to discover new methods.

Some people employ only one method of applying make-up, representing different characters in a similar way, or making them up without taking into account the features of their times and the tastes and interests of the people. This is wrong. People's appearances change as the times change, they look different depending on the contemporary national sentiments and customs.

Therefore, if characters are to be made up in keeping with the requirements of the times and the aesthetic sensibilities of the people, the make-up art must develop a profound understanding of both the actor and the character and, in addition, possess a thorough knowledge of period surroundings and national customs. The deeper this understanding is, the more effective will be the choice of a variety of appropriate methods for applying make-up and the more likely new methods are to be discovered. The discovery of new methods in the course of developing new characters makes it possible to create vivid and individual character portraits and to represent their life and times accurately.

It is also essential for the make-up to be adequate to the technical requirements of the film. The lens of the camera captures details which cannot be immediately discerned by the human eye, so the make-up artist needs to be well aware of these technical aspects of film, and work in accordance with both technical and artistic requirements. If he considers only the artistic requirements to be important and ignores the technical ones, the make-up will not be sufficiently accurate. Only a character faithfully made up to be as real as a living person will linger in the minds of people.

COSTUMES AND HAND PROPS SHOULD CONFORM TO THE PERIOD AND THE CHARACTER

Costumes and hand props reveal various aspects of the personality of the individual who wears, uses and handles them, as well as the features of the period in which he lives and the stage of development of his society.

Characteristic features of the period and national sentiments can be detected in the texture, forms, patterns and colours of the clothes a person wears. An individual's living conditions and personality are also clearly evident from his clothes. People's attire varies just as their individual personalities do.

The objects used by people in their daily life are also engraved with the personalities of the people who handle them and traces of their life. They reflect the distinctive features of the period, the social and economic situation, the standard of culture and the customs of national life.

These features of clothes and other objects make cinematic costumes and hand props an essential means in the characterization of the times and people.

If costumes and hand props are to be used effectively in a film, the representational level of the art design must be high. If the art design fails to produce costumes and hand props to suit the personality of the character and the period, the actor can hardly be expected to act well.

Cinematic art design, geared towards the making of costumes and hand props, is a refined art which helps to form the personality of the character portrayed by the actor. Therefore, when producing costumes and hand props, the artists should make quite sure that they express the class position and mental state of a character clearly and uniquely.

In an exploitative society poor people cannot afford to have clothes made from good-quality fabric or to use good quality things in their everyday lives, whereas landlords and capitalists can do so. The artists should therefore clearly express the class position of a character through his economic circumstances, which are revealed through his costumes and hand props.

The class position and ideological and mental state of a character are all clearly revealed in the forms, patterns, ornaments and colours of his costume and hand props. A character's economic circumstances as reflected in his costume and hand props make his general class position clear, while his tastes and hobbies again as manifested in the forms, patterns, ornaments, and colours of his costume and hand props, demonstrate his class character and ideological and moral state in subtle detail.

In an exploitative society the workers and peasants cannot afford to have their clothes made from good material or to use good things like the rich; their dress and the things they use are functional, and the patterns and colours of these things are sober and simple enough to express the beautiful and noble spiritual traits of working men and women. However, the clothes and personal effects of landlords and capitalists are a mixture of crude forms, vulgar patterns, base colours and ornamentation, and they expose the degenerate and dissipate mentality of the exploiting classes. Film art work should therefore direct its energies to revealing a character's tastes and preferences in precise detail and pay close attention to clearly expressing his economic circumstances.

Special attention should be given to the costumes and hand props of the positive characters, particularly those appearing in a film which reflects the reality of socialism. When they see a film, people try to learn from and imitate not only the words and actions of the positive characters, but even their costumes and hand props.

The costumes and hand props of positive characters can be popularized as model for imitation if they conform well to the characters' personalities, the requirements of the times, and the people's new aesthetic tastes. Film art work should therefore avoid any tendency to restore the old and return to the past, or to fall into a Western style, and advocate "modernization"; it should correctly assimilate the positive aspects of our national heritage and accurately reflect the requirements of the new age, thereby producing novel costumes and hand props which are a true expression of the life of our working people and are adequate both to the personalities of the characters and the requirements of the socialist way of life.

Costumes and hand props should be individualized to match the personalities of the characters. Even people of the same class origin, with the same aspirations each have an individual manner of dressing and using their personal effects. By creating appropriate costumes and hand props, film art work can reveal the personalities of individual people in vivid detail and clearly express the distinctive differences in their personalities.

The artists working on films should have a profound understanding of the characters' individual personalities. They should closely observe their tastes and preferences and the manner in which they express them, and use this knowledge to ensure that the personalities of the characters are expressed in a coherent and truthful manner through the various features of their costumes and hand props. They should not carelessly lump together disparate elements which have no relationship to the common characteristics of a definite class or stratum of people, on the excuse of maintaining the character's individuality. The depiction in depth of a character's essential individuality requires that the various features, major and minor, of his costume and hand props should be blended into a harmonious unity which reveals a single, individual personality.

The use of costumes and hand props as a visual means of characterization can only render a character authentic if the features of the period in which he lives and of his national life are reflected accurately.

Man is a social being, and he cannot live divorced from his times and his nation. Man embodies in himself the features of his times and his nation since he lives within a definite period and defined national boundaries. These features assume a definite form in a person, appearing in his words and actions, expressing themselves even in his clothing and his use of personal effects.

In the past, under the colonial rule of Japanese imperialism, our people were poorly dressed. But today our people have become masters of the country, they are all decently dressed and prosperous.

Since it is impossible to separate a man from his times or a character's personality from his attire and personal possessions, there is a direct link between the times and people's attire and the things they use in their everyday lives. Artists should closely examine these relations in real life, and express the traces of history that are contained in people's clothes and the things they use, in order to create characterizations which clearly express their individual features. It will then be possible for them to depict faithfully the personality of a character who is typical of the times in which he lives.

It will not do to give the same features to all the pieces of costume and all the hand props, on the grounds that the features of the period should be consistently maintained. Artists should have a sharp eye for detail in order to identify what is most essential among the various traces of history which are reflected in clothes and personal effects, and they should be able to generalize in order to characterize a period through a single telling feature.

A person's clothes and personal effects also contain traces of national life. One can easily find national features that have been acquired over a long historical period, not only in national costume and implements but also in people's everyday clothes and other possessions. To cite an example, the way a Korean makes a Western-style suit of clothes is different from the way a Westerner makes it; their briefcases, too, are made differently. Clothes and personal belongings reflect the features of the climate, manners and customs and economic life of a nation. These all blend together to produce the national features of clothes and personal belongings.

The principles of history and modernity should be strictly observed in determining the national features of clothes and hand props. Since national features are constantly changing and developing in keeping with the social system and the life of the people, the national features of the age in which a character lives must be reflected accurately in the costumes and hand props. We cannot mechanically transfer features that have been formed in our own age to the costumes or hand props in a work that depicts the past, nor can we revive traces of the past in the costumes and hand props of a work which reflects socialist society. The national features that are embodied in a person's character must be conveyed through historically accurate costumes and hand props.

Costumes and hand props should not only be appropriate for the personality of the character and his times, they should also suit the actor. Costumes, in particular, must suit the actor since he has to wear them in playing the part.

If the costume suits the actor, his outward appearance is considerably improved and even his physical shortcomings can be concealed. In daily life, too, clothes that suit a person enhance his personality. Hence the proverb, "Clothes make the man."

In a film the costumes should contribute to enhancing the actor's personality. Costume designers should make good clothes which suit the actor's face and body and allow him to represent the character of a person more subtly.

The personality of the character must not be ignored here, on the grounds that the clothes should suit the actor and enhance his outward appearance. Even a costume that suits an actor perfectly will look unsightly if it does not clearly express the personality of the character. Since the aim of making a costume that suits the actor is to create a truthful portrayal of the character's personality, the clothes that are made should suit both the character's personality and the actor's body.

Costumes and hand props should be made so as to portray the outward appearance of a character and contribute to the visual form of the scenes.

The artistic designer must not simply think of the features of the times, the character and national life while ignoring the form of the costumes and hand props, nor must he emphasize the form alone and lose sight of the fundamental requirements of authenticity. If his only interest in using forms, patterns and colours is the visual form of the scenes, he will end up by separating content from form, weakening the meaning of the content, and eventually reducing the costumes and hand props to mere outward show. It is true that the formal beauty of costumes and hand props is inseparable from a harmonious balance of form and a harmony of patterns and colours. However, these elements can only be meaningful when they accord with the requirements of the period and the character.

In a film it is essential to harmonize both the costumes and hand props of each individual and the costumes and props of all the characters. Seen separately, the forms and the colours of the costume and hand props of one individual may appear attractive and beautiful, but if they are conspicuously out of tune with the costumes and hand props of other characters, they will destroy the overall formal beauty of the cinematic production.

The representational harmony of costumes and hand props in a film as a whole can only be achieved when the costumes and hand props of all the characters are all well matched and yet vividly express the individual personalities of the characters. In fundamental terms, harmony is achieved when different things accord well with each other. If similar things are brought together, not only is it difficult to achieve harmony, it is impossible to avoid repetition and extremely difficult to depict the individual personalities of the characters in bold relief. Costumes and hand props should therefore be carefully harmonized, and yet clearly distinguished from each other according to the characters' personalities.

The costumes and hand props should also match the colours of the make-up, the scenery and natural settings, so that the visual form of the image on the screen is enhanced and the personality of the character is vividly expressed. If costumes do not conform with the colours of the make-up, the characters give the impression that they are wearing someone else's clothes, which do not suit their own personalities. If this happens, the audience will not believe in the actor's characterization, no matter how skilfully he may act. Only when the actor's clothes and hand props conform perfectly with the colours of the make-up does the audience perceive a vivid human portrayal on the screen and accept it as real.

The character's costume and hand props should not be too conspicuous, but should conform with the colour tones of the scenery or natural settings, without being so hard to discern that they are lost in the latter. The harmonization of costumes and hand props with the elements making up the surroundings should be handled with caution, because this is a problem related to the fundamental requirement of authenticity, and the question of how, according to what principle, the relationship between the character and his surroundings should be determined as the character is developed.

The effectiveness of the costume and hand props in portraying a character finds clear expression in the actor's characterization. The art designer should therefore fulfil as accurately as possible all the requirements of portrayal by means of costume and hand props. The art designer alone is responsible for making the costume and hand props an effective means of sustaining the personality of the character, instead of reducing them to an outward show for the actor. Whenever he draws a line or marks a dot, he must carefully picture to himself the personality of the character. It is only possible to create honest and vivid artistic portrayals which clearly express the character of the times and the individual's personality through careful consideration and persistent inquiry.

THE SETS SHOULD REFLECT THE TIMES

If make-up, costume and hand props are the basic formal means for depicting the personality of a character, then the sets are the basic means for portraying the period and the surroundings in which he lives.

In a film the surroundings are transformed into a visual image on the screen through the art of set design. This art draws together onto a single roll of film the natural and social conditions which make up the surroundings of life, thus expressing the social and class position and economic circumstances of the characters, their standard of culture and education, their customs, ideas and emotions.

The art of set design creates the surroundings of the characters' lives and it is important that these circumstances of their lives and personalities should be depicted accurately.

In some films, however, these principles of set design are not always observed properly. In one old film the house of a musician who was suffering every manner of humiliation and insult under the colonial rule of Japanese imperialism was arranged in a manner that did not conform with his standard of living. It contained an expensive piece of embroidery and a huge mirror, which were actually only appropriate to the living standards of the rich at that time.

The houses of working people and those of capitalists and landlords cannot be the same, and even those of the former cannot all be arranged in a uniform way, divorced from the character of the times and the social system. Sets which do not distinctly reflect the personalities of the characters, their living conditions and the period in which they live can make no contribution to a faithful representation of life.

The art of set design should concentrate first of all on a vivid and faithful visual representation of the period and the surroundings. Just as a person's personality alters with the changing times and the pattern of life, architectural forms, furniture and ornaments all change and develop in various ways.

The houses of today are different from those of the past and the furniture and ornaments of today are not the same as those of olden days. The architecture of our times is developing along the line of an appropriate combination of socialist content with national form, and furniture and ornaments are being made which conform with the socialist pattern of life. The work of set design for the cinema must be carried out in accordance with the life of the times represented.

Sets must be typical of the life and times.

We should not mechanically transfer real houses or furniture onto the screen without any adaptation on the pretext that we are making our settings look real. When real objects are mechanically transferred into set designs it becomes impossible to make the surroundings appear authentic, and this makes it impossible to give an accurate portrayal of the features of the period and the characters' attitudes towards life. Naturalist tendencies in the art of set design confuse the point of a work, undermining the audience's comprehension and the film's educational function.

A primary requirement of the art of set design is to make the forms and colours of the sets conform to reality. The art of set design should not be confined merely to reproducing the outward appearance of a house or of furniture, but should clearly display the essential features of the period and the social system which they reflect, thereby rendering each setting authentic. When the essential features of the times and the social system are clearly evident, the settings will appear realistic and impressive, and people will be able to form a correct understanding of the times reflected in the work, even from a single item in the set.

Sets and props should not be exaggerated on the grounds that the essential aspects of life have to be clearly and sharply expressed. This inevitably leads to the beautification and embellishment of life, and the cinematic portrayal of reality loses its truthfulness and vividness.

The art of set design should not beautify, embellish or vulgarize life. A poor set which is out of keeping with the true situation distorts life and is devoid of pictorial value.

The art designer should strive to overcome any shortcomings in his creative work and conscientiously create settings which adequately represent the times and the social system depicted. He will then be able to design realistic and truthful surroundings for the characters to move in, and to provide people with an accurate understanding of the nature of life.

As well as depicting the period, the settings should unambiguously portray the personality of the characters who lived at that time.

Everyone lives in specific social surroundings in a definite period of history; he is both influenced by these surroundings, and, at the same time, reshapes them according to his own ideals and requirements. Hence the surroundings reflect the personalities of the people who live in them. This is clearly indicated by the fact that even people who live in the same period and under the same social system each construct their surroundings in their own way.

In our society, too, everyone has a different way of arranging his rooms. In some homes people are fond of goldfish bowls or flower pots, while in others they like to hang pictures and embroideries on the walls.

Everyone has his own tastes and preferences, so he arranges his rooms in his own way.

Set design in films should always depict the surroundings in accordance with the features of the characters' personalities. If sets or props only emphasize the features of the times and social system, while failing to offer an accurate representation of the personalities of the people portrayed, the surroundings cannot possibly give a truthful impression and the personalities of the characters cannot come to life.

The surroundings portrayed in artistic works are essential for the portrayal of people's characters in various circumstances, and they only acquire meaning through being subordinated to this portrayal. No setting in a film should be simply an ornament which is divorced from the personality of the character.

Film sets, no matter how insignificant in scale, are essential elements of the film that are closely interwoven with the personality of the character, and they must be inseparably related to his life. Furthermore, each setting should reflect profound traces of the characters' lives and bear the distinctive marks of their particular personalities. To be truly effective in revealing the characters' personalities settings must be closely linked with their destiny.

The sets are thus determined by the requirements of the characters' lives and subordinated to the clear expression of their personalities. But if this aspect is overemphasized and they fail to provide an accurate reflection of the characteristic features of the social system of the times, they will also fail to portray life truthfully and make the surroundings appear authentic.

In creating settings, the art designer should not make the requirements either of life or of the personality absolute, nor should he ignore either of them, but combine them both harmoniously. The settings can only become significant means of depiction which are true to the surroundings and the characters' personalities by combining the requirements of life and those of the personality in one pictorial frame.

In order to clearly present both the features of the period and the personalities of the characters in the sets, the set designer should emphasize the objects which are central to the creation of authentic surroundings and which reveal the personalities of characters in a particular scene, and omit secondary elements. Scenes in films are quite frequently complicated and loosely structured because various items are arranged in a disorderly manner and the ornamentation is too elaborate.

The set designer should impart a clear form to the surroundings. In films, authentic surroundings only become meaningful if they are given a formal structure. Even if the characters' houses and their everyday implements are made to reflect the period, they cannot acquire distinctive visual life of their own unless they are given form.

To give the general surroundings form, one has first to ensure that the form of their individual elements, such as sets, properties and ornamental objects, is fully defined. In order to create an adequate portrayal of real life the set designer needs to be skilled in formal composition, and he must pay careful attention to the form and colour of the sets.

When people build houses or make furniture, they combine practical and aesthetic elements. Likewise, every film set should be both functional and aesthetically refined.

In the art of set design it is essential to ensure not only the harmony of each individual element which is used in creating the surroundings, but also the harmony of the overall visual image. Creating harmony in one element and not in another does not indicate talent. The formal beauty of the individual elements of settings cannot guarantee the beauty of the whole image as long as they lack integral harmony. Thus, the formal beauty of the individual parts is only valuable insofar as it contributes to the formal structure of the image as a whole.

Even excellent settings cannot be regarded as well-designed if the everyday tools and ornaments used are selected inconsistently. "Unique" props and impressive ornaments which are out of tune with the settings and fail to harmonize with the surroundings, only serve to shatter the authenticity of the scene.

In order to enhance the visual form of a scene, it is imperative to ensure the perception of three dimensions by creating effective perspective in the settings and lay them out in a balanced fashion. Even when the perspective is right, the sets cannot provide a harmonious screen image if this balance is not achieved. Harmony should be created not only in the arrangement of the sets and properties but also in the forms, colours, patterns and ornaments of all the settings which are used in building up the surroundings.

The successful fulfilment of the technical requirements of set design is essential to the faithful cinematic representation of the characters' surroundings. Set design involves the coordination of a wide range of complex creative tasks, such as the director's use of space, the movements of the camera and the free movement of the actors. However excellent the form of the sets may be, the actor and the cameraman cannot properly implement their plans for the depiction of the scene if the actor is restricted in his movements and the cameraman cannot also move freely.

The camera shows an object's form and even its surface quality as vividly as in reality. Therefore, if sets and properties are not realistic in appearance, the entire screen portrayal is falsified.

If all the settings are created so as to reflect the period, the personalities of the characters, and the distinctive features of the film, the surroundings will be authentic and living human portrayals of the characters will emerge.

SCENES AND MUSIC

"Films without music and song hardly deserve to be called films. A film without songs gives one a feeling of loneliness and is tantamount to a play with only dialogue. A truly fine film which will appeal to the people, must always have good songs."

KIM IL SUNG

A FILM WITHOUT MUSIC IS INCOMPLETE

If a film is to be enjoyed by the people, it should possess a profound subject, rich content, and good music and songs.

A film without music and songs is incomplete.

Both the requirement of life itself and the distinctive features of film make it quite natural to include music and songs in films.

Music is essentially the art which is closest to the people, since it has emerged from their work to transform nature and society, and has developed in the course of life. All arts emerge from life, but music, in particular, and also dance, are more closely linked to life than any other art because they have emerged directly from the work environment and have been practiced and enjoyed there.

Wherever there is life, there will always be music and songs. In our socialist society in particular, where the people are masters of the country, work itself brings the joy of creation and life itself is a beautiful song.

Wherever we go in our country today, militant and revolutionary songs echo loudly in the people's homes and work places. Our people have been extremely fond of songs and dance from ancient times. They provide a clear expression of their national character as they have been formed through the ages, and a reflection of their noble artistic aspirations.

If we are to make a film which conforms to our people's national sentiments and preferences, we should include in it many excellent songs which the masses can sing with joy. If a film has no music and songs, the life presented in it will become too sterile and stiff for people to appreciate, and they will not enjoy the film.

Good songs and music make an immense contribution to the ideological and artistic quality of a film.

Music is a noble art which clearly reveals a person's inner thoughts and experiences and evokes a warm, passionate response, instilling rich sentiments and a pulsating vigour into human life. Music in a film intensifies the emotional side of life and contributes to the ideological and artistic qualities of the production.

People can grasp a film's ideological content from its images, but if music is added, their emotional response is heightened and their aesthetic involvement is increased. The ideological content of a production will then make a deeper impression on them and their feelings will be thoroughly roused. Lacking this element, a film produces the impression of a dialogue play.

When the music in a film is good, the production abounds in passion and sentiment and the clarity of its ideological content is enhanced.

Furthermore, music allows the thoughts and emotions of the characters to be portrayed more subtly and the development of their personalities to be depicted more vividly.

The feature film *The Sea of Blood* contains a scene in which the mother, who has been languishing in jail is on her way home. This particular scene has neither dialogue nor any conspicuous action, but the audience is made vividly aware of the mother's unbounded loyalty to the revolution by the song which is sung "My Heart Will Remain Faithful".

Music in films also plays a major part in expressing the essence of the period depicted and its social system and national features. The social and historical environment in a film is presented graphically and delicately by the artist, but his art cannot match music in the emotional expression of the essence of the period and its social system, and in deftly plucking at the heartstrings of the people.

In films it is also possible to present a clear image of the features of the period, its social system, and the living conditions of the characters by using music that is already well known to the public. When a scene depicting life in the period of the anti-Japanese armed struggle or life during the Fatherland Liberation War uses songs which people were fond of singing in those days, the audience vividly recall how they lived at the time and recall all manner of details.

Including good music in films is extremely effective in making the music widely known to the masses. The excellent songs sung in films become extremely popular with our people, who feel that they live, work and fight together with the heroes and heroines of the films, as they sing these songs.

We should use music and songs as much as possible in our films. However, we should not randomly include poor songs or songs which are inappropriate to the content of the film and the requirements of the scenes, simply because a lot of music and songs is a good thing. Music which lacks any clear object or aim and is not in harmony with the environment depicted in the scene, cannot contribute to the enhancement of the film's ideological and artistic qualities.

Our films must contain militant and revolutionary music, the beautiful and noble music of the people, which is congenial to the tastes and the aspirations of the people of our times, which makes them aware of the real truth of life, vigorously encouraging them to strive to create a new life. We can only regard a film's music as genuine when the songs have rich and sweeping melodies which reflect the people's noble aspirations and beautiful sentiments, songs which everyone can easily understand and enjoy singing.

Films must not use songs which lull the ardour of a turbulent revolutionary life and the struggle for progress by arousing images of a tranquil life. Films must use plenty of music which is vibrant with the fighting spirit which sweeps away the obsolete and the reactionary, the revolutionary passion which moves people to strive to defend what is new and noble.

It hardly needs to be said that cinema music should not emphasize the militant theme exclusively, abandoning every element of lyricism. But the lyrical elements in music should always resonate with the inner minds of our people, with their great revolutionary passion and noble sentiments. And the militant elements should not be reinforced by meaningless, empty shouts, but by the expression of noble ideas and emotions and beautiful sentiments. Only by doing this can the art of film music become a powerful force which guides people into a worthy life of struggle and endeavour.

If film music is to enhance the ideological and artistic qualities of a film as well as effectively rousing the masses to creative endeavour and innovative struggle, the composer must himself be a pioneer of the times, an ardent revolutionary. The truth and power of a musical representation of reality derives from a noble ideological consciousness, from burning passion and rich sentiments. A composer who fails to involve himself passionately in the times depicted and express his love of man and of life, who has only a conceptual grasp of the personality and life of the hero, will only be able to sketch a generalized musical image. Only a composer who is ablaze with noble sentiments and has a clear understanding of the nature of man is capable of creating profound and excellent music which can move millions of hearts and which the people will sing.

Film songs should be good enough to pluck at the heartstrings of the people, so that they can be sung by many people and serve to link the film closely with the masses. Fine songs allow the content of films to linger longer in the minds of people.

A SONG WITH UNFAILING APPEAL IS A TRUE MASTERPIECE

An excellent film always contains good songs, which help in their turn to make the film still more famous. Good songs not only enhance the ideological and artistic qualities of a film, they can also play an important educational role because they become so popular among the masses.

Everyone knows the song "My Heart Will Remain Faithful" from *The Sea of Blood* and the song "The Red Flower of Revolution Is Kept in Full Bloom" from *The Flower Girl*. Many people began to sing these songs as soon as they appeared. The more one heard them, the more one wanted to hear them, and the more one sang them, the more one wanted to sing them. Films should contain musical masterpieces like these.

A song with unfailing appeal is a true masterpiece.

The fusion of noble ideas and burning passion is the distinguishing feature of excellent music and songs.

The "Revolutionary Song" created amid the fierce flames of the anti-Japanese revolutionary struggle is a masterpiece which is still sung today: it is a powerful source of inspiration to our people in the revolutionary struggle and the work of construction. When singing this song, one feels cheered and invigorated by the passionate and vibrant expression of an important idea.

Music and songs should possess profound meaning and powerful emotional content so that they will grip the hearts of people and imbue them with unflagging strength and courage. However beautiful and tender a musical composition may be, it cannot become a really popular tune that everyone sings unless it expresses a meaningful idea with a lyrical force that moves people's hearts.

The true value of a musical representation of reality lies in the idea it contains. However, if music is to pluck at the people's heartstrings a meaningful idea has to be blended with a burning passion which evokes a lyrical response. The unique appeal and eternal vitality of a masterpiece lies precisely in the fact that a noble idea is expressed with burning passion.

Music should also be composed with passion. The passion that lends force to music's ideological content and vital life to its portrayal of life, springs from the composer's own ardent heart. However, not all composers possess this passion. Unless he faces up to reality squarely, and adopts a positive attitude towards life, a composer cannot experience this all-consuming passion. Only if he possesses a passionate love of life and defends it resolutely can he experience the powerful urge to sing of life with all his heart and produce first-class music which can move the people's hearts.

Songs should have gentle and beautiful melodies which are pleasant to hear and easy to sing and endear them to the people.

Some people consider that the artistic value of songs lies in their complexity, but like all other arts, music is for the masses and the basic criterion for assessing the quality and value of songs and melodies is whether the masses like them.

Songs are written for the people. A song which is incomprehensible or difficult to sing will not earn the love of the people, and it will not win enduring popularity. If the endeavour to produce a song with high artistic value results in melodies which are unnecessarily complicated or include extremely high or low notes, and are therefore hard for the masses to understand, then these songs have been written simply for their own sake and they will not win the appreciation of the people.

The innate preference of our people has always been for gentle and quiet songs, and not for music which is complicated and difficult or flamboyant and pretentious.

The artistic sentiments peculiar to our people have developed over a long historical period of time and they find their clearest expression in ballads, that is, in popular music. Good ballads are short, simple, easy to understand and easy to sing. They contain no extraneous elements of ornament or style, no caprice or whimsy. The distinctive features which express the genuine artistic value of popular songs lie in the fact that on hearing them, one feels drawn to sing them and the more one sings them, the more profoundly and freshly one senses their meaning.

Many of the revolutionary songs which were created during the anti-Japanese revolutionary struggle are still sung today, and provide great inspiration to our people by celebrating their struggle for the victory of the revolution and construction. Composers should pay close attention to the distinctive features of the revolutionary songs produced by the communist fighters amid the flames of the revolutionary struggle and bend all their efforts and talents towards emulating them in creating excellent songs which are truly revolutionary and popular.

If film music is to become a real masterpiece and pluck at the heartstrings of the audience, then the song must be built on the fine structures of popular verse.

In the perspective of musical development, the present era could be called the age of the verse form or stanza. In a revolutionary age, an age of socialist and communist construction, priority must be given to the development of militant songs with simple verse forms which the broad masses can appreciate and enjoy singing.

The stanzaic song is the finest form of Korean popular song which, for many centuries, has given simple yet refined expression to the people's sentiments and aspirations. This stanzaic form must be employed in the composition of film music in order to produce good tunes that the people will love. Music which harmoniously blends beautiful and noble feelings and ideas into a popular form can be a true masterpiece.

It is also essential for music to combine content and form harmoniously and to achieve a balanced blend of ideological and artistic elements.

In a really good song, the content is in perfect agreement with the form and the words fit also the music perfectly, so that if one reads the words, the music comes naturally to one's mind and when one plays the music, the words emerge of their own accord.

A masterpiece always has words which express a rich content and a profound meaning but are themselves both simple and refined. If the words are not truly poetic and produce the impression of a speech delivered from the stage, then the music will seem like a dialogue song. In order to grasp and develop a fresh and excellent musical idea the composer must explore life in depth, seeking a wealth of experience and responding genuinely to the poetic spirit of the spoken word.

The words of a song should be a beautiful and refined poem. Words which express complicated and fussy ideas have too many syllables and are difficult to set to music; even if they are provided with a melody, they are incapable of evoking any emotional response. But when every word is filled with profound meaning and a great idea which stirs people to action is expressed within the space of a couple of lines, they can easily be set to music which also expresses profound meaning and powerful emotion.

The words and music of a song should form a harmonious artistic unity. This is a fundamental requirement in the composition of stanzaic or popular verse songs, the most important factor contributing to the songs' tenderness and beauty.

True harmony of words and music can only be achieved by bringing the ideas expressed and the emotional tone into full accord with each other, by making the musical rhythm conform with the rhythm of the words, and the pitch of the music with the intonation of the words.

The songs and music for films should be enjoyable even when one is not watching the cinema screen. A piece of film music should be perfected as an independent work of art and yet still serve to support and enhance the film's portrayal of its theme. This applies even more so to songs. Songs in films are always related to the theme and derived from the dramatic content of the scene, and yet each is a complete work of art in itself, a genuine song that can be sung quite apart from the screen action. The finer a song is, both ideologically and artistically, the greater its independence from the context of the film. A truly great song can be sung off the screen, and yet still serve to reinforce the message of a film.

Truly fine music which expresses an abundance of beautiful and noble ideas and emotions will naturally emerge from the warm feelings in the heart of a composer who lives among working men and women. This passion which burns in his heart could never be developed by sitting at a desk or at the keyboard of a piano.

The composer's creative passion will emerge in full force when he has a full mastery of the view of the world implicit in the concept of Juche, and explores the life of the masses in depth, emulating the revolutionary spirit and indomitable will of the working class, loving life and fighting for the revolution just as they do. A piece of music can be regarded as great when the melody is replete with meaning and passion which have been born out of a revolutionary attitude towards life and an ardent love for the people.

The composer should centre his work on the composition of popular songs and spare no time and effort in emulating the creative wisdom of the people.

Popular music is the embodiment of the people's musical talent. The forms of popular music provide a magnificent portrayal of a person's profound and complex inner thoughts and can induce laughter or tears at will. Popular melodies are not only filled with cheerfulness, optimism, tenderness, elegance, delicacy and rich emotion, they also possess immense expressive power and vitality. All of these qualities give people strength and courage.

The composer should make creative use of these fine features of popular music in order to produce splendid revolutionary music suited to the new era and congenial to the tastes and sentiments of the Korean people.

A masterpiece is the fruit of talent and hard work. Good music is not created by chance.

The composer should be painstaking in his efforts to create even a small piece of music such as a popular song. It is by no means easy to compose a popular song, for popular songs are the basis of all musical art and express the essence of musical thought.

To develop the ability to define a beautiful and expressive melody, the composer should explore reality in depth and constantly inquire into the nature of life. To develop a mastery of vivid, expressive musical language, he requires not only a profound understanding of the requirements of the new situation of our times, but also the modesty to learn from the musical heritage of mankind. Then he will be able to create a new musical language which surpasses all that has been created before, and compose the unique melody demanded by a new situation.

The composer should take such a serious attitude to his creative work that of every hundred melodies he composes, he will perfect only one. If he studies his craft so carefully as to finally accept only one musical note from a hundred he has written and only a single stave out of a hundred, his creative talent will develop and he will generate novel and powerful melodies.

A composer who does not work hard to develop his talent can never create a masterpiece.

A MELODY SHOULD BE UNIQUE

The appeal of truly fine music lies in a beautiful melody which expresses positive feeling.

The composer must work hard on a melody in order to create good music which suits the film and is conducive to the people's ideological and emotional education. The creation of the melody is the composer's main artistic task, since it uses the form of music to express the concept he has developed from the requirements of the seed of the film and the requirements of the scenes and it contributes directly to the ideological and artistic quality of the production.

Melody is the basic means of expressing the ideological and emotional content of a musical composition, and it is the fundamental factor determining the ideological and artistic quality of the musical portrayal of reality. The value of a musical composition is determined by the beauty, positive emotional tone and unique form of the melody.

Melody is a crystallization of human ideas and emotions. In real life people often feel an urge to sing of their own ideas and emotions. Even those who have no knowledge of music sing softly to themselves when something pleasant happens and are moved to sing in a forlorn tone when grief overwhelms them. Melody is thus a manifestation of emotion which springs from human ideas and feelings. If a composer wishes to reflect the inner spiritual world and the diverse lives of characters vividly in his film music, he must turn his attention first to the creation of a unique and expressive melody.

The ideological and emotional content of music is expressed in the melody and is unimaginable apart from it. The natural flow of powerful and expressive melodies gives the music of a film its intellectual and emotional content.

Of course, the words of a song are the direct expression of its ideological content, but without a tune they remain lifeless. The melody of a song provides the basic means of expressing the ideological content which is reflected in the words. A song arranged for an instrument creates as strong an impression as when it is actually sung, because the melody actually reinforces and sustains the ideological and emotional content of the words by musical means. In short, the vitality of a piece of music resides in the melody. Hence, the composer's work on the melody is always fundamental to the creation of music.

The composer should create beautiful, noble and positive melodies which the masses will love and enjoy singing.

Music of a high ideological and artistic standard always has melodies which are beautiful, noble, tender and fresh. The beauty and richness of a melody express the beauty and richness of the ideas and emotions possessed by a true human being. In order to create exquisite and rich melodies, the composer must explore life in depth, striving for genuine experience of the noble spiritual world of humanity so that he may discover the seed of his melodies in life itself. When composing film music, the composer should study both real life and the ideas, emotions and life of the characters depicted in the work. It is particularly important for him to have a good knowledge of the personality and life of the hero. Developing a profound insight into the hero's noble ideas, emotions and aspirations and a true appreciation of his life will enable him to identify the seed of a melody that is suited to the content of the film.

Though the range of melodic images offered by life may be diverse, the composer must be guided by the requirements of the film in identifying the seed of a melody which can most clearly express the ideas and emotions of which he is to sing. This seed may not always immediately seem to be perfect. However, if the composer pursues his study of life and ponders the matter seriously the seed can be realized in a melodic form with quite distinct ideological and emotional tones, unique forms and structures. A melody will only be truthful, beautiful and unique if it springs from the heart of a composer with a genuine and warm love of life and a wide experience of its variety.

In order to be original a melody must have a clear emotional tone and its own distinctive features. The tones of music and songs vary according to their type and the moods they express, but, even when pieces of music are of the same type and mood, they each acquire their own unique emotional tones depending on the composer's attitude towards life and his artistic tastes. For instance, some people build their marches on powerful, militant melodies, others build them on lively and optimistic ones, and still others imbue them with lofty emotional content.

While maintaining his creative individuality the composer should always take care to introduce into his melodies the emotional tones that are suitable to the scenes of the film so that the ideological content of the film may be distinctly expressed.

Let us suppose there is a scene in which a scout active behind enemy lines is parting with an underground operative at a crucial moment, before going to the enemy's lair in an effort to safeguard the advance of the People's Army. Through sharing danger and the threat of death, and carrying out their revolutionary duties together in the difficult situation behind enemy lines, they have become very close as revolutionary comrades. But they have to part in order to carry out their respective tasks. What are the implications for the emotional tone of the music?

If the composer does not take into account the central ideas, emotions and aspirations of the two characters but merely emphasizes the grievous feelings of parting, the message of the music will become vague. The two characters share the noble aspiration to dedicate their all to the sacred battle to crush the enemy and hasten our victory in the war.

Therefore, as one departs for the enemy's lair, ready to die in the performance of his combat mission, and the other sees him off without a word their emotions can by no means be sentimental. The underground operative must experience the most profound sympathy for the heroic action of his comrade-in-arms as he departs on his mission regarding his self-sacrificing effort for the revolution as the highest honour. He clearly feels an ardent comradeship, and the earnest desire for his friend's success. The composer should imbue the melody with the sublime revolutionary spirit and ardent sentiments of the heroes and emphasize this emotional tone. Then he will be able to give faithful expression to their ideas and emotions and match the emotional tone of the music to the requirements of the scene.

Film music should provide a clear emotional characterization of the ideological content of the production and the ideas and emotions of the characters. Music which does this will be quite distinctive, and its emotional tone will be unequivocal. If film music which sings of the working class only employs militant melodies, it will not be totally distinctive and will fail to add a fresh and distinctive emotional tone to the film. According to the personalities of the characters and the logical development of the plot there should be melodies which are militant, lyrical, noble or merry. The content of the film and the emotional tones of the melodies will then be fused into one, and the music will be attractive and pleasing to listen to.

In musical composition it is important to employ new and varied means and techniques of expression.

The composer's musical conception arises from his individual experience of life, but it can only be made into a musical representation of reality by his skilful use of definite means and techniques of expression. Even if he has grasped a unique musical conception, the melody will not bear the imprint of novelty unless the conception is presented through new means and techniques.

The true emotional tone of a melody cannot be concealed. If the composer does not strive unstintingly to discover new melodies and instead mixes elements of melodies copied from other works, no matter however skilfully he does it, they will not be original melodies. When one hears a piece of music that is not truly original, one gets the impression that one has heard it somewhere before. The composer should continually seek to discover new musical means and techniques and use them in an original way, in order to ensure that each melody expresses something fresh and new.

However, he must not follow the policy of absolute priority for technique on the grounds that the melody should be unique.

Music for music's sake, music which overemphasizes form rather than content, is not loved by the people. Likewise, film music which is written for its own sake, which is inconsistent with the content of the production, is pointless. The skill of the film music composer lies in creating beautiful and positive melodies which conform to the content of the film and are also flawless musical compositions.

The music for every film scene should be exquisite, gentle and positive in tone. The composer should respect the national character of our people. Songs which are too high in pitch or dragged out for too long for no reason, lack tenderness and gentleness, they are not only difficult to sing, but also difficult to appreciate, and our people do not like them.

Songs should be beautiful, tender and gentle and they should flow smoothly, so that they are easy to appreciate and easy to sing. If a composer is to write songs which the people will love and enjoy singing, he must compose them in our own Korean manner. Our songs are songs which accord with our people's sentiments and preferences, songs which the masses are fond of singing.

The composer can only write our kind of songs if he creates new melodies which are based on traditional national melodies and yet are congenial to contemporary aesthetic taste. Our traditional national melodies clearly embody the noble ideas and emotions and sentiments of our people. The composer should devote close study to the characteristic features of the traditional national melodies created and refined by our people over our long history, and use them as a basis for creating new melodies to meet the requirements of our times.

A new and distinctive melody can only be produced out of the composer's own individual experience of life. If he is unable to harmonize his own individual view of life with the spirit of the times, a composer can neither maintain his creative individuality nor compose a unique and impressive melody.

Good music makes a film unique. The composer should work with a genuine and positive appreciation of life, devoting all his energies to creating unique melodies which are congenial to the sentiments of our people and consistent with the spirit of the times.

GOOD LYRICS MAKE GOOD MUSIC

The song is the smallest of musical genres, but it has greater power to move people than any other musical genre. Orchestral music produces a different impression on each listener and is interpreted in different ways by different people. But a song expresses ideas and emotions directly and concretely through the words supported by the melody. It can therefore easily be understood by people and has a more direct and powerful effect on them.

In life a song is never far from us; it may be sung anywhere, at any time and it is never forgotten. A song has such a great ideological and emotional influence on people that it stirs people's hearts and inspires them in the struggle to create a new life. It is therefore very important to create good songs for film music.

In order to produce good songs, good lyrics should be written first.

Lyrics are the ideological and artistic basis of music. Good lyrics make good music. Masterpieces are always based on good lyrics.

The lyrics should be poetic and, at the same time, rich in ideological content. In blending together noble artistic qualities and exalted ideological content in the lyrics of a song it is absolutely essential to present a rich ideological content in a beautiful and refined poetic form.

The vitality of lyrics derives from the exposition of significant ideological content in a refined poetic form. The quality of the lyrics and the ideological and artistic value of the music of a song are determined by the ideological content and its poetic presentation.

The lyrics in film music should have a revolutionary content which accords both with the nature of our films and the ideas and emotions of the people of our times, the builders of socialism and communism. The words may either reflect the noble and happy life of the people or sing of the joy of nature, according to the content of the scenes.

However, if only joy and happiness are stressed in singing of the happy life of the people, the lyrics may be tainted with hedonism. While they sing of this life, the lyrics should ensure that people do not forget their former miserable plight, and so inspire them with the burning desire and the enthusiastic commitment to hasten towards a brighter future.

When singing of the joy of nature, too, lyrics should reflect the advantages of the socialist system and the noble life of our people, emphasizing their revolutionary spirit. Good lyrics about a beautiful landscape may please people, but there is more of value in lyrics which reflect the people's proud life and struggle and portray their pure and sublime spiritual world in a meaningful manner.

No matter which scene of the film the song may be included in, the lyrics should mainly reflect what is new, beautiful and revolutionary in the life of the people. Lyrics which accurately reflect the essential nature of life and people's beautiful inner thoughts and feelings have true ideological depth and emotional content so that the more one hears them, the more deeply one is affected.

The fact that lyrics should address new and significant problems raised by life itself does not mean that one should restrict one's interest entirely to the present age. If only the present is emphasized in writing the lyrics for songs, they will not be able to express a broad generalization of the developments and changes of life. A song that is written to be sung only today has no great value as art. A song which people can sing today and tomorrow, which is passed on throughout the trials of history, may be called truly valuable art. The creation of such a valuable song requires not only good music but also the expression in the lyrics of a particularly significant problem of human life and its expression in general poetic terms of a high standard.

In addition to excellent ideological content lyrics must possess a high artistic quality. Even the finest ideological content will fail to move people deeply if it is not supported by a high artistic quality of expression.

The lyrics of a song should constitute a fine poem. Poetry is the life of a song and a song without poetry cannot give rise to a beautiful melody. From ancient times, fine poems have been loved by the people and transformed into songs.

Words that possess poetic quality are lyrical. In poetry, the ideas should flow as they express the emotion, for the strength of poetical depiction is its ability to elicit an emotional response.

To make poetry means to create a refined poetical form that is replete with genuinely warm feeling. A mere arrangement of the rhythms and lines in keeping with the rules of poetic form will not imbue each word with passionate emotion and a dry ideological appeal will not contribute to the emotional impact of the poem.

However, it is not acceptable to avoid political expressions on the grounds that one is using words poetically. The attempt to enhance poetical depiction by avoiding political expressions is based on ignorance of the essence of poetry. Even political expressions may have strong emotional appeal and persuasive power and pluck at the people's heartstrings, when they express the poet's genuine passion in a truly poetical fashion. If some words are clearly inappropriate because they bluntly expose a political bias, this is because the ideological content has not been emotionally digested.

The more concise the lyrics, the better. The ideas and emotions they express should be clear and their expressions succinct, while the meaning should be profound.

The song is a musical art form which, despite its formal limitations, is capable of expressing people's ideas and emotions in a natural poetic flow. The verbal structure must therefore be extremely compressed and succinct if it is to be readily set to music and sung with ease. If the words are not properly structured in verses, the poetic content cannot be adequately expressed while remaining consonant with the features of the musical structure, and the ideological depth and emotional content of the song will be impaired.

To render the words concise, one requires to take a firm grasp of the kernel of the idea which is to be conveyed and to hold fast to it. If the ideological nucleus cannot be maintained and a variety of different ideas are unfolded, no one idea can be adequately sustained and the content of the words loses its impact. Of all the emotions they have experienced poets should only include the essential ones in the lyrics and present them in concise poetical terms.

Even when the words do express an essential ideological and emotional content it cannot be expressed concisely if it is described in the style of prose. An extended description in words can never express the idea with adequate force; it destroys the poetic effect. Furthermore this roundabout route which cannot provide a clear, emotional expression of the ideological essence significantly reduces the expressive power of the words themselves.

In order to write succinctly one needs to polish one's poetical words carefully. In real life it is possible to express an idea or an emotion in several different ways. But this is not the case with written words. If the words of poetry are ambiguous and their emotional tone is not clear and distinct, they cannot be regarded as truly poetical words. Whatever the idea or emotion expressed, the emotional tone only becomes distinct when the expression is sensitive, delicate and sharp.

When working on the words of a song, it is important to compose poetical sentences that are consistent with the flow of the music, while carefully selecting one's poetic words. Even poetic vocabulary will not reveal the true meaning intended if the words are not positioned properly. The sentence construction should be simple, plain, gentle and rhythmical, and it should provide expressive support for the kernel of the idea and emotion which is to be depicted. Descriptive sentences should not be included in the words of a song. In poetry descriptive sentences are taboo.

Our beautiful and rich language is an inexhaustible source of genuine poetic words. The Korean language possesses a vast wealth of expressions and is capable of subtly expressing any idea or emotion, however complex and diverse. Lyricists should master the Korean language and should continue to learn the new, beautiful and cultured words that have been refined in use by the people. The words used by people are genuinely poetic words. Relying firmly on the words used by the people is the best way for the poet to render their verbal expressions subtle, rich and refined.

In writing words that are to be sung it is essential not only to select good poetic words but also to arrange the rhythms and rhymes well. A poem without rhythm and rhyme lacks emotional force. Whereas a lyrical poem is a poem to recite, the lyrics of a song are a poem to sing. The rhythms and rhymes should therefore be arranged in a smooth and natural manner so that the song can be sung while allowing the melody to flow along. The flow of the words should not be too fast or too slow, it should not be broken or intermittent. Even easy words make awkward poetic sentences if they fail to flow along with the rhythm.

When the rhythm of the words flows too hastily, it does not allow time for meditation, it cannot engender a feeling of tenderness and this produces a frivolous song. On the other hand, if the rhythm is too slow, it cannot articulate the flow of emotion, and this makes the song seem stale.

In writing lyrics for songs we must guard against alien or restorationist rhythms which are over-complex or whimsical, or which produce a feeble, droning effect inconsistent with the spirit of the times. By their nature, our people do not like breathless pitch or slack and weak rhythms. The poet must continually create new rhythms which are powerful, noble and vibrant, rhythms which suit our revolutionary age.

The words of a song should be easy to understand and to sing in tune with the music. Only then will the song become a masterpiece and be loved by the people.

However good the ideological content of a song may be, if it cannot be understood and sung with ease by the people, it cannot exert educational influence. For a song to be acceptable to the people, the music should be good, but, above all, the words should be easy to understand and to sing. If the words become complicated, the music will also inevitably become complicated.

The important thing in writing popular words is to express the profound ideological content in plain terms. All the revolutionary songs created during the anti-Japanese revolutionary struggle have a significant ideological content which is social and political in nature, but anybody can understand their meaning with ease.

The words in songs should be selected from amongst those that are loved by the people, in order to express the meaning accurately. Then anybody will be able to understand the song easily and sing it without difficulty.

It is important to select easy words and arrange the poetic phrases in a natural fashion. The words of revolutionary songs are drawn from a popular vocabulary that is familiar to the people, and are arranged in accordance with their everyday usage so that they are easy to understand. The poetic phrases produced are similar to the words of a conversation and yet they make natural use of rhythms that are peculiar to poetry. Thus they share the magnetism of everyday language and people want to recite them constantly.

In films the words of a song should be in accord with the content of the screen image and the action of the scene. Since the song should always define the emotional tone of the film's ideological content, the words should be written so as to suit the visual and dramatic content of the screen and scene, so that the music will also naturally conform to them. But if the words are confined to mere repetition of the content of the visual image or the action or to direct explanation, they will not contribute to clarifying the depth and scope of the content and, as a result, they will not enhance the ideological quality of the film.

The words of a song should not directly express the ideological content portrayed on the screen, but give it greater depth. When the words add an artistic flavour to the content they can complement the content of the screen in many respects, thus adding depth to the theme of the film and also creating a song which will be sung and loved by the masses.

The words should express an essential idea, while depicting content in a way which supports the screen image and the action of the scene. One scene may raise different ideas, but they cannot all be expressed in the words. If they are, the words will be reduced to an explanation of the scene. If the words repeat the characters' lines and are restricted to explaining their actions, the song will add nothing to the presentation of the scene's main idea. Only when the words add to the depth and scope of the main idea of the scene will they enhance the overall ideological quality of the film.

Good words make good music and a good song improves a film.

MUSIC SHOULD BE APPROPRIATE TO THE SCENES

The music in a film must be suited to the content of the scenes and the circumstances of life depicted. Even good music will not be successful if it is not in harmony with the content of the scenes. Fine cinema music is music that matches the scenes and is flawless in itself.

The use of music which suits the scenes is extremely important in producing a good film in which ideological and artistic qualities are properly combined.

Every situation requires its own particular musical expression. One requires a labour song for when one is at work, and a militant song for when one is fighting the enemy. This is why from ancient times there have always been labour songs and war songs. Only when film music both conforms with the spirit of the times and suits the specific situation depicted can it pluck at the people's heartstrings.

No piece of music can be appropriate for every scene in a film, because the precise ideological content of each scene varies and a different aspect of life is represented. However good the music may be, it cannot enhance the ideological and artistic qualities of a film unless it is appropriate for the particular scenes and the context of life in which it is used.

Music which expresses a character's ideology and emotions and flows naturally out of life adds a great deal to a film and moves the spectators profoundly. Music that is consonant with the scenes elevates the ideological and artistic level of the film and makes a powerful artistic impression on people, so that they sing it all the time.

Above all else, the music in a film must accord with the content of the script.

In films a variety of songs are used in different scenes. This is quite natural, because characters with different personalities appear in turn and each scene presents different incidents and circumstances.

In order to write music that accords with the content of a film one must, first of all, compose good themes. The theme song is central to cinema music. Therefore, the manner in which the theme song is written and used is essential in determining the general level of a film music and its emotional tone.

Theme music that suits the content of a film must vividly convey the central theme of the work and the spiritual world of the hero. A film contains various shades of ideology and emotion, but the fundamental elements among them emanate from the life of the hero. The theme music must therefore be composed to match the tone of the hero's emotions and ideology if it is to contribute to a clear expression of the central theme of the work.

However, the individuality of the hero should not be exclusively stressed simply in order to give prominence to his emotions and ideology. Theme music can also add profundity to the central theme of the film by reflecting the essential nature of the period depicted and the social system in which the hero lives, and by clearly expressing the sentiments and aspirations of the class to which he belongs.

A composer should take into account the characters' ideology and feelings while focusing his portrayal on the elucidation of the social environment which gives rise to this ideology and these feelings. If he places too much emphasis on the ideology and feelings of an individual, he will not be able to give a broad-based depiction of essential character, or to portray the period and its people accurately. If music embodies the central theme of a film and portrays the thoughts and feelings of the hero in depth, then it is excellent theme music which conforms with the content of the work.

If the theme music is to enhance the content of the film it must be well composed and effectively used in the scenes where it is required.

The dramatic line requires the support of theme music when the emotions of the hero, who plays the central role in the exposition of the film's central theme, surge to a climax at some time in the course of his life. Theme music should be used at important points in the film, when the central theme of the work is expressed particularly clearly, but it cannot be used where there is no definite emotional event in the hero's ideological and spiritual development. In order to use the theme music effectively, therefore, the director and the composer should decide beforehand on the scenes in which it is to be used; at the same time they should structure the dramatic composition and the expression of sentiments so that the theme music can be played to match them.

The repeated use of fine piece of theme music in various forms is one way of maximizing the role of music in a film. Using the theme music repeatedly is a method of accentuating the effect of a film by adding clarity to the central theme, and effectively probing the inner thoughts and feelings of the hero.

There may be several stages in the drama's development at which the hero's ideological awareness and emotions are heightened. If we understand these emotional highlights of the film correctly and make effective use of the theme music, we can represent them in a subtle and effective manner.

In the film *The Sea of Blood,* the theme song is repeatedly used in an original way so that it continually emphasizes the concept and theme of the work in a way which matches the development of the drama and enriches its ideological and emotional content, so that people are profoundly moved.

All the music in a film, not just the theme music, must be played in a way which suits the scenes.

If the music is naturally derived from the plot of a story, it will be adequate to the requirements of the content of the film and the individual scenes. Therefore the music should be initiated and developed so as to match the development of the plot, and the music and the plot should be mutually supportive. If the music does not flow with the development of the character, or it does not match the change of scenes, the incongruity of the music and the action will be obvious.

If the music is not built up towards the climax in step with the dramatic development, through a series of important events, but is only suddenly heard when a dramatic collision occurs, the audience will find it hard to accept. And if the music is made to play for a long time or stopped awkwardly, regardless of the flow of the plot, it will impede the emotional response of the audience and mar their impressions of the film. If the music in a film is not closely linked with the plot, it will have an adverse effect on the portrayal of the theme.

We must not try to adapt music to the content of the scenes in a straightforward and mechanical fashion, simply for the sake of having music in the scenes. Music has its own particular part to play in a scene's portrayal of the theme. Music plays its part in the general representation through its own peculiar language, and if it is used to explain the content of scenes in a straightforward manner or simply repeats it mechanically, then it is failing completely to meet the specific requirements of film as a collective art form. The music should always be in line with the ideological and emotional content of the scenes, and it should serve to deepen and heighten the dramatic content.

There is no rule which states that when the hero is in a difficult position and is having a hard time the music should be matched to the scene by being melancholy and pathetic. To emphasize the fact that he is capable of overcoming the ordeal although he is now hard pressed and that he is impelled to rise up despite the terrible hardship he is suffering, the music must be pathetic yet militant and passionate. The content of the scenes and the music must always tally.

The music in a film should also correspond to the flow of the plot. The general harmony of the film requires that the flow of the plot and the flow of the music both start from the same point and combine to express the same pattern of life. If the music does not flow along with the plot, but remains independent of it, not only will the harmony of the work be destroyed, but its content will be obscured.

Although music possesses its own inner consistency it must also conform to the development of the plot and provide subtle emotional shading.

Appropriate music in a film may complete the perfect artistic expression of great passion, breathtaking tension, and sweet joy. People can accept these emotions more readily with the assistance of the music.

Different characters have different thoughts and emotions and ways of life, and are portrayed in different ways in the scenes of a film. The musical score must therefore use various forms and methods in order to conform to the film.

Composers should carefully consider the forms and methods they will use in the music for a film. Some of them are frequently unsuccessful because they are unable to discover the forms and methods required to make the best use of music which has been well composed.

The problem of how to use music and in what form should be solved in accordance with the requirements of the scenes involved. If one merely tries to make the music successful, without thinking of the requirements of the scenes, and adopts forms that are incongruous with these requirements, neither the film nor the music will turn out well. When the forms of the music are correctly selected and used as required by the action of the scenes, the music will fit the film and provide a clear and emotionally powerful interpretation of its theme.

The composer should therefore decide on the form of music to be used—solo, chorus or orchestra—according to the scene's ideological content, action, and flow of emotions. Deciding on a musical form which accords with the flow of the plot and the action of the scene so as to enhance its artistic portrayal of life is a creative undertaking which requires precise and delicate skill.

Just as the director edits scenes, so should the composer be able to edit the music which is used. Musical editing by the composer involves deciding how to use songs and music that match the flow of the story and the action of the scenes and how to link and present the various melodies and songs. The composer has to see to it that the music and songs are presented in forms which blend well with the various scenes, so that they help to breathe life into the ideological and emotional content of the film.

The music in a film should not conflict with the acting and must allow the actors to give a natural portrayal of the characters' lives and personalities. Film is an animated art, so the characters' actions should stand at the focus of attention of the various scenes. The composer must always take these features of the film into consideration and should not make actors sing for no particular reason or use a large musical form such as a choir or orchestra, which will dominate the actions of the characters, on the pretext of making diverse use of music.

In our Korean films it is a good idea to make extensive use of the *pangchang,* rather than making the actors themselves sing or pretend to do so, with a professional singer dubbing their words. If the *pangchang* is used properly, in accordance with the situation, to suit the actions of the characters, it can provide a subtle psychological description and reinforce their emotions in line with the logic of the action.

However, the actors in films can be made to sing themselves in certain circumstances, and a song sung by a character in response to specific circumstances produces a special impression on the audience. But forcing an actor to sing may hamper his acting. Our style is to create a natural portrayal of a character's general psychology, his ideas and feelings, by means of the *pangchang,* thus enriching the ideological and artistic content of the film.

The music in a film should be used as necessary and show flow harmoniously. When the satisfactory use of music has not been planned in the script or in the director's plan, the composer should offer his own views on the inclusion of a good piece of music in the film. However, he must not attempt to create events merely for the sake of the music. If there is no music where it is needed, the composer should call attention to this fact, but he should not insist on rehashing the composition of the whole work in order to lay emphasis on the music. When music is introduced into the film in a forced manner contrary to the flow of the drama, neither the drama nor the music will achieve the desired results.

The musical score of a film can only be successful through the collective efforts of conductor, singers, and musicians, as well as the composer. It is particularly important for the composer and conductor to cooperate in producing a good interpretation of the score. They must work together to create good music that meets the requirement of the film.

Good music is essential to a film's success; when the film as a whole is a success, the music's quality is still further enhanced. The composer's creative fulfilment and joy are derived from the harmony of the scenes and the music.

MUSICAL ARRANGEMENT IS CREATIVE WORK

There are many cases in which the same music is used repeatedly in different scenes of the film. The theme music may be repeated in the form of a solo, a chorus or an orchestral piece. When one and the same piece of music and song is repeated in various forms and styles according to the requirements of the various scenes, the quality of their contribution to the theme's representation depends on how they are arranged.

It is impossible to achieve a really fine standard in film music if musical arrangement is neglected. Some composers write good pieces of music, but they fail to make effective use of them, largely as a result of careless musical arrangement.

Musical arrangement is creative work which is extremely important in enriching the ideological and artistic qualities of the music and in providing a profound and delicate interpretation of the songs. The expressive content of the same piece of music differs according to its arrangement. A good arrangement should render the flavour and colour of the original music more subtle and avoid damaging its ideological and artistic qualities.

Only good musical arrangement is capable of lending clarity to the thoughts and emotions expressed in the music and adding diverse and distinctive emotional tones to the score. It may therefore be said that the expressive content of music and songs depends directly on the musical arrangement.

In order to arrange a song well, one requires, above all else, a complete grasp of all the features of the original. Whether arranging a song written by others or by oneself, one must always adopt the correct attitude for dealing with a new song, and analyse the features of the melody and its emotional tone in detail before starting to arrange it. If one does not have a correct understanding of the ideological and artistic features of the original song, one cannot arrange it properly, however talented one may be.

The key to the arrangement of a song is to follow the original musical conception and to expand and enrich it. When the original conception is maintained, its ideological and emotional colours can be expressed still more fully and the general quality of the music improved. If the original conception is not maintained, the musical arrangement will neither properly express the thoughts and emotions of the original, nor give it a new flavour, and will be reduced to the level of imitation.

When he understands the original concept correctly and makes an effort to create a more subtle and precise interpretation, the composer can throw the essential elements of the original music into bold relief by expressing them in a quite distinctive fashion. To create an original musical arrangement requires profound creative meditation. Some composers may arrange two or three songs in a single night, but this is not the way to create a unique and original interpretation of a piece of music.

The art of musical arrangement is certainly neither straightforward nor easy. Cinema music in particular ought to be arranged on the basis of the general requirements of musical arrangement, the distinctive ideological and artistic features of the film, and the specific requirements of the scenes in which music is used. When the music is arranged, therefore, it is important to draw up a correct overall plan for its interpretation and ensure that the musical arrangement always maintains the basic melodies and enhances the ideological and artistic qualities of the film. The more adequate the scope and depth of the composer's plan is to the complex problems of the simultaneous interpretation of the music and the film, the better the arrangement will be.

The fundamental principle of musical arrangement is to express the basic melody more effectively. The manners in which the basic melody is modified is decisive to the general musical arrangement.

Making it hard to appreciate the melody by twisting it or complicating it, or senselessly pitching it too high or too low is not our style of musical arrangement. Senselessly changing the tunes to make the song complicated is a bad habit which obstructs the smooth flow of the song and obscures its ideological and emotional tonality.

The arrangement of a song should render its flow concise and easy to understand. Only in this way can the listeners be drawn naturally into the world of the music and recall the original song.

Musical arrangement should retain the basic features of the original song while giving it a new flavour. Just as every element in a score must be fresh, so must the musical arrangement. This will ensure its effectiveness as a musical interpretation of the film's theme. The music in a film should be subordinated to the profound elucidation of the work's theme and its ideological content. It is necessary, therefore, to develop the original music so as to evoke new shades of feeling.

In order to arrange music in an original manner the composer has to rely on his own opinions and create something new. A new interpretation cannot be achieved by simply making a tune complicated without any creative input, or by retouching only some parts of it.

The selection of new means and methods of musical portrayal and their original use is an important way of adding freshness to the initial theme. Nothing new can be created by simply borrowing the means and methods which are often used by others. Although the musical content may be new, if the form used in interpreting it is not, the music will not actually give the impression of originality. The musical arranger must therefore endeavour to create a new form that is suited to the content, while maintaining the basic melody. The most important skill here is to suit the arrangement to the character and mood of the music, and to make it varied and interesting.

It is important for the accompaniments to film songs to be well arranged. Since each film requires several songs, the proper arrangement of the music to accompany them is a major factor in ensuring the general quality of the film music.

In arranging the accompaniments of songs it is important to maintain the basic melody while also embellishing it to render the songs more gentle. Musical accompaniment only acquires meaning by adding life to the basic melody. It must avoid hindering the listeners' understanding of the words and enhance the overall impact of the songs. If an accompaniment fails to project songs smoothly, support them and enrich their ideological and emotional content, it will contribute nothing to the score, and will rather tend to disrupt it.

An accompaniment should be arranged in such a way as to enrich and improve the general texture of the music by adding a new flavour to the basic melody.

Music should be arranged with an eye to achieving a good performance. The quality of the performance depends largely on the musical arrangement.

The musical instruments which are selected and used in a musical arrangement and the roles they are made to play is not simply a technical matter. Each musical instrument has a unique quality of tone that can be exploited in a piece of music. What is more, musical instruments in many respects reflect the features of national culture so they can be quite effective in expressing national sentiments.

The unique timbres and distinctive national characteristics of our own woodwind and string instruments suit the tastes and sentiments of our people. The arrangement of music should therefore be based on the selection of instruments which suit the features of the melody, for the main part our own national woodwind and string instruments. Woodwind instruments, which can serve to enhance the music's national characteristics, should be accorded an important role.

The problem of selecting instruments to form a Western-style orchestra should be solved in the same way as it is in the case of a Korean orchestra. But it is imperative to maintain the distinctive features of

Western music while allowing the Korean tune to predominate throughout. For these purposes it is a good idea to use mainly soft string instruments in arranging Western orchestral music and to refrain, as much as possible, from using the brass and woodwind instruments which sound too harsh or dull.

It is not our style to give a piano a lot of melodies to carry in a musical arrangement. The dogmatic approach of using only a piano for solo accompaniment should be eliminated. The use of the electronic organ should be restricted from its present level of overuse, and it should always be used instead for the effective enhancement of the national flavour of our music.

The correct combination of national instruments with Western ones is extremely important in the formation of an orchestra. Some experts argue that if national instruments are combined with Western ones, the unique tone of our national music is blurred, but this is a one-sided view. Of course, it is difficult to produce a distinctive national tone by combining entirely different musical instruments.

However, the dances "The Snow Falls" and "The Azaleas of the Homeland" put an end to the old practice of using only Western instruments to accompany songs. The dances were performed to the accompaniment of the Korean national instrument the *haegum,* violins and Korean woodwind instruments. As a result, the national tonality of the music was actually brightened and unique sounds suited to the tastes and emotions of our people were created. This may serve as a good example of the fact that sounds are not debased when national musical instruments are combined with Western instruments. The problem is the principles according to which the Korean musical instruments are combined with the Western ones.

When we speak of combining Korean and Western musical instruments we have in mind laying the main accent on the former, subordinating the latter to the Korean music, emphasizing the specific features of our woodwind instruments so as to make the unique tonality of our national instruments clearly audible and properly combining the different kinds of musical instruments. If the principle of Juche is not observed in forming an orchestra, and various kinds of instruments are mixed together on an egalitarian footing, the sound will become confused and make it impossible to preserve the unique national tonality of our music. If Korean and Western musical instruments are to be properly combined, the main stress must be placed on the preservation of the Korean timbre and the rational formation of an orchestra in accordance with the features of the music and the functions and sounds of the different instruments.

When musical instruments are chosen for an accompaniment, the quality of the vocal sound and the mood of the song should be taken into consideration. The principle guiding the use of instruments in the arrangement of an accompaniment is to use every possible means to make the songs as distinctive as possible. In general, therefore, it is good for an orchestra that plays the accompaniment for film songs to be small in scale, since a small ensemble will allow the songs themselves to predominate.

In arranging film music a composer should always carefully consider the specific stills and scenes which require music. He can produce a varied musical portrayal of the action to meet the requirements of each still and each scene, but in order to perform its proper function the arrangement must adequately express the intent of the original music in a manner which accords with each scene. Even when the intentions of the original music have been satisfied, an arrangement is meaningless if it is not in harmony with the scene. In arranging film music a composer must distinguish the various voices and form the orchestra so that they conform effectively with the ideas, feelings and forms of the different scenes. He must give serious consideration to the various musical forms and methods of musical interpretation before deciding which to use.

Musical arrangement is the creative work of developing music and songs afresh and thereby adding subtle emotional shading to the human life described in the scenes on the screen. A composer who regards the original music as an end in itself and neglects the art of musical arrangement is an artist who does not know much about music. The key to the success of a musical score lies in the arrangement. Only a composer who is good at both writing and arranging music can truly be called an excellent composer.

ART AND CREATIVE ENDEAVOUR

"You, the film makers, must thoroughly revolutionize yourselves and fight on devotedly for the Party and the revolution, for the victory of the cause of socialism and communism. This is the way to prove yourselves worthy of the Party's consideration and the trust it places in you."

KIM IL SUNG

THE PROCESS OF CREATIVE WORK MUST BE THE PROCESS OF MAKING CREATIVE ARTISTS REVOLUTIONARY AND WORKING-CLASS

Whether or not writers and artists are able to make themselves revolutionary and working-class comes down to the question of whether or not they are determined to continue with the revolution and go on to communist society. This is therefore one of the fundamental questions in deciding the destiny of our developing socialist and communist art and literature.

Making writers and artists revolutionary and working-class means developing them into communist revolutionaries with a firm grasp of the Juche outlook on the world, into revolutionary writers and artists of a new type.

It is extremely important to remodel them on a revolutionary and working-class pattern in view both of the special role they play in the revolution and construction and of the special features of literary and artistic work.

Writers and artists find themselves in charge of one front of the Party's ideological work and directly responsible for the development of a socialist, national art and literature. In participating in this work they draw on their professional knowledge and artistic talents to contribute to the training of all members of society as communist revolutionaries of the new type who have an unshakable grasp of the concept of Juche.

The role of writers and artists acquires greater significance as socialism continues to be built in depth. Following the establishment of the socialist system art and literature are confronted with the task of producing a greater number of revolutionary works capable of making an active contribution to the development of people's communist world outlook. With the establishment of the socialist system the economic foundation which engenders outmoded thoughts is eliminated. However, since the development of people's consciousness lags behind change in the material conditions of society, outdated ideological remnants of the exploitative society linger in their minds for a long time. Writers and artists must therefore create greater numbers of revolutionary works which are very effective in instilling the communist ideology in people's minds.

If writers and artists are to produce works capable of effecting people's revolutionary education, they themselves, the creative artists, should acquire revolutionary and working-class qualities and become communists before anyone else. Revolutionary works can only be produced by writers and artists who have fully established their own revolutionary world outlook.

A work of art or literature accurately reflects the artist's world outlook. Writers and artists analyse and assess the realities of life from their own class standpoint and on the basis of their ideological tendency, which are represented in their works. Their world outlooks exert an active influence upon the whole process of creation—from the selection of seeds in life to their finalised portrayal. The final artistic products may therefore be either working-class and people-oriented or bourgeois and anti-popular, depending on the artists' ideologies. Thus the fundamental condition and decisive guarantee of the development of socialist art and literature that is Party-oriented, working-class and genuinely popular, is for the writers and artists to make themselves thoroughly revolutionary and working-class.

The past lives of the writers and artists and the distinctive features of artistic creation also make it imperative for them to transform themselves in a revolutionary manner and model themselves on the pattern of the working class. In their past lives the older generation of writers and artists was more affected by outmoded ideas than any other people. Even the younger writers and artists have been engaged in mental labour, and largely divorced from the physical labour of production, so they have had fewer opportunities of training themselves in revolutionary struggle than other working people. In addition to this, objective conditions leave them open to the influences of capitalist culture. In this situation, a ceaseless struggle must be waged to make writers and artists revolutionary, in order to eliminate from their minds all sorts of outmoded concepts and capitalist ideas such as individualism, egoism and latitudinarianism, as well as dogmatism and revisionism, and accelerate the process of the revolutionary transformation of the whole of society and its assimilation to the working class.

Revolutionizing our writers and artists and assimilating them to the working class is not only an urgent task of our revolution, it is also a mature requirement for the development of art and literature.

Socialist art and literature can only be properly developed by a new and revolutionary system and method of creative work which are appropriate to the intrinsic nature of socialist society. However, art and literature still retain quite a few remnants of the old system and method of creative work left over from the class society, and their forms are also in great need of renovation. Therefore, if we are to develop our art and literature in a way which is adequate to the requirements of the age of Juche and the intrinsic nature of socialist society, art and literature must be made to undergo revolutionary transformation. To this end, the writers and artists must transform themselves in a revolutionary fashion.

How, then, should they be made revolutionary and working-class?

In view of the importance of the revolutionary transformation of intellectuals in the context of making the whole of society revolutionary and working-class, and taking into account the distinctive features of the creative activities of writers and artists, the Party long ago advanced the policy of making the creative process itself a process of the revolutionary transformation of artists and their assimilation to the working class.

This is the most important means of making the writers and artists revolutionary.

For writers and artists their creative work and the process of revolutionary transformation are inseparable. They are two aspects of the struggle to achieve a single objective.

In revolutionizing writers and artists, the Party aims to arm them effectively with a Juche-based world outlook so that they will produce excellent revolutionary works conducive to people's re-education along communist lines, and to lead them on to a communist society. Their revolutionization can only proceed energetically and art and literature can only be developed on a sound basis when their creative work and the effort to achieve their revolutionary transformation are advanced in a coordinated fashion. Separating these two aspects is detrimental both to the revolutionary transformation of writers and artists and the development of art and literature. Their separation will result in the Rightist deviation that rejects the ideological training of writers and artists and encourages the attitude that artistic creation is all important, or the Leftist deviation that neglects the artistic aspects of creative work and emphasizes only the ideological training of the artists. If these deviations arise, it will be impossible to accelerate the process of making the writers and artists revolutionary and working-class or to successfully develop the new, communist art and literature. The Party's policy of making the process of creative work a process of revolutionary transformation is a scientific and realistic policy which accords with both the basic requirement of revolutionary transformation and the nature of revolutionary creative work.

Revolutionary practice is tremendously important for the restructuring of people's consciousness and the promotion of their revolutionary transformation and assimilation to the working class.

The great leader Comrade Kim Il Sung instructed us that revolutionary practice is a powerful means of reforming people's ideology.

People generally develop into revolutionaries through the ceaseless training provided by the complex and exacting practical struggle to transform nature and society. In similar fashion writers and artists can press on with their own revolutionary transformation through their creative work in art and literature, through participation in theatrical performances, and carrying out their duties.

It is by no means an easy task to produce works of revolutionary art and literature. Artistic creation is an extremely difficult and complex revolutionary task that requires a high degree of mental effort and enthusiasm, a strong will, persistence, steely organizational discipline and a lofty collectivist spirit.

Revolutionary creative practice amply provides the conditions and opportunities required for the revolutionary transformation of writers and artists and their assimilation to the working class. The Party has exploited these conditions and opportunities in putting forward its policy of converting the process of creative work into a process of making them revolutionary and working-class. Writers and artists should clearly understand the revolutionary essence of the Party's policy and implement it in full.

If they are to undergo total revolutionary transformation in the process of their creative work, writers and artists must, first of all, transform it into a process in which they cultivate boundless loyalty to the Party and the revolution through adherence to the spirit of the Party, the spirit of the working class and the spirit of service to the people.

The creation of works of revolutionary art and literature and the production of theatrical performances are the first and foremost revolutionary duties and glorious combat tasks assigned by the Party to our writers and artists. It is precisely by fulfilling these duties and carrying out these tasks with credit that they prove themselves loyal to the Party and worthy of its high political trust and expectations. Only, therefore, when they cultivate their loyalty to the Party and train their Party spirit throughout the entire process of creative work can they transform it into the process of their own revolutionary transformation.

If writers and artists are to make the process of creative work into the process of their own revolutionary reformation and assimilation to the working class, then they must live, work and struggle throughout the whole cycle of creation like the heroes of the revolutionary works they create.

The heroes of our art and literature are model revolutionaries who have taken a firm grasp of the great concept of Juche and are fighting devotedly to implement Party policy. Writers and artists may create the images of these revolutionary heroes, but not all the creators have attained the same level of the spirit as their creations. Heroes in fictions are sometimes regarded by the masses as inferior to their counterparts in real life. This disparity occurs when the artists' spiritual level is lower than that of their heroes.

The greater the writers' and artists' ideological preparedness to equip themselves firmly with the Juche-based world outlook and to live, work and struggle in the manner of revolutionary heroes, the loftier will become the mental world of the characters depicted in their works and the greater the ideological depth of the works themselves. Writers and artists must first earnestly strive to learn from their own heroes and work hard at their own ideological training. Those who are only revolutionaries when they are writing or acting on the stage but revert to their former selves in daily life, and live in a slovenly fashion, are not capable of creating exalted portraits of revolutionaries or of effecting their own revolutionary transformation and becoming fused with the working class.

Creative work is not a mere job, but an honourable revolutionary task. An artist who derives a sense of proud dignity from serving the Party and the people in his creative work should ponder whether or not he is prepared, politically and ideologically, technically and practically, to describe the revolutionary character he is going to deal with, whether or not he has qualities as noble as those of the hero who ventures through fire and water to fulfil the demands of the Party and the revolution, whether or not he has attained the height of the hero's personality. And then he must strive to be equal to his task. To achieve this goal, all our writers and artists must strive purposefully, consciously and persistently with one will throughout their creative work to realise the slogan "Let's live, work and struggle like revolutionary heroes". Only in this way can they achieve their own revolutionary transformation into writers and artists who breathe, think and act like revolutionary heroes and really transform the process of creative work into one of revolutionary education and ideological training.

In order to make the process of creative work a process through which they themselves become revolutionary and working-class, writers and artists must play a greater part in their revolutionary organization through their work and must reform their individual lives on revolutionary lines.

Their ideology cannot be separated from their lives. People who have undergone revolutionary transformation apply themselves to creative work and live in a frugal and cultural manner. An artist's ideological viewpoint and his style of life find full expression in his creative practice. A person who is not sound in his daily life cannot be sound in his creative life.

Writers and artists can only prepare themselves to be genuine revolutionaries when they regard the process of creative work as a process of ideological and revolutionary training and participate earnestly in the life of their organization. Each one of them should faithfully fulfil the creative assignments allocated to him by the organization, voluntarily observe the ethics of creative work and make it a rule to produce his works and conduct his life in a revolutionary manner under the guidance and control of the Party organization.

The most important thing here is to organize, plan and execute creative work under strict discipline. The Party has already put an end to the obsolete, conservative system of creative work and established a new revolutionary system, even defining a daily routine. In all circumstances and conditions writers and artists must strictly adhere to a routine of producing works and living which is in keeping with the requirements of the system of creation and the standard of life established by the Party. Any practice of creative work and manner of life which violates established order and discipline should be subjected to an intensive ideological struggle.

In our society, works of revolutionary art and literature are not the brain childs of a few people; they are the results of the joint efforts, collective intelligence and voluntary discipline of writers and artists who are deeply conscious of their mission. Their high level of political consciousness, iron discipline and collectivist spirit in creative work are the major conditions which guarantee their success.

Particularly in a collective form of art such as the cinema, opera or drama, the group's unity of ideology and purpose and discipline are vital. The entire creative staff must think and act with one idea and a single intention, and strive as one to complete their works of art, assisting each other and pulling together, under the slogan "One for all and all for one".

In order to improve the quality of the works produced and achieve the group's unity of ideology and purpose, the process of creative work itself should be made a process of strengthening the artists' organizational life and firmly establishing the communist ethics of creative work. This is the only way to transform creative practice into a blast furnace for ideological tempering and an outstanding school of revolutionary education.

An intensely critical approach is essential for turning the process of creative work into one of the revolutionary transformation of the creative staff and their assimilation to the working class.

The revolutionary practice of creative work is a process of struggle and innovation intended to boldly eradicate all outmoded thoughts and behaviour left over from the exploitative society in the field of art and literature and renew both fields in accordance with the requirements of the concept of Juche, thus creating a new communist art and literature commensurate with the intrinsic nobility of the working class. In the course of this renewal all manner of unsound ideas will raise their heads.

Therefore, an uncompromising critical struggle must be waged against every unsound element and shortcoming revealed in the process of creative work.

Criticism must always be frank, principled and comradely. Everyone must take a principled attitude towards criticism and perform sincere self-criticism in order to frankly disclose his own shortcomings and remedy them. In this activity he must regard the masses as his mirror. At the same time, he should employ effective comradely criticism in the effort to correct others' defects and shortcomings. When an atmosphere of revolutionary criticism prevails in the group, the creative work will be performed efficiently and artists will be stimulated to grow and develop faster.

Party leadership is the precondition and essential guarantee for the transformation of the process of creative work into a process that makes artists revolutionary and working-class.

A successful revolutionary transformation in writers' and artists' creative activities and daily life can only be brought about under correct Party leadership. Writers and artists who are ready to contribute to the revolutionary cause of the working class must all strive to become stalwart communists under Party leadership.

They must closely follow Party guidance, entrusting their destiny entirely to the Party and placing their unswerving faith in it. In order to be able to entrust one's all to the Party one must open one's heart to it. Those who entrust everything to the Party and follow its guidance always thinking and acting as it instructed, can become revolutionary more quickly.

When the situation is difficult writers and artists must defend the Party all the more stoutly and must be all the more candid in admitting their own errors. They must firmly believe in the Party and follow it without the slightest vacillation, no matter what wind is blowing at any time and from what direction. Such is the position and attitude of those who are faithful to the Party. These people can always succeed in everything they undertake and even if they commit errors, they can rectify them quickly and continue to make progress.

It is not easy to realize the goal of making writers and artists revolutionary and working-class through their creative activity, still less in the course of the creation of one or two works. People should continually revolutionize themselves throughout their entire lives. Even those who have been steeled in the arduous revolutionary struggle will lag behind the times unless they continue to undergo relentless revolutionary training and steel themselves in the practical struggle.

If it requires a hundred doses of medicine to cure a man's disease and restore his health, he must take all the hundred for them to have the desired effect. If he skips the last one, all the other 99 doses will have been wasted. Likewise, writers and artists must not be half-hearted in their efforts to revolutionize themselves, nor must they give up the effort after only a short crash programme. A man cannot become a revolutionary in a couple of days, nor can he become revolutionized by reading a few books or by making a few innovations in his work and his life. The struggle for revolutionary transformation must be waged with stubborn patience to the last.

The most important task for the writers and artists who create socialist and communist art and literature is to become revolutionary. Our writers and artists must support the Party's policy of converting the process of creative work into one of making them revolutionary and working-class, by earnestly endeavouring to become truly communist writers and artists of the new type.

A MAN SEES, HEARS, FEELS AND ABSORBS AS MUCH AS HE CAN UNDERSTAND

Man's potential understanding knows no limits. There is no object and no phenomenon in the world that cannot be understood. Things which are still beyond the range of understanding will be easily understood as our society develops and science attains a higher level. The depth and scope of human understanding varies from person to person because of individual differences in their consciousness and their ability to understand.

Human consciousness is a reflection of reality, but not an automatic, unmediated reflection. Man understands reality through a process of active thinking. Therefore, his understanding cannot surpass the limits of his experience. As a man accumulates more knowledge, he is able to understand reality in greater scope and depth. But if he has only seen and heard a little and only experienced a little for himself, his vision will inevitably be so much the narrower and his ability to perceive reality will inevitably be limited.

The scope and depth of a person's cognition depends, in the final analysis, on the level of his world outlook and his individual ability to understand. A man sees, hears, feels and absorbs as much as he can understand. Therefore, everybody should study diligently and constantly add to his store of knowledge.

However, not all forms of knowledge enhance one's cognition and practical activity. Knowledge that cannot serve one's practical purpose is merely knowledge for the sake of knowledge, and it is useless however much of it one may have.

The real value of knowledge is defined by its accuracy in reflecting the truth of nature and society and its effectiveness in practical activity. Only knowledge that has been derived from the requirements of practice and the truth of which has been tested in practice can be an effective force for the transformation of nature and society.

That one sees, hears, feels and absorbs as much as one can understand and is prepared for, means that a wealth of experiential knowledge is required in order to be able to see, feel and absorb objects and phenomena correctly and then proceed to correctly defined action.

A person's knowledge must be integrated with a revolutionary outlook on the world if it is to be a powerful tool of analysis and action. A world outlook is a person's general view on nature and society; it defines his position and his attitude towards reality, and regulates his cognition and practical activity. Therefore, when he possesses a correct world outlook, he can perceive and absorb reality correctly and manage his practical activity without error.

These same relations between the objective world and cognition and between cognition and practice are reflected in the creation of works of art and literature.

Genuine art and literature attempt to provide people with a correct understanding of the world and equip them with a revolutionary world outlook, a practical weapon for the transformation of nature and society. This goal can only be achieved if literary works raise important human issues and describe in detail and in depth the process by which people's revolutionary world outlook is formed, through the profound representation of various aspects of social life. This indicates that an artist can only succeed in his creative work when he has taken a firm grasp of the revolutionary world outlook of the working class.

An artist also sees, hears, feels, absorbs and expresses as much as he can understand. The breadth and depth of his understanding of nature and society, of human beings and their lives is revealed in his work. If he possesses an ample knowledge and experience of life, he will be able to describe people and life so that they appear as varied, rich and vivid as they are in reality.

Any piece of art work reflects both the political views and the artistic skill of the author. Reality is the source of artistic creation and the basis of all portrayal. But not all aspects of reality are the objects of art, and reality is not reproduced in works of art exactly as it is.

Everything represented in a work of art has been analysed and assessed by the author on the basis of his own ideological and artistic views, and the form of the work has been created by him in keeping with its content. Everything in a work has to be filtered through the author's subjective view. The same object and the same life can be described in different ways, according to the ideological and artistic levels of different writers. It is therefore necessary for artists to possess advanced political views, artistic skill and a wide range of knowledge which will assist them to perceive objects and phenomena correctly and depict them truthfully.

First of all, an artist must possess advanced political vision. Political vision means seeing with the eye of the Party and judging all phenomena shrewdly from a revolutionary point of view.

If an artist possesses advanced political vision, he can perceive the true essence of a problem in which diverse aspects of reality are interwoven in a complex fashion, he can analyse them and deal with them in keeping with the requirements of the Party and the interests of the revolution. If an artist lacks a correct revolutionary standpoint in his experiences of reality and creative work, he cannot clearly depict the essential nature and significance of the events that occur in reality, and in depicting reality he ultimately distorts it.

An artist's political vision is the factor which determines the political and ideological quality of his works, and it plays a major role in ensuring their artistic value. When he has highly developed political vision, the artist is able successfully to apply the principle of the truthful representation of life in his creative work and judge accurately whether his portrayal of character is adequate.

Because he serves the Party and the revolution through his creative work, an artist must possess a high level of artistic skill in addition to his developed political vision. A person with a low level of technical skill cannot make an excellent technician and a person with a low level of artistic skill cannot be a genuine creative artist. A high level of artistic skill and highly developed political vision are the two major requirements for becoming a revolutionary artist.

The artist's skill is the important factor which combines exalted ideological content with refined artistic qualities in a work of art. Only talented artists are able to realize correctly their descriptive goals. Although a writer may have selected a socially important seed from the experience of life and be aglow with creative ardour, he will not be able to describe it effectively if he lacks sufficient descriptive ability. Because a seed possesses ideological substance and provides the soil in which the elements of description can strike their roots, he will only be able to describe it beautifully if his political horizon is high and his artistic skill is well developed.

Artistic skill is only a genuine creative force in combination with highly-developed political vision. A person who knows only art and does not know the Party's policies cannot be a revolutionary artist. He cannot create a valuable work of high ideological and artistic qualities with his skill alone. Art of a high quality can only be created by an artist who holds a correct view of all aspects of the revolution and construction, is knowledgeable about both nature and society, and is endowed with true artistic talent.

An artist should achieve mastery of his creative work through varied training and preparation. Art represents reality in a comprehensive and integral way. An artist should therefore possess a broad and profound knowledge of life and an extensive and varied knowledge of the world.

An artist requires expert knowledge of all spheres of nature and society. Only such knowledge will enable him to create any artistic image he writes without error or difficulty. Film artists, and people involved in group forms of art, in particular, should master the techniques of all spheres of art.

An artist must be a devoted scholar who studies and learns tirelessly under all circumstances applying all available means and methods and exploiting every opportunity.

Books are a storehouse of knowledge which provides indispensable mental nourishment for artists. From books artists can obtain diverse and detailed knowledge of aspects of society and nature such as politics, the economy, science, culture, military affairs and morality. Everyone needs books, but artists in particular cannot live or engage in creative work without reading. Books must become their life's companions and respected teachers.

Artists must also learn all the time from their practical activity. For artists creative work is a highly significant form of social practice. Artists must develop advanced expertise through their creative practice, ceaselessly polishing their talent and deepening their wisdom. As practice is the starting-point and the basis of cognition, it is most rational for artists to acquire expertise and skill through the actual process of creative work.

Film artists need to have a theoretical knowledge of films, but they cannot produce fine films if they only master the theory. The theory of film is indeed indispensable for artists, involved in film making, but it cannot provide satisfactory solutions to all the problems arising in creative work. True knowledge of film production and practical skill can only be fully ·acquired through actual creative work.

This creative work provides artists with experience in the diverse skills of their trade and in applying the general methods used in an artistic portrayal of life. It also allows them to extend and consolidate their theoretical knowledge and test its validity as they acquire still more knowledge and experience.

Artists should learn from the experience of other creative workers. While drawing on their own experience and the lessons of creative work, they should be willing to learn open-mindedly and sincerely from the practical experience of other artists. In this way they can accumulate the wealth of knowledge and experience they require.

Artists must study diligently all their lives so that they need never feel regret for wasted time. Tireless study opens up the high road to success in the arts.

BE LOYAL TO THE PARTY AND PROVE YOURSELVES WORTHY OF THE TRUST IT PLACES IN YOU

Writers and artists must justify the lofty political trust of the Party by working loyally and devoting their artistic skill to its service. This is the new requirement established by the Party for the revolutionary transformation of writers and artists in accordance with the requirements of the endeavour to build socialism and communism and for the raising of the ideological and artistic level of art and literature to new heights.

The political integrity of writers and artists and their professional fate are bound up with the question of justifying the great political confidence of the Party by living a loyal life and working with great skill.

The Party's political confidence is the greatest honour and happiness for writers and artists who have entrusted their destiny entirely to the Party and devote themselves to the Party and the revolution. Writers and artists can only achieve political integrity through the political confidence placed in them by the Party, and to add lustre to it they must justify this great trust. The political integrity of writers and artists is unthinkable apart from the confidence of the Party.

Writers and artists should strive to obtain not only the Party's political confidence but also its professional confidence. The professional confidence of the Party means that the Party believes in their ability to produce excellent works of art and literature with noble ideological content and high artistic qualities and that they are capable of satisfactorily completing whatever creative tasks they may be given, no matter how difficult. To enjoy the professional confidence of the Party, writers and artists must possess advanced political vision, a wide range of knowledge and great artistic talent.

Our Party requires absolutely that writers and artists strive to raise their political and ideological standards and develop their artistic talent, and it provides them with excellent conditions for improving their political and professional qualifications. Its intention is to revolutionize thoroughly all writers and artists and lead them all onward to communist society without losing a single laggard on the way. Writers and artists should therefore always bear in mind that the Party requires them to undergo thorough political and professional training because it loves them and places great confidence in them. They must loyally strive to justify its confidence and love.

Writers' and artists' loyalty to the Party must find concrete expression in their works rather than in their words. Writers and artists can justify the great confidence of the Party by producing revolutionary works with elevated ideological and artistic qualities which meet the challenge of the times and accord with the aspirations of the people.

Ideologically and artistically excellent works can only be created by writers and artists who are thoroughly prepared politically, ideologically and artistically. They must help to establish the Party's monolithic ideological system, improve their artistic qualifications and prepare themselves fully to carry out whatever creative tasks they may be given by the Party.

Study and training is the basic means of raising the level of their political and technical qualifications. Anyone who fails to apply himself effectively to study and training can never acquire a high level of political and professional qualification. Lofty political vision and artistic talent can only be developed through tireless study and training.

Writers and artists should work to raise the level of their political and technical qualifications on the principle of combining theoretical studies and practical training.

In theoretical studies it is important to make the correct links between political theories and theories of art. If creative work is to be conducted on a high ideological and artistic level it is necessary to master both political and technical theories. If an artist is not versed in political theories and knows only the theories of art, he will not be able to produce works which are of value to his society and his people. It is obvious that an artist who does not understand the revolutionary times in which he lives is unable to conceive an art which embodies the noble spirit of the times and the profound idea of the revolution, and that an artist who lacks a well-rounded training is unable to create an accurate depiction of the complexity and variety of human life.

The principle that must be observed first and foremost in study and training is to give priority to political study and its intensification.

The most fundamental requirement of political study is to master the great concept of Juche. It is fundamentally important for the establishment of writers' and artists' revolutionary world outlook, their acquisition of professional skill and knowledge, and their actual creative work, that they should be equipped with a thorough grasp of the concept of Juche.

Writers and artists must also equip themselves with our Party's Juche-orientated ideas and theories of art. These ideas and theories offer a profound and totally adequate insight into all artistic problems, ranging from the fundamental principles and means of developing socialist and communist art and literature to the various practical questions involved in creative work. If writers and artists have an unshakable grasp of the Juche-orientated ideas of art and literature, they will encounter no difficult or insoluble problems in their creative work, and will not be liable to deviations either of the Left or the Right.

In their study of theories of art they may read different kinds of reference books in order to grasp in greater depth and breadth the essential nature and profound accuracy of the Juche-orientated ideas of art and literature and to acquire a correct understanding of the real nature and harmfulness of "theories" which contradict the Juche-inspired idea of art and literature. But if they should fail to achieve a firm grasp of the Juche-inspired idea of art and literature and read indiscriminately, accepting everything, they will not be able to distinguish right from wrong and will develop a distorted view of the world, so that they will be liable to go astray. They must always keep this danger in mind.

Writers and artists must base their study of art on training themselves as well-rounded communist artists. Socialist and communist society requires everyone to become a competent worker who possesses ample knowledge, a sound morality and a healthy body. Artists should not only be versed in their professional specialism to the extent required by the new society, they must also acquire profound knowledge and practical ability in other fields, develop lofty political vision, noble moral qualities and healthy bodies.

They must subordinate the study of art to the successful implementation of their immediate creative tasks, and conduct it systematically in order to achieve long-term goals. An actor who tomorrow has to play the part of a tractor-driver ploughing the fields cannot afford to spend his time improving his qualification by learning to play a musical instrument. The study of art only produces good results when it is undertaken in combination with actual creative work.

The study of art by writers and artists must contribute to their long-term objective of training themselves as harmoniously developed artists with a wide range of ability, and should not detract from the immediate requirements of their creative work. If the pressure of his creative work lends an artist to the study today of only what is immediately needed, and if tomorrow he only prepares himself for his part because it is urgent, and he finds no time for anything but this ceaseless creative work, he will be unable to develop his artistic skills systematically and harmoniously. Although a short-term study plan and daily routine may serve as a stop-gap, they will not save him from the impoverishment of knowledge and skills which will overtake him with the passage of time. If he studies persistently, progressing by stages towards well-defined objectives he will find his study interesting and rewarding.

Study must be directed towards the accumulation of knowledge which can be applied. Theoretical study must therefore be combined effectively with practical training in order to improve creative skills, and practical training must be conducted scientifically on the basis of theoretical study. This is because theories of art provide the scientific basis for improving practical skills and practical training is the process of consolidating theoretical knowledge into applied knowledge. Artistic skills can serve creative work effectively only when theoretical and practical knowledge are thoroughly integrated. If a man is able to express something in words and conceive it clearly in his mind, but is unable to put it into action, then he cannot be called an actor.

Without exception, all writers and artists must vigorously pursue their skills training in order to improve their qualifications. However, most writers, directors, cameramen and fine artists are less enthusiastic about skills training than actors and musicians. They evidently hold a mistaken view of the nature of this training. Some people seem to think that skills training is only needed by beginners or those who lack professional qualifications. But writers and artists who are determined to work for the Party and their fellow citizens must, without exception, strive throughout their lives to improve their skills.

Even from the strictly professional point of view writers, directors, cameramen and composers cannot deny their need for proficiency in the skills of their art. A film-writer requires knowledge of directing, the art of acting, camerawork, the fine arts, music and everything else related to motion pictures. A director must be better qualified in both theoretical and practical matters than his actors. A cameraman who is skilled only in filming will be unable to capture a scenario on film adequately, and a composer who is ignorant of literature and poor at playing an instrument will not be able to compose fine music for a film.

A public exhibition of skills is a good example of a training method which improves artistic qualifications. It is an effective form of training not only because it involves all the elements which contribute to the attainment of the ultimate goal, but also because a large number of people can participate in it or watch it and learn from it. It is also a form of training which can be arranged regularly.

If an exhibition of skills is to be successful, items must be selected which are rich in political and ideological content and suited to the improvement of the various aspects of the skills involved, for instance, major scenes from films, one-act plays, stories, poems, dramatic sketches, humorous dialogues, songs, instrumental performances and other pieces.

Both the content and form of the exhibition of skills must be genuinely educational so that it will contribute to improving the skills of the performers and also teach the spectators a great deal by arousing their interest. The exhibition must not be conducted like a contest of skill in which only highly-qualified artists take part, nor should it only include artists with relatively low skills. If it is oriented to high levels of skill, those with a low level of skill will lag still further behind; if it is oriented to low levels of skill, it will fail to stimulate those who have already attained a relatively high level and, worse still, it will even have a bad effect on the performers themselves, retarding the improvement of their qualifications as a group and undermining the quality of their creative work.

Yet another major form of skills training is a small troupe performance. This is an important artistic activity because it provides skills training in the process of linking art closely with life, and the artists closely with the masses.

Skills training is effective if it is conducted by combining group practice such as exhibitions of skills with public performances and individual training.

It would be difficult for all the artists of a collective to participate in a group training session at the same time. Training must be given on a regular basis, not merely when an exhibition of skills or a public performance is due. Group training can only be successful if the individual participants are well prepared.

Individual training must be conducted tirelessly with a scientific training system, using specific tasks to achieve definite objectives, under the guidance of the organization and with the assistance of the group.

A properly organized daily routine for artists must effectively combine study and training with creative work. One day may only be a moment in the course of a person's life, but artists must manage their day-to-day life effectively, bearing in mind that every moment is significant in the task of paving the road to a distant future goal.

This daily routine should be a plan for establishing a revolutionary style of life and work, and devoting one's life to militant struggle. As such it cannot be implemented unless all outmoded habits are eliminated. It is impossible to establish a new revolutionary style of life properly where outmoded notions and customs persist. Our artists must launch a powerful campaign to make a clean sweep of all outmoded, undisciplined, loose and disorderly practices. They must always live energetically and ambitiously and demonstrate a high degree of political enthusiasm.

If writers and artists are to work and live in a revolutionary manner, they must structure their daily routine on the basis of regular, organized habits. This is essential if writers and artists are to accelerate their revolutionary transformation and assimilation to the working class and forge ahead in their creative work.

If a writer plans and organizes his life, he can conduct his work and his life purposefully and achieve something of value even if he were only to live a single day. If he lives in a slipshod manner, without any plan, he will not be able to make effective use of his time and will waste every day that passes. A desultory and careless life lacking any definite objective leaves many requirements unfulfilled and lacks structure, thus allowing undesirable elements to infiltrate and cloud the person's mind, leading to his eventual degeneration.

To arrange one's daily life on a basis of regular habit one must organize all of one's study, creative work, and political and cultural activities according to a plan and regard its implementation as an essential element of the natural process of life. Precise planning and a high level of organization in action are the distinctive qualities of a communist, and these qualities must find impeccable expression in his life.

Creative work holds the central place in the daily routine of artists. Political and organizational activities and social work, to say nothing of studies and cultural activities, must all be subordinated to the successful practice of creative work, their basic duty. In planning and implementing the daily routine emphasis must be placed on creative work, intensifying the political life of the organization, the regular daily study of art to improve one's qualifications and the combination of social and cultural activities with all the above. If an artist procrastinates and neglects his politico-organizational life and studies simply because his creative work is his main interest for, not only will he be unsuccessful in his creative work, his political development will also suffer seriously. A revolutionary must know how to work according to his plan and make effective use of his time even under pressure of work.

The life of an artist must always be a process of strenuous and conscious revolutionary effort and artistic creation. The day's work must begin with studies and end with an organizational review of the day's work and the confirmation of the plan of work for the next day. The life of an artist must be a continuous process of new advances and progress in which today is not the same as yesterday and tomorrow is not the same as today. We can say that artists who are engaged every minute of everyday in creative work for the Party and the revolution are living a noble and meaningful life, proving themselves worthy of the Party's consideration and the great political trust it places in them by working loyally with an advanced degree of political consciousness and high professional skill.

SPEED CAMPAIGN IS FUNDAMENTAL TO THE CREATION OF REVOLUTIONARY ART AND LITERATURE

In recent years a speed campaign[6] has got well under way in the field of art and literature, resulting in an unprecedented upsurge in creative work, and a great many works of high ideological and artistic quality have been produced. The effectiveness of the speed campaign has been fully demonstrated in the course of producing a film version of the classic work, *The Fate of a Self-defence Corps Man,* and other films dealing with contemporary subjects from our life, and also in the creation of revolutionary operas of a kind similar to *The Sea of Blood.* Experience has clearly demonstrated that the speed campaign is, indeed, a fundamental revolutionary form of creative work which enables us to develop art and literature rapidly in order to meet the requirements of the present day and significantly raise the ideological and artistic standards of works of art.

The speed campaign in the creation of works of art and literature is a fundamentally revolutionary mode of creative work providing the basic structure for artistic endeavour. It allows writers and artists to fulfil the requirements of the Party's ideological work promptly, by encouraging them to display the maximum of political awareness and creative enthusiasm and produce successful works of high ideological and artistic quality in the shortest possible period of time.

An energetic campaign of acceleration in the areas of art and literature is a sure guarantee that they will produce prompt and correct responses to the challenges thrown up by reality in its accelerated development and raise their own militancy to the highest possible level.

Art and literature must always run ahead of reality, playing the role of a stimulus and motivating force in each period and at each stage of the revolutionary struggle. In order to play this role properly, they must produce works representing the Party's policy for each period as soon as it is published.

Their buoyant revolutionary enthusiasm for the complete victory of socialism in the northern half of the Republic and the reunification of our nation at the earliest possible date, has stimulated our people to the achievement of new and miraculous successes and the introduction of unprecedented innovations, every hour of day. In this great movement of progress, communist people of the new type are being cultivated in large numbers. The situation in which we live, whereby things which were new yesterday become outmoded today, constantly sets new goals to art and literature.

If timely solutions are to be found to the pressing questions raised by our revolutionary situation, it is necessary to eliminate the outmoded viewpoints and attitudes which find expression in a sluggish approach to work and in talks about "mentalities" and "inspiration".

The campaign of acceleration not only reflects the essential requirements of socialist art and literature but also the intrinsic features of the actual work of creating revolutionary art and literature.

As a matter of principle, creative work cannot be successful if it is dragged out unnecessarily. The secret of success in creative work is not in the amount of time involved, but the noble conception and high enthusiasm of the artist. If he is ideologically mature and is fired with creative enthusiasm, he can tackle any task, no matter how difficult, with daring and confidence and complete a work, no matter how large, in a short period of time.

Art is a product of thought and enthusiasm. Profound thinking, burning enthusiasm and intensive and persistent creative endeavour are the decisive factors in achieving an incredibly high speed of creative production and raising the level of a work's ideological and artistic quality to an incomparable height. If the artist is roused to persist in his bold endeavours, by a high degree of political awareness and creative enthusiasm, he is sure to attain good results even in a short period of time. On the contrary, a creative artist with a low level of political consciousness and no creative enthusiasm is unable to produce a good piece of work no matter how long he may take over it.

In fact, we ourselves have had valuable experiences of providing ineffective artists with ideological sustenance, encouraging them to great revolutionary enthusiasm and requiring them to work in the exalted spirit of the campaign of acceleration and seeing them redouble their efforts and produce good works. The campaign of acceleration is not only in accord with the intrinsic nature of the work of creating revolutionary art and literature, it also provides the ultimate guarantee of improvement both of the political and professional qualifications of writers and artists and the ideological and artistic quality of their works.

The allegation that the campaign of acceleration will lower the quality of work is nothing but a capitalist, revisionist sophistry that in effect advocates "libertarianism" in creative work.

In socialist society, there is ample scope for the rapid development of art and literature to a high level. Art and literature can be developed quickly in this society because all the essential preconditions for their development can be enlisted under the Party's monolithic guidance, and creative efforts can be effectively organized and planned. In this society the state also provides writers and artists with adequate material conditions for them to live and pursue their creative work, so that they can concentrate on this work and apply the full measure of their energies and talents to improving the quality of their output and accelerating the creative process.

In socialist society, the Party's intelligent leadership and meticulous care are the decisive factors in the rapid development of art and literature in the correct direction. In each period and at each stage of the revolution's development, the Party indicates to writers and artists the correct direction for the development of creative work, and provides scientifically-based answers to the theoretical and practical questions arising in the course of their creative endeavours as they pursue that direction. The Party helps them to improve their political and professional qualifications by providing intensive ideological and artistic education, and it guides their creative activities so that they are able to improve the quality of our art and literature and develop them rapidly.

In socialist society, the capacity for the continuous high-speed development of high-quality art and literature steadily increases as the Party's leadership of art and literature is strengthened, the political and professional abilities of the writers and artists are improved, and better material and technical conditions are provided. Whether or not the campaign of acceleration is able to draw on the strong basis of existing favourable conditions depends on how writers and artists engaged in creative work, and those who guide their creative efforts, understand the revolutionary essence of the campaign and implement its requirements in practice.

The essential requirement of the campaign of acceleration in creative work is to mobilize all forces and forge ahead with creative work as fast as possible, while ensuring that the ideological and artistic quality of the works produced is of the very highest level. In other words, the speed campaign requires that maximum success, both in terms of quantity and quality, should be achieved in the shortest possible span of time.

Speed in artistic creation presupposes the very finest quality. Speed without regard for quality, speed for its own sake, is meaningless.

Creative work must not be slowed down allegedly in order to improve its quality. Slackening the speed of creative work is proof that creative enthusiasm and confidence are lacking. An inadequate understanding of life and hesitant confidence in the works produced are the factors that slow down creative work; a slow speed of production means that the quality of the works is low.

Conversely, the quality of works should never be reduced in order to increase the speed of production. If a film is produced in one month to satisfy the requirement of speed and then three months is spent in upgrading it not only will the problem of quality remain unsolved, but large amounts of materials, funds, time and labour will be wasted and considerable loss will be incurred. The speed of artistic and literary creation must not be accelerated for its own sake, but in order to enhance the ideological and artistic quality of the works produced. Only the proper combination of constantly high speed and high quality satisfies the requirements of the campaign of acceleration.

In order to launch a campaign of acceleration in creative work, it is essential to select a proper seed and acquire a full understanding of the work to be produced. The selection of the right seed for the creative endeavour is a prerequisite condition of a speed campaign; it enables the writer to discover the correct solutions to the ideological and artistic problems arising in the course of his creative endeavours and provides him with a distinctly defined attitude towards the results of his work. When the writer concentrates all his ability on his work with a firm confidence in the results of his creative endeavours, he can both work at high speed and improve the ideological and artistic quality of his output.

A perfect literary piece which contains the right seed is indispensable for the conduct of a successful campaign of acceleration in the creation of a work of group art such as a film or an opera. The creation of films and operas can only be undertaken full steam ahead if the literary groundwork has been prepared, so no attempt should be made to launch a speed campaign with works which are not perfect. If a speed campaign is launched on the basis of an immature work, many adjustments have to be made in the course of the production. This will inevitably slow down the speed and impair the quality of the work.

If speed campaign for the creation of a work of group art is to be effective, the entire creative staff must acquire a total understanding of the perfect literary work that has been prepared. Each member of the staff which is to produce a film or an opera must study the ideological and artistic features of the literary work thoroughly and in depth and come to an agreement with the others on all problems arising in the course of their creative work. Without a full understanding of the literary original and unanimity of the creative staff, the creative endeavour will end in confusion. Therefore, they must all make it a rule to study their scenario and script thoroughly until they understand them and hold serious discussions on the creative intention of the work, so that every member of the creative group acquires a complete understanding of it.

When the members of the creative team have selected the right seed and mastered the meaning of the work, they must launch a bold, lightning campaign and rapidly complete their creative tasks one after the other. When one has set a clear target and developed unshakable confidence, one must advance boldly and persistently towards one's goal until decisive victory is achieved. This is the militant attitude to work and the revolutionary working method of a communist. When a good seed has been selected for the work of artistic creation every effort must be focussed on it, and creative work must be pushed forward with a strong will and ardent commitment. In this way it is possible to advance at a very high speed and improve the quality of the artistic representation of life.

A speed campaign can only be successfully launched when the requisite material and technical conditions for a lightning creative campaign have been prepared. Launching a speed campaign without any advance arrangements can only result from a craving for fame or a perfunctory attitude to creative work. This tendency in creative work must be rejected, and also the slothful attitude of those who simply complain of poor working conditions must be combated uncompromisingly.

All the creative workers must work hard in the revolutionary spirit of self-reliance to complete the necessary material and technical preparations for the speed campaign. Of course, the Party organization and the administrative staff of the creative collective will also be required to make strenuous efforts in order to provide the material and technical conditions for creative work. But the writers and artists are responsible for their creative work so they themselves must be capable of making the arrangement for their creative work. If the writers and artists display the revolutionary spirit of self-reliance, and do not wait for other people to provide conditions for them, they will be able to change unfavourable conditions into favourable ones and develop an audacious and successful speed campaign.

The most important condition for success in a speed campaign is the definite precedence of political work and its support by means of an intensive ideological campaign.

In order to press on with a speed campaign, one must solve the three problems of ideology, technology and guidance. The most important of these is the problem of ideology. This matter must be settled satisfactorily before the other two can be settled.

The positive ideological and spiritual condition of the people who produce works of art and literature is essential to success in the speed campaign. Even if adequate material and technical conditions have been provided, a campaign to attain both high speed and high quality will not be successful unless the ideological and spiritual condition of the creative workers is positive. Therefore it is essential in dealing with any creative endeavour to give definite priority to political work and to launch a dynamic ideological campaign.

Political work has to be conducted with people. It is important in creative work for the creative workers to be encouraged to display a high degree of political enthusiasm and creative zeal and to commit themselves totally to the speed campaign. To achieve this the creative staff should be given a full grasp of the goals of the speed campaign, its methods, and the significance of the work of art to be created for the revolutionary education of the working people. Each of them will then be sure to fulfil his own assignment.

Furthermore the creative staff should be welded in a close unity of ideology and purpose so that they will fulfil their creative task through a well-concerted effort. A speed campaign can only be successfully carried out by a group which has promptly and accurately accepted the requirements of the Party's policy and whose hearts are solidly united in loyalty to the Party and determination to implement its revolutionary assignment unfailingly. If the creative group is held closely together by unfailing loyalty to the great leader Comrade Kim Il Sung, a sense of responsibility for their duty, and a unity of ideology and purpose they will manifest revolutionary enthusiasm, unbreakable will and the strength to press ahead and overcome any crisis whatever in order to bring the speed campaign to successful conclusion.

The major requirement of the political work for a speed campaign is that the creative staff should acquire the revolutionary trait of unqualified support for the great leader's instructions and the Party's policy. New miraculous and innovatory successes in creative work will be achieved continually if the creative workers are imbued with the unqualified revolutionary spirit which achieves the most brilliant of results by displaying total devotion and boundless creative energy, by regarding the great leader's instructions and the Party's policy as the letter of the law and remaining firmly determined to deny themselves all rest and even deny the right to die until they have fulfilled their revolutionary duty.

Since a speed campaign is intended to ensure the fulfilment of the creative task no one, once he has committed himself to action, should be allowed to change the objective and plan of the campaign, which have been discussed and decided collectively, or to violate the established daily schedule. The objective and plan of the campaign are discussed and decided collectively by the Party committee concerned, which represents the Party's intentions and the collective will of the masses themselves. The day's planned quota of work must be fulfilled within the day come what may, and the daily and weekly work plans must be fulfilled at the highest level of quality.

A speed campaign only becomes a meaningful campaign of creative work when it is a process of the revolutionary transformation of writers and artists and their assimilation to the working class.

A speed campaign is a means of struggle to eliminate all conventional, outmoded habits and attitudes to work and to establish new ones. A speed campaign involves the intensive struggle between the new and the old, that is, between progressive and conservative, between innovation and stagnation, between forward advance and marking time. Therefore, a speed campaign implies an ideological campaign directed at rooting out the remnants of outmoded ideas from the minds of the writers and artists and imbuing them with revolutionary and working-class ideas.

If a speed campaign for developing creative work is to become a process of the revolutionary transformation of writers and artists and their assimilation to the working class, then it must be, above all, a process by which the Party's monolithic ideological system is established among them. All the workers who participate in the campaign must be encouraged to develop to a high degree the revolutionary trait of accepting the Party's orders and directives unconditionally and carrying them out to the end and simultaneously eliminate from their own minds all remnants of outmoded ideas. Only then will the speed campaign become a process of genuine re-education.

If a speed campaign is to be conducted successfully, the revolutionary organizational life of the workers must be improved and they must be induced to display the highest possible level of collectivist spirit and noble communist morals. The Party organizations concerned must provide substantial assistance to all the workers in launching and conducting an uncompromising ideological struggle by means of criticism, in the course of which they steadily make themselves more revolutionary and working-class.

A speed campaign must be a campaign of regular creative work for all film studios and for all creative groups. A speed campaign which is conducted on the basis of providing a few selected groups with specially favourable conditions will be of no help in raising the level of artistic work as a whole, and, worse still, it will produce a negative effect on those artists who cannot participate in the campaign. Furthermore, if a speed campaign is limited to solving a few problems of the present moment, instead of being conducted on a regular, continuing basis, the second effort will not be successful, even though the first may have been victorious, and it will actually be impossible to launch a third campaign.

Since a speed campaign should be a regular form of creative work, it must, on no account, be conducted under the terms of a crash programme. Even if a campaign is intensive, your organizational life must be tightened up, study must be set on a regular basis, work must be conducted in a revolutionary manner, life must be cheerful and include organized cultural recreation. If you exclude the meetings, put off studies and neglect the arrangement of rest and recreation because of the pressure of the campaign, it will be impossible to enthuse people to continue working with unflagging creative energy.

Despite all the challenges and pressures of the speed campaign, creative work and life must be closely scheduled so that everyone is cheerful and energetic, learns a great deal and makes rapid progress. If this is done, the second piece of work created will be better, and the third one better still. Thus, both the people and the art will develop apace in the course of repeated speed campaigns. It is only when a speed campaign produces good results that everyone really enjoys living and working and creating in a revolutionary manner, grows accustomed to it and committed to it, to the extent that they feel a genuine need to continue the speed campaign.

The speed campaign must be a highly organized, well planned, intensive creative endeavour. However high the level of people's political enthusiasm and creative zeal may be, success cannot be expected unless the organizational work is well structured.

In order to provide a strong impetus to the speed campaign, the administrative section must draw up a scientific plan based on an accurate assessment of personnel, materials and technical requirements, organize the productive efforts to the last detail and radically improve the work of supervision in step with the requirements of the developing situation.

In order to secure the artists' high political enthusiasm and creative zeal and the creative group's unity of ideology and purpose, the Chongsanri spirit and method and the Taean work system must be thoroughly applied to the work of organizing and supervising film production. In this connection it is important for the administrative section to establish a unified, collective system of organizational supervision under the leadership of the Party committee, and to effectively combine political leadership and artistic guidance.

Senior officials must probe deep into the process of film production, identify problems in good time and solve them in a responsible manner. This is a principle that must always be observed in the organization and supervision of a speed campaign.

The organizational supervision of production must be managed in a way that ensures the unfailing implementation of the plan of creative work and encourages people to introduce creative innovations. The officials must therefore be precise and punctual in providing the creative workers with materials, funds and equipment and also with sufficient consumer goods to allow every member of the creative group to concentrate all his energies and talents on the successful production of films of high ideological and artistic quality in a short span of time. Organizing and mobilizing the intensive work of the creative forces, operating all the equipment at full capacity and utilizing materials efficiently require the active commitment of everybody, from the senior officials of the film studio to the workers, and the energetic employment of all facilities, from film cameras to projectors, in the creative endeavours.

Under the leadership of the Party, our revolutionary film artists have thoroughly implemented the revolutionary policy of the speed campaign and created the "Work Mode of the Paekdusan Production", which consists in the application of the great Chongsanri spirit and method[7] and the Taean work system[8] to the sphere of art and literature. The "Work Mode of the Paekdusan Production" is a new communist mode of creative work employed by the revolutionary film artists trained by the Party in their work of adapting classic works to the screen in line with the revolutionary policy of the speed campaign.

The essential revolutionary feature of the "Work Mode of the Paekdusan Production" is that all the artists forge ahead with the speed campaign, producing films of higher ideological and artistic quality more quickly by developing a firm grasp of the concept of Juche and working as required by the Chongsanri spirit and method and the Taean work system.

The lifeblood of the "Work Mode of the Paekdusan Production" is the unfailing loyalty of the film artists who have thoroughly grasped the Party's monolithic ideology to the great leader Comrade Kim Il Sung. "Let us become the guards and death-defying corps unfailingly loyal to the great leader!" is the revolutionary slogan and the inalienable creed that united the members of the Paekdusan Production with one mind and purpose and encouraged them to act as one. Precisely because they possess such high political awareness and positive principles to live by, the Paekdusan Production have been able to fulfil splendidly in a very short time the onerous task of creating film versions of the classic works, *The Sea of Blood, The Fate of a Self-defence Corps Man* and *The Flower Girl,* films of great significance in the history of our art and literature.

As the principle of the speed campaign has been implemented the "Work Mode of the Paekdusan Production" has spread widely in all fields of art and literature and resulted in miraculous successes. In the field of opera, for instance, the revolutionary opera *The Sea of Blood,* which ushered in a new epoch of revolutionary opera, and other masterpieces have been created in a very short period of time. This is the excellent fruit of the speed campaign, a new revolutionary principle of creative work put forward by the Party and a great innovation in the creation of art and literature.

GUIDING THE CREATIVE PROCESS

"When the Party's line and policies are correct and proper means and measures are adopted for their implementation, success in the implementation of the revolutionary tasks depends entirely on what work methods and styles the officials directly responsible for their implementation employ and on how they mobilize the broad masses in this work."

KIM IL SUNG

REVOLUTIONARY CREATIVE PRACTICE REQUIRES A NEW SYSTEM FOR GUIDING THE CREATIVE PROCESS

Following the victory of the socialist revolution, the working-class Party is faced with the task of creating fully-developed communist art and literature.

Communist art and literature are the endeavour to describe model examples of a new type of person who strives devotedly for the building of a socialist and communist society, in order to help develop the revolutionary outlook on the world of all members of society and impart a strong impetus to the people's revolutionary struggle and their work of construction, in the course of which they transform themselves, society and nature in accordance with the principle of Juche. Whether this historic task is carried out successfully or not depends entirely on how the Party guides the work of art and literature.

The working-class Party is the General Staff and sets the pace and guides all aspects of the revolutionary struggles for independence, sovereignty, socialism and communism. The destiny of the Korean people and the eventual victory of the Korean revolution depend entirely on our Party's leadership. The steady improvement of our Party's leadership in all fields of the revolution and construction is a sure guarantee of the triumph of our revolutionary cause.

In the field of art and literature, too, the historic cause of creating and developing working-class art and literature which accord with the intrinsic nature of socialism and communism can only be successfully accomplished under the leadership of the Party. Only when the Party leadership of art and literature is strengthened and writers and artists sincerely accept Party leadership can the onerous yet honourable task facing art and literature be carried out with credit.

In order to provide proper Party leadership for our art and literature in their new stage of development, it is necessary to establish an appropriate work system and method which are in keeping with the requirements of the concept of Juche. Whether or not the superiority of communist art and literature is displayed properly depends on the principles, system and method of Party guidance which are established.

Some people today deny the need for the Party leadership of art and literature, while they claim that they are building communist art and literature. They are weakening the controlling functions of the state administrative organs, the organs of proletarian dictatorship, which are in charge of art and literature, and transforming the Unions of Art and Literature, the artists' organizations, into social clubs. They are also failing to provide political guidance for the creative activities of writers and artists and completely "liberalizing" the work of art and literature. Because Party policy on the work of art and literature is misleading in some countries, art and literature there are at a low ebb, and the danger of a return to capitalism has even emerged.

Historical experience demonstrates that in order to develop art and literature in accordance with the intrinsic nature of socialism and communism, it is imperative for the working-class Party to establish a new revolutionary and communist system and method of guidance and strengthen Party leadership.

Of paramount importance in the Party leadership of art and literature is the establishment of the system of Party guidance.

This means that the work of art and literature is organized and carried out under the monolithic guidance of the Party so that the Party's policy on art and literature is thoroughly implemented. In other words, it means that the Party members and artists establish as the norm the revolutionary attitude of accepting unconditionally the instructions of the great leader Comrade Kim Il Sung and the directives of the Party and ensuring their unconditional and thorough implementation, so that all creative activities are conducted under the monolithic guidance of the Party centre.

The work of art and literature is a very important undertaking which constitutes a part of the Party's ideological work in dealing with people's way of thinking and has a far-reaching political and ideological effect on them. It must therefore only be conducted under the Party's monolithic guidance.

Only when the system of Party guidance of the work of art and literature has been established is the Party's Juche-orientated idea of art and literature sure to be implemented thoroughly in all circumstances without the slightest vacillation and our art and literature sure to develop into Juche-orientated art and literature, and become a model of communist literature and art, which brilliantly carry forward our Party's glorious revolutionary cause through the coming generations.

Only when the system of Party guidance has been established will the work of training Party members and artists in the field of art and literature to become ardent communist revolutionaries, equipped with the Juche world outlook, be more successful, and the unity of writers and artists in ideology and purpose in striving towards their goal be strengthened.

Since in our socialist society all the means of art and literature are in the hands of the Party and the state, and they play a great role in the ideological education of the working people, our Party has made it an unshakable principle to provide its monolithic guidance to the work of art and literature. This is the Juche-orientated principle of leadership applied by our Party, which trusts the writers and artists and encourages them to entrust their destiny entirely to it, and wholeheartedly commit themselves to its policy on art and literature, in order to develop our art and literature as rapidly as possible into revolutionary ones that serve the people, accelerate the progress of our revolution and thereby make an active contribution to the world revolution.

Our art and literature have been able to grow and blossom resplendently as they do today entirely because the Party has kept art and literature under its direct control and has provided them with monolithic guidance. We must continue in the future to give pride of place to the work of establishing the system of Party guidance in the field of art and literature and developing it in greater depth.

If the system of Party guidance is to be firmly established all questions that arise in the work of art and literature must only be dealt with in accordance with the decisions of the Party centre, and the projects undertaken by decision of the Party centre must be realized without fail.

In order to enhance its role of leadership in art and literature, the working-class Party must clearly define the position and role of the state administrative organs in charge of art and literature and those of the Unions of Art and Literature, drawing a distinct line of demarcation between their functions, and destroying all outmoded patterns of work.

The outmoded conventional system and method of work have deep roots in old traditions and the old social order that were formed over a long historical period. It is therefore no easy task to reform them to suit the new situation. Only by adopting a proper position and a correct attitude to art and literature is it possible to eliminate the outmoded system and method of guidance in creative work, which retain numerous remnants of capitalism, and to establish new system and methods that accord with the distinctive features and requirements of socialist art and literature. The system and method of work are an expression of people's ideological viewpoint and their style of work. Therefore, the establishment of the new system and method of guidance in creative work requires above all else the correction of people's ideological viewpoint and style of work.

In socialist society, the prospects for the development of art and literature are boundless. Our country's highly advanced socialist system provides writers and artists with all the necessary working conditions and a solid mass foundation for the rapid development of art and literature.

The advantages of the socialist system will only be fully expressed when writers and artists link their efforts and work willingly and creatively to produce fine works of Party-orientated, people-orientated art and literature. The willingness and creative response of the writers and artists will not be displayed spontaneously, they will only find full expression under the correct and meticulous guidance of art and literature by the Party.

In guiding the work of art and literature, our Party has made unremitting efforts to enhance the function and role of the organs which guide this activity and the Unions of Art and Literature in a manner which accords with the intrinsic nature of socialist society and fulfils the requirements of creative work.

A long time ago, our Party advanced the policy of the three organizations—the Party, the Ministry of Culture and Art and the General Federation of the Unions of Art and Literature—working together to improve the system of guidance and assistance in the work of art and literature. This is a correct policy, since it enhances the Party's role of leadership in art and literature, enhances the functions of the Ministry of Culture and Art as an administrative and organizational body and those of the General Federation of the Unions of Art and Literature as an educational body, and mobilizes collective efforts to the maximum, so strengthening the political and ideological unity and cohesion of the ranks of literary workers and artists and encouraging highly successful creative work.

In socialist society, the state administrative organ in charge of art and literature, as an institution of the proletarian dictatorship, must constantly strive to improve its performance in organizing and controlling the implementation of the Party's policy on art and literature, and seek to provide writers and artists with working conditions in a responsible manner.

The General Federation of the Unions of Art and Literature, as the link between the Party and the writers and artists, must provide serious ideological and artistic training for writers and artists in accordance with the Party's policy on art and literature, unite them firmly behind the Party and provide collective support for their creative work.

By enhancing the role of the Ministry of Culture and Art, which is the executor of the Party's policy on art and literature, and also the administrative body guiding their development, and by enhancing the role and the functioning of the General Federation of the Unions of Art and Literature as an educational establishment, our Party has ensured the provision of profound and effective Party leadership in all aspects of art and literature.

In order to develop our art and literature to a higher stage, however, we must completely eliminate the outmoded system and method of work which still linger in the sphere of art and literature, and be careful to avoid a mixed jumble of systems and methods which are neither capitalist nor socialist. Officials of the bodies appointed to guide art and literature still have a tendency to deal with the guidance of creative work in an administrative and technical manner, and various aspects of the creative activities of writers and artists are still hindered by the subjective and arbitrary bureaucracy of the officials working in the artistic organizations.

Bureaucratic and formalistic methods of work will not encourage writers and artists to display a high degree of political awareness and creative talents. It is imperative to root out the outmoded systems and methods of work in view of the especial importance of art and literature after the establishment of the socialist system. If this is not done, it will be impossible to develop them more rapidly. The high standard of art and literature required by the new age can only be adequately achieved when the new system of guiding creative work has been completely established in accordance with the intrinsic nature of socialist society and the distinctive features of socialist art and literature.

The new system for guiding creative work is intended to realize the thorough implementation under the Party's monolithic leadership of the revolutionary mass line in art and literature and creative work and to guide all the writers and artists to adopt the attitude of masters of society in the unfailing fulfilment of their revolutionary duties. The new system considers the writers and artists to be responsible for the creation of art and literature and therefore puts the major emphasis on the definite priority of political work, work with people, which increases their political awareness and creative enthusiasm, and on the timely fulfilment of the revolutionary tasks facing art and literature by relying on the masses and mobilizing their energies. The speed and quality of artistic and literary creation depend on the political awareness and creative enthusiasm of the writers and artists. Therefore, the new system for guiding their work must always give pride of place to political work with the people involved, with the writers and artists.

The most important thing in the new system of guidance is the collective guidance of creative work and the Party committee's collective leadership of all the work of art administration.

The manner in which the production of works of art and literature is guided is a very important issue in the development of monolithic Party guidance. The critical examination of the works produced is one of the major levers for applying direct Party guidance to art and literature. It is essential to the work of helping writers substantially to produce their works in accordance with the Party's policy on art and literature.

In socialist society, the Party leadership of art and literature must be realized first of all through the steering of work orientation and the guidance of the content of the work. In order to ensure the proper development of art and literature, the working-class Party must clearly define the direction of development of creative work in each period and at each stage of the revolutionary struggle and provide correct guidance concerning the ideological content of the works produced. The definition of the correct tendency and the effective guidance of content is the only approach that can ensure that art and literature will develop without deviating to the right or the left and that works of sound ideological and artistic quality are produced in large numbers.

If it is to provide thorough guidance concerning the content of art and literature, the Party must strengthen the institution which examines the works under its guidance, and must improve the system and methods of examination to meet the requirements of the current situation.

In socialist society, both the people who create works of art and those who assist and guide them share a common ideology and aspiration, and they strive to implement the Party's policy on art and literature thoroughly and produce works of high ideological and artistic quality for the people. In our society, therefore, works can never be examined by the censorship method of old society, the method of simply stamping them "approved" or "rejected".

In socialist society, works of art and literature must be examined, under monolithic Party guidance, by the senior officials in charge of the area in consultation with professional workers who are well qualified in politics, ideology and practical artistic matters, in order to apply the principle of offering the creative artists ideological and artistic assistance and helping to achieve perfection in the work. Only when works are examined in a spirit of solidarity and cooperation and strictly in accordance with the Party's policy can art and literature really be developed soundly and quickly to serve the Party, the revolution and the people.

We must also establish a well structured system for the conduct of artistic and literary work under the collective leadership of the Party committee. The work of creating the Party's own art and literature and the Party's own films can never be the exclusive monopoly of a few senior officials or individual creative artists. For all practical purposes, it must be the work of the Party committee, the highest leadership body of the artistic organization. The collective leadership of creative work by the Party committee is capable of eliminating both the outmoded system of work still lingering in the field of art and literature, and the bureaucratic and formalistic method of work, and achieving the full implementation of the Party's policy.

In order to enhance the collective leadership function of the Party committee in creative work, it is important to staff the committee with well-qualified people and strengthen its militant role. The Party committee should be composed of people who are well-versed in both Party policy and art. If these people work with the artists, the Party organization will be able to supervise creative work effectively and guide it correctly.

A major requirement of the Party leadership of creative work is the elimination from the artistic organizations of the outmoded pattern of administration so that the higher organizations will assist their subordinates in a responsible manner and creative work can forge ahead in a unified and planned way in accordance with the Taean work system.

The creation of the works of group art such as films and stage production is, by its very nature, a complex undertaking involving the participation of a large number of creative artists and large amounts of equipment, materials and technical support. All the participants in such an undertaking must be united in their activity by strict revolutionary order and discipline and interact with each other according to a scientifically-based and dynamic plan and under unified command. To achieve this end, creative work in the arts must be administered in a coordinated and planned manner under the guidance of the Party committee.

This requirement of film production has been met by establishing a unified staff system for the administration of creative work in the arts. The staff of an artistic organization is composed of the chief of staff, who is responsible for all its internal affairs, and of officials with a good knowledge of administration, art, technology and production. The staff also has a unified system of command and a flexible information system. Therefore, the administrative staff can always obtain a clear picture of the entire process of creative work and the situation at all its departments, and is always able to give every department meticulous guidance.

The new staff system is a system of life and work capable of eliminating subjective arbitrariness, departmentalism and libertarian apathy in creative work and of providing it with scientific, rationally planned guidance. It is capable of strengthening the administrative links between all sectors and also their creative and productive ties, and enabling all the workers to pull together with one ideology and will in their efforts to complete their production.

If the advantages of the new system for guiding creative work are to be given full expression, officials, writers and artists must take a firm grasp of the revolutionary work method and the popular style of work and apply them in practice. When our Party's revolutionary mass line and the Chongsanri spirit and method, the embodiment of the mass line, are fully implemented, the new system of guidance of creative work will acquire still greater vitality.

CREATIVE WORK MUST BE GUIDED BY THE METHOD OF SINGLE COLLECTIVE ASSESSMENT

In order to identify successful solutions to the problems arising in the course of the revolution and construction, it is essential to enhance the Party's leadership role and allow free play to the revolutionary enthusiasm and collective resourcefulness of the masses.

In artistic and literary work, it is also the case that complex problems can always be solved successfully, no matter how difficult they may be, if experts come together to pool their efforts and talents under the leadership of the Party.

The organization and mobilization of the joint efforts of writers, artists and experts is the most reliable guarantee of success in practical creative work.

The assessment of works is a major aspect of artistic and literary activity which requires collective endeavours. In socialist society the creation of art and literature must always be conducted along the guidelines of the Party's ideological work and in order to meet its needs. Creative work should therefore be conducted in a planned and organized manner under the monolithic leadership of the Party.

An important aspect of this organized approach is the collective assessment of works by artistic and literary workers under monolithic Party guidance.

The assessment of works in order to guarantee their ideological and artistic quality to the Party and the state and to ensure their production within the time appointed is a heavy responsibility. It cannot, therefore, be taken care of by one person or a few people, nor can it be dealt with at the discretion of individual officials. Works must be examined collectively by experts who have a good understanding of the Party's policy and possess lofty political vision and an ample knowledge of art.

The system of single collective assessment not only ensures the monolithic Party guidance of art and literature, it also strengthens comradely cooperation and unity in creative work and provides substantial support to creative workers, enabling them to produce works of great ideological and artistic value in a short period of time. It also makes it possible to eliminate subjective and bureaucratic tendencies in the guidance of creative work, observe the principle of democracy and allow the creative artists' individuality maximum expression.

This system also enables creative workers and officials to improve their political and ideological qualifications and their artistic skills. Since the works are examined by officials well-qualified in both Party policy and theories of art and by experienced artists, their collective guidance and support help to broaden the creative artists' vision of Party policy and extend their knowledge of art. On their part, the examiners can probe deep into practical work of creation, identifying problems promptly and offering effective support to the creative artists.

The most important factor in the collective assessment of works is adherence to the principles of loyalty to the Party, the working class and the people. The essential function of the assessment of works is to guide and assist creative artists in representing the Party's policy correctly in their works and creating images that champion the interests of the working class and the people and accord with the tastes and sensibilities of the working masses.

The assessors must assist the artists in every way possible to produce works of high ideological and artistic quality which serve the interests of the Party, the working class and the people. Their first and foremost duty to the Party is to express prompt and sharp criticism of the slightest element which is contrary to Party policy, to help the creators to correct it, and to fight resolutely to prevent the infiltration of any ideological poison from reactionary art and literature.

In assessing the works they must offer effective political and artistic guidance. Political and artistic guidance is fundamental to the assessment of works of art.

It is of paramount importance that effective political guidance be given definite priority in the assessment of works of art. By political guidance we mean assisting and guiding the creative artists in the choice of politically significant seeds from the milieu of life and their proper description in accordance with the Party's policy. Effective political guidance makes it possible to select seeds in keeping with the Party's political direction and the requirements of each period and stage of the developing revolution, to describe these seeds properly and raise the ideological and artistic standards of works produced, so that their educational role is enhanced.

In order to provide effective political guidance, the assessors must not only be well acquainted with the Party's policy relating to the content of the work concerned, they must also study the Party's policies on other areas in detail and in depth. After they have acquired a profound knowledge of the Party policy, the assessors must consider how the creative artists understand Party policy, how the questions they raise relate to this understanding, and how they resolve these questions. In the discussion of the issues, they must help the creative artists to polish their good points and correct mistakes or make good gaps, by convincing them completely.

Creative artists must be given political guidance throughout the processes of correcting their plans of work, helping their work of description and analysing their products. This will strengthen the creative artists' political conviction, inspire them with creative enthusiasm and guide them along the straight path. If the assessors only examine a work in its first and final stages, and do nothing but find fault, the artist may be too embarrassed to complete the piece. Since it is always the creative artists themselves who are responsible for their work, they must not be cowed into always reading the faces of their assessors and helpers in a defensive frame of mind.

Although it is important to give definite priority to political guidance in the assessment of works of art, this alone is not enough to provide substantial guidance and assistance to the creative artists. Even when the seed of a work has been selected in accordance with the Party's policy and the subject has been established in such a way as to enhance its political significance, the work will not make a profound impression on people unless its characters and its depiction of life offer them a vivid artistic picture. Even when the right seed has been chosen and the subject has been established properly, life can be distorted and characters can be obscured unless the portrayal is presented in accordance with life's essential nature and logic, and in accordance with the laws of art. In the assessment of works, therefore, political guidance, while given priority, must be appropriately combined with artistic guidance.

By artistic guidance we mean assisting and guiding creative artists in the satisfactory artistic representation of the ideological content of their works by cultivating artistic qualities derived from Juche-orientated ideas and theories of art and literature. In offering artistic guidance it is important to adhere to Party principles and standards. Artistic guidance must not be confined to purely technical and administrative assistance. The question of description in art is always essentially an ideological one. Since there can be no artistic portrayal devoid of ideological content, it is important in artistic guidance to offer the creative artists real assistance in representing the ideological content satisfactorily.

If they are to provide effective artistic guidance, the assessors must first acquire a profound knowledge of our Party's Juche-orientated ideas and theories of art and literature. These ideas and theories provide profound solutions to all problems, great and small, which arise in the course of artistic creation. Only when creative work is closely guided in accordance with these ideas and theories can the artists be effectively assisted to produce fine works of art.

If the assessors each counsel creative artists in their own way, offering their own disparate suggestions, without any reference to Party principle or theoretical standards, and imply that artistic description may be carried out one way or the other at will, they will end up by imposing their own individual tastes on the creative artists and the works involved will get out of hand.

The assessor's examination of a work can only be considered successful if he convinces the author completely, both from the point of view of ideology and of theory, and inspires him with creative enthusiasm so that the author himself can discover the best way of writing his description.

The process of creation is a process of energetic enquiry, filled with mental excitement and creative passion. A creative artist can only produce an original work of art when his heart is fired with such creative zeal that he is unable to contain his desire to speak to the people and society of his time about justice and truth, about the great, the noble and the beautiful. A creative artist who lacks a profound knowledge of the life of his own period and does not feel passionate sympathy for it, will be unable to produce a fine work that matches the aspirations of the period and the challenges of life.

The same principle applies to the person responsible for guiding creative work. If he simply dictates to the creative artist in an administrative and technical fashion, demonstrating a cold and uninterested attitude, doing nothing but find fault with the work and assert his own demands, then he will never attain good results.

To restrict oneself to evaluation of the work and the asserting of demands is a bureaucratic method of censorship. The method of censoring and controlling creative work, instead of carefully guiding it, is not only in conflict with the intrinsic nature of creative work, it also has nothing in common with the Party method of guidance of artistic work. The assessor should enlighten the creative artist and assist him in his work, but he must not order him about or dictate to him. A relationship based on obedience to orders will not be conducive to successful creative endeavour.

In seeking to enlighten a creative artist it is important to inspire him with creative enthusiasm and stimulate him to profound thoughts and energetic use of his imagination.

From the rich and varied images of life, creative artists choose only those which excite them and contain the message they wish to convey. Since their choice is based on their own convictions and the logic of life as they perceive it, they are firmly convinced that their own thoughts are the most just and the most reasonable.

The assessors must recognize these features of creative work and refrain from expressing their own logic and tastes in counter-suggestions which they impose upon creative artists, simply because they do not like the manner of their descriptions. Artistic portrayals of reality, whether good or bad, are based on the artists' faith and logic. It may, therefore, be necessary to correct their faith and logic, rather than restructure their works at a stroke.

However good it is in itself, a counter-suggestion will prove useless unless it is accepted by the writer and fits in with both the artistic logic he has expressed throughout the work and with specific situations. It is much better for the creative artist to be roused to seek a new mode of description.

If creative artists are to be enlightened as to their shortcomings and guided to produce proper artistic portrayals, they must be offered guidance and assistance which suit their level of preparedness and their individual personalities. Writers' personalities must be respected, whether they are veterans or beginners, and they must be given proper assistance in the accurate assessment of the quality of their work and their own level of political and professional maturity. This is the way to produce good results.

Arousing creative artists to this awareness requires, as a matter of principle, that the assistance offered to creators should allow them to complete their works by their own efforts, and in doing so improve their ideological and artistic qualifications. So there should be no question of another writer finishing the work of one whose works are not satisfactory.

You can make a desk for another person, but you cannot write for an author.

The less well-developed an artist's ability, and the less satisfactory his portrayal of life, the more patient and the more sincere you must be in convincing him. If, instead, you write for him, you will not be helping him, and in the long run you will lose both the writer and his work.

The assessment of works of art is not restricted entirely to the works themselves; it involves working with the people who produce them. Assessors must, therefore, not view problems in a short-sighted fashion simply pointing out the merits and demerits of a work. They can only offer effective assistance to creative artists when they have become familiar with them as people. A correct understanding of an artist's political vision, artistic qualifications and creative individuality is the most important factor in helping him to succeed with the work in hand.

In order to attain a correct understanding of an artist's political and practical qualifications, the assessors must systematically study his history of creative work. Knowledge of the good points and shortcomings revealed in his works overall, and acquaintance with his creative individuality and work habits will enable the assessors to define the defects of the work in hand and take appropriate measures.

In the work of artistic guidance it is important to respect the individuality of the creative artists and guide them to create fresh and original images. The goal of collective assessment is not only to ensure adherence to Party principles in creative work, to eliminate unjustifiable subjective individualism and prevent possible errors in creative work, but also to assist the artist in displaying their initiative to the maximum and to accelerate the production of fresh and original works which accord with Party policy and meet its needs. Hence the artist's individuality must not be undermined for the sake of the collective principle. If an artist's individuality is suppressed, he will not produce an original work. When the right seed has been selected and an appropriate subject has been established, the writer must be allowed to portray them as best as he can.

Creative artists must be encouraged through the assessment of their works and inspired to write in an original way, discovering vivid descriptive techniques and fresh expressions which have not been used by others. This will stimulate them to a higher sense of responsibility and creative initiative and increase the variety of mood in our works of art and literature.

Assessors must be prudent and discreet with the results of the artists' painstaking efforts. If they declare their judgement on the spot following a cursory glance through the work in hand, their assessment will not inspire confidence. The first impression of a work is very important in its evaluation, but the assessors must always consider it a second time. The work must be examined sincerely. If it is good, the assessors must ponder exactly why it is good; if it is bad, they must consider why it is bad and what is the remedy.

An assessor must not forget that a single rash word from him may cause great deal of harm to the Party, and result in the confusion and failure of the artist's creative endeavours. He must carefully think things through ten times before he makes a single point, and ponder ten possible counter-suggestions before he advances one.

The need for deep thought by the assessors does not imply that they should cling to their own subjective views. Subjective views are liable to be one-sided in most cases. People who have a firm understanding of the Party's policy and are resolved to implement it thoroughly will say, "In the light of the Party's policy", rather than "in my opinion".

When dealing with a work, the assessors must also consider it from the author's point of view. If they demonstrate to him that they can understand his difficulties, grasp the essence of his problems and are prepared to endeavour together with him to find creative solutions, their assessment and assistance will meet with a sympathetic response.

If assessors are to educate a creative artist, they must be better informed and more advanced than he is. A wide range of profound knowledge will enable them to convince the artist easily and guide him quickly onto the right path. If the advice they give him reflects a sound understanding of the problems of creative work, they can help add flesh and blood to his portrayal of life and help him to understand ten things by considering one.

The assessors are responsible to the Party and the state for the work of art and literature. They must discuss issues sincerely and open-mindedly with the creative artists so that they are united in one purpose. They must always see the good points first and then offer constructive suggestions to correct shortcomings, while preserving the good points. If they work in this manner, no fortress in creative work will be able to resist their assault.

The principle of collectivity must be strictly observed in the assessment of works of art.

In the course of a work's creation disagreements may emerge between the artist and the assessors, and between the assessors themselves. In this case the assessors must discuss the matter sincerely and openly and then offer an agreed opinion. If each offers the artist his own particular opinion the artist will be confused, and the work will come to nothing. A boat that should have been launched in the sea will attempt to climb a mountain. Therefore, when a work is assessed a consolidated opinion, agreed through adequate collective discussion, must be offered to the artist, and sincere consultation must continue until the creator is convinced of its correctness.

In the assessment of works of art and literature, there should be no question of placing one individual's opinion above the collective opinion agreed upon through comprehensive discussion. In this work, an arbitrary approach would be contrary to the Party principle of assessment. Once arbitrary individual tastes are tolerated in the guidance of creative endeavours the unity of collective examination will be totally undermined, and creative work will get out of hand.

The work of assessment must be conducted in a purposeful and planned manner. If the first process of artistic creation, writing, and the work of its assessment are not planned, then films cannot be produced in a planned manner.

The assessment of works must always precede the actual work of their creation and must be conducted as a regular activity under a long-term plan. There should never be any question of examining works only after they have been produced and doing nothing in this area while they are still in production. Until such time as the work is finished everyone must help in the creative effort; they must not just sit and wait for works to be finished, but assist them towards completion in the shortest time possible.

The assessment must be a creative endeavour which develops art and literature steadily and effectively translates the Party's policy into creative work.

THE REVIEW OF CREATIVE WORK MUST PRODUCE GENERALIZED MODELS

The results of any work must be properly summarized before a new task is undertaken. This is the way to advance confidently to a higher level. Communists should work by distinguishing between good points and bad points through a painstaking review of the work that has been done, and then advancing by developing the good points and rectifying the bad points.

In art and literature also an accurate review must be made of a work when it has been finished. This assessment is capable of distinguishing successful and unsuccessful elements, drawing lessons from experience, generalizing the successful points and laying a strong foundation for further success.

The review of a work of art is the final stage of work in which the creative endeavour that has gone into the work is summed up. It cannot therefore be separated from the actual activity of creation. It is the final conclusion of the effort to create a work of art, and the starting point of the endeavours to produce the next one.

The use of a review to produce an accurate analysis and generalization of experience is essential for the continuing development of art. It is only possible to produce a work of art better than the previous one if the lessons learned from the experience of the previous efforts are adopted in a creative fashion. Art is advanced and enriched in the process of adapting and reworking the experience at all levels of previous creative endeavours, from the overall creative method to the individual means of expression.

However wide your experience in artistic creation may be, you will be unable to create a truly original work and will simply repeat your previous experience unless you grasp the essential point, which is that you must digest and absorb experience in order to be able to draw on it in your work. Writers and artists must thoroughly review their creative work and make good use of every valuable element of experience.

In order to review their work effectively, writers and artists must discard the conventional, time-wasting method by which each analyses and evaluates his own works in his own way, without any standard of comparison.

If a review meeting is transformed into a kind of debating club where everyone is involved in the pointless arguing of pros and cons, with ten people saying ten different things, all irrelevant to the purpose of the review and needs of the creative artists, no clear lesson will be drawn from experience, and it will not be possible to determine the appropriate measures to be taken in the future.

Seminars and meetings for the collective criticism or review of works which are conducted without any definite standard will only provide a forum for eloquent people to demonstrate their knowledge. At meetings like this creative artists will become discouraged and confused. These meetings will inevitably generate an atmosphere of distrust, fault-finding, jealousy and other undesirable feelings which are harmful to the ideological unity of the ranks and their unified purpose. This is all a pernicious remnant of the artistic life of the old society, and it must not be tolerated in the work of our revolutionary art and literature.

A long time ago we rejected this obsolete method outright and established a new method of reviewing creative work, by which the whole process of creative activity and its results are thoroughly summarized in accordance with Juche-orientated ideas on art and literature, and the creative artists' understanding of the Party's policy in this area is improved.

Creative work must be reviewed by the same method which is used at meetings for the study of Juche-orientated ideas on art and literature.

From the point of view of Party work, this implies the application of the Chongsanri spirit and method to the sphere of art and literature. This is a form of political work used to review the activities of the writers and artists in implementing the Party's policy on art and literature by the standards of Juche-orientated ideas on art and literature.

This method of review makes it possible to correctly analyse, assess and generalize what has been newly created in this area through the implementation of the Party's policy, what new experience has been gained in the process, what success has been achieved and what lessons learned in the attempt to implement the Party's policy of converting the process of creative work into one of making creative artists revolutionary and working-class.

This method also enables creative workers to develop a more profound understanding of the essential nature of Juche-orientated ideas on art and literature through the lessons of practical experience, and to improve their political and practical qualifications. In the course of analysing the results of their work and distinguishing its merits and demerits and their respective causes, the creative workers will attain a better understanding of the essence and validity of our Party's policy on art and literature and develop a political vision based on Party policy which is capable of accurately assessing all the major and minor problems arising in their creative work.

Creative work must be reviewed in the light of the norms of Juche-orientated ideas on art and literature. These ideas provide the basis of all creative work, the guidelines for the entire process of creation and the standards for its review. Only when works are created and analysed and reviewed on the basis of these ideas will our art and literature be developed in genuinely Juche-orientated and revolutionary forms. Juche-orientated ideas on art and literature are the only ones that can serve as the yardstick for assessing the process and the results of creative work. If a problem is not analysed and judged according to these ideas, not only will the tendency to return to the past be revived and sycophancy and dogmatism raise their heads, but capitalist and revisionist ideas will infiltrate our art and literature.

The most important thing in reviewing creative work is to demonstrate the validity and vitality of our Party's Juche-orientated ideas and theories of art and literature. The review, therefore, must analyse and generalize in the light of these Juche-orientated ideas and theories of literature and art every question arising in the process of creation, even those concerning political studies, skills training and Party organizational and political work directed towards converting the process of creation into one of making the creative artists revolutionary and working-class. Only when this is clearly stated as the goal and the content of the review of creative work, will the discussions make substantial progress in the right direction, allowing a great deal to be learnt in a short space of time.

In the review of creative work model works must be widely publicized. Since the aim of the review is to help all writers and artists to absorb Juche-orientated ideas on art and literature and increase the production of high-quality works, the participants in the review must earnestly discuss how to develop creative work, with a view to teaching and learning from each other. The review must therefore emphasize the successful works which are fine examples of Juche-orientated ideas on art and literature and the experience gained in their creation. It must also stress the generalization of these examples.

If such typical pieces are put forward as models, the creative artists who have produced other pieces will not only clearly see their own shortcomings in the light of the models, but will also experience and learn enough from the models to make a firm resolve to improve their own work and take appropriate measures to correct these shortcomings.

If the review is to give prominence to typical pieces and draw general lessons from them, it must clearly distinguish the new and excellent elements from the other aspects of the work, concentrate on the scientific analysis of the factors that have contributed to its success, and demonstrate them logically and tangibly so that everyone is convinced. We must eliminate the practice of dealing equally with every aspect of a work in the manner of a business routine, by debating a good point for a certain time, and then a bad point for the same length of time without any discrimination of emphasis.

If a positive result achieved in creative work is overlooked or not commented on, it will never become widespread in our art and literature. Brilliant successes and positive experience gained by painstaking efforts should naturally be given greater attention, thoroughly analysed and widely publicized.

The review of works must be undertaken on a regular basis. Regular review will make it possible to analyse and summarize the successes and shortcomings of creative work before it is too late and to develop it smoothly by encouraging the good points and rectifying the defects as early as possible. Good results cannot be expected from reviewing a multitude of accumulated works in a few days under a crash programme, or from working without the necessary preparation, regarding the review as a humdrum daily routine that continues the year round.

As a matter of principle every piece of work must be reviewed separately and several together once or twice annually.

If the review is to be successfully conducted the participants must go over the work under review beforehand. If they are shown the various works all at once in the course of the review, they will not be able to prepare themselves properly for the occasion.

If they go over every piece as soon as it is finished and participate in its review, they can share the experiences of the creative artists and the lessons they have learnt, they can offer them real help in their creative endeavours and forestall possible deviations in their future efforts. If, in addition to the piece-meal review, the whole process of creative work is summarized annually or semi-annually the officials and artists will be able to share their experiences and the lessons they have learned against a broader perspective and advance confidently to the creation of new works, with a clear understanding of the direction on which art and literature are developing, a loftier political vision and a greater wealth of experience.

In the comprehensive and intensive review of creative work, it is important to set clearly defined major objectives for each creative group, for each piece of work and for each problem and to produce a considered summary of the items which will add to the significant lessons of experience.

If the central point of the review is not made clear and the questions raised are obscure, it means that the preparations were not thorough enough and consequently not much will be learnt from the review. Even an inadvertent error in the course of the creative process must be taken up and clearly summarized so that it will serve as a lesson from experience.

The review can raise questions such as the manner in which the author has perceived and understood the reality, what he intended to portray and how, why the portrayal has fallen short of his intention, what are the reasons for the poor results, and what are the measures to be taken. If these questions are clarified, both those analysing the works and those listening will derive valuable experience and lessons from the debate. A lengthy discourse on general principles or a dry business-like account of the process of creation will entirely miss the point of the review process. Pointless debates are uninspiring and tedious.

It is important that the review of creative work should generate a vibrant creative atmosphere in which all the participants in the debate are unified by a single purpose, united in the sincere and open attitude of teaching and learning from each other, and the desire to introduce genuine innovations in creative work.

The officials and the artists participating in the review must share the common aim and desire to develop art and literature more quickly under the leadership of the Party and strive sincerely to learn from each other. No one among them should regard himself exclusively as an assessor or someone who is being assessed; it is everyone's duty to learn and everyone is entitled to teach. They can only learn a lot in a short period of time when they strive for the same objective, teaching and learning from each other, helping and leading each other forward.

All the officials and artists must think and act as one, in keeping with the Party's ideas and will, rejoicing over the successful works as though they were their own, sincerely regretting the defects in other works, learning from every good point, and seeking together to correct mistakes. The review of creative work will then be a very effective undertaking. A man who does not feel bitter regret at an artist's shortcoming will be unable to accept a success and champion it warmly.

The review of creative work must provide an ideological summary of the artists' views, their mode of thinking, attitude to creative work and their artistic style. To be successful the review must be founded on an ideological struggle to equip writers and artists with a firm understanding of Juche-orientated ideas on art and literature.

A meeting for the review of creative work is not an occasion for the complacent applause of success or self-praise, still less is its function to single out a few individuals and shower them with praise. The greater a success is and the better the work is going, the higher should be the demand made, and the greater the efforts to which people should be exhorted. It must always be remembered that, if a success in one campaign is simply applauded and the mental preparations for the next campaign are neglected, the eventual result will be failure.

If a review of several works is carried out at one time, not only positive elements but also backward elements will be discovered. If those defects are connived at as being inevitable in the course of progress, the artists infected with them will be encouraged to remain as they are and will lag further and further behind until they become irredeemable. It is therefore very important to express sharp criticism of shortcomings and rectify them before it is too late, for the sake of maintaining the general advance, and encouraging collective innovations.

All reactionary ideological trends and elements such as capitalist, feudalist and revisionist ideas and sycophancy towards great powers are contrary to the concept of Juche, and form the first target of intensive criticism at the review. Even the slightest element of these outmoded ideas or inclination towards them which is revealed in creative work must not be tolerated, but combatted and eliminated once and for all.

Slothfulness and conservatism revealed in creative work must also be overcome through uncompromising struggle. These ideological tendencies find their expression in the fear of taking responsibility for creative work and in paying mere lip service to creative initiative in practical work. They are a pitfall in the development of film art. Slothfulness and conservatism are therefore a major target of struggle that must be criticized and overcome if art and literature are to develop rapidly to a higher level.

The strong spirit of criticism in a review of creative work must derive from the Party attitude of raising the standards of all creative groups and every creative worker to the standard of the model that has been put forward, and developing art and literature more quickly. If the essence of mistakes and shortcomings is illuminated from the ideological point of view, and if the struggle to overcome them leads every one to the right path, the quality of creative work will naturally improve.

It is important always to express criticism in a way which maintains the integrity of the concept of Juche and to strike hard at reactionary ideas, in order to redeem one's comrades and create perfect works of art. In order to achieve this, the critical analysis must be sharp, and there should be no question of mere fault-finding or stigmatizing writers and their works ideologically and ostracizing them politically. Criticism is not only a means of overcoming outmoded ideas, but also a powerful means for cementing the ideological unity of the collective behind a single purpose and increasing the strength of the organization.

If criticism is to be effective, typical shortcomings must be analysed in detail and in depth, and time should not be wasted on secondary defects. If criticism is diverted to defects which are not essential, major shortcomings may be overlooked, and substantial lessons will not be learnt. If criticism is directed to one thing or another indiscriminately, merely for the sake of strengthening the spirit of criticism, nothing will be gained and the results will actually be harmful.

An ideological struggle which champions the positive and combats the negative is the most rational and effective way of conducting the revolutionary education of writers and artists. It is extremely important in the revolutionary transformation of writers and artists and their assimilation to the working class. Meetings for the study of Juche-orientated ideas on art and literature will not only teach writers and artists the knowledge and techniques indispensable for the creation of revolutionary art and literature, but also train them to acquire the revolutionary attitude and traits of ardent champions of the Party policy who implement it so that they become better qualified as writers and artists of the new type who have firmly established their own quality of Juche.

The review of creative work will have justified itself if it brings forth fresh innovations and new advances by making good things widely available and overcoming mistakes through criticism.

A meeting for the study of Juche-orientated ideas on art and literature is an important element in the endeavour to encourage energetic efforts by all writers and artists to advance our Juche-orientated art to a higher level, to encourage them to take great pride in their participation in the creation of revolutionary art and literature and maintain a high degree of political awareness and creative enthusiasm.

NOTES

1   **Chajusong**—an attribute of man who desires to live and develop independently as master of the world and his own destiny

Because of Chajusong inherent in his nature, man, unlike animals which are subordinated to their environments, desires to live free from the fetters of nature and society and is the master who dominates the world

Chajusong is the life and soul of man, the social being Physical life is the life of man as a living organism, and socio-political life is the life of man as the social being

If a man has no Chajusong in society, he is as good as dead for a social being, even if he is physically alive Only a man who has Chajusong and exalts his socio-political integrity can be a truly worthy social being

Human history is a history of struggle of the people for Chajusong

This is so essentially because the masses desire Chajusong and struggle for it

The transformation of society, remaking of nature and remoulding of man are the important contents of the masses' struggle for Chajusong

The Chajusong of a country and a nation is the prerequisite for the Chajusong of the popular masses, and the struggle for the Chajusong of a country and a nation is precisely the struggle for the Chajusong of the masses

The Korean word "chajusong" is given as it is pronounced because there is no suitable English word to correctly express such a profound meaning and wide connotation of the original   p 1

2   **The class and mass lines**—the political lines which are maintained by the Workers' Party of Korea

The class line is one of the fundamental principles guiding the activity of the working-class party, which fights for the working class, the leading class of the revolution, and in defence of its class position

The mass line is also one of the fundamental principles guiding the activity of the working-class party, which fights for the masses and carries out its revolutionary tasks by allowing full rein to the strength and creative wisdom of the masses

In order to achieve its historical mission, the working-class party must properly combine the class line with the mass line   p 28

3   **Their revolutionary transformation and assimilation to the working class**—an important task which the working-class party and state must carry out after the establishment of the socialist system The revolutionary transformation of people means eradicating the remnants of outmoded ideas from their minds and arming them with the communist ideology, so that they become ardent revolutionaries, men and women who have a genuine revolutionary world outlook Their assimilation to the working class means that the working class which has seized power transforms society on its own pattern in every sphere of the economy, culture, ideology and morality In other words, it involves raising the ideological level of all members of society and their technical and cultural standards to those of the working class and establishing the single ownership of the means of production by the people as a whole by transforming cooperative property into public property In this way, class distinctions between the workers and the peasants will be eliminated and all social relations reorganized completely on the pattern of the working class   p 33

4   **The Fatherland Liberation War (June 1950-July 1953)**—the just war of the Korean people to repulse the invasion of the US imperialists and defend the freedom and independence of their fatherland, and an anti-imperialist, anti-US struggle against the allied forces of the US imperialists and other world reactionaries

The US imperialist aggressors, the sworn enemy of the Korean people, and their stooges the puppet clique of Syngman Rhee rejected the realistic and reasonable proposal of the Democratic People's Republic of Korea for peaceful national reunification, and launched a surprise invasion of the northern half of the Republic at dawn on June 25, 1950 The US imperialists brought millions of troops to the Korean front, including one-third of their ground force, one-fifth of their air force, most of their Pacific Fleet, the troops of 15 satellite countries and the south Korean puppet army as well as large amounts of the latest weapons and equipment Moreover, during the Korean war they resorted to the most brutal methods of warfare, including bacteriological weapons However, rallied closely behind the great leader Comrade Kim Il Sung and under his wise leadership, the Korean people inflicted an ignominious defeat upon the US imperialists and their stooges and won a historic victory   p 46

5   **The anti-Japanese revolutionary struggle**—the struggle of the Korean people waged for 20 years from October 1926 to August 1945, under the guidance of the great leader Comrade Kim Il Sung, against the Japanese imperialist aggressors in order to win national sovereignty and independence and to achieve the class liberation of the oppressed working masses   p 51

6   **The speed campaign**—the basic form of actions to perform all tasks of socialist construction at a lightning speed It is a revolutionary principle of building socialism always by leaps and bounds and making miraculous successes continually by drawing on the high political awareness and creative activity of the masses The basic requirement of the speed campaign is that, through the mobilization of all available forces, every piece of work should be performed as quickly and as best as possible   p 291

7   **The Chongsanri spirit and method**—the idea and method of mass leadership which the respected leader Comrade Kim Il Sung created by applying and developing the revolutionary mass line, a tradition of the Workers' Party of Korea, in conformity with the new situation of socialist construction in February 1960 when he was directing the work of Chongsan-ri (now Chongsan-ri, Kangso District, Nampo City) and of the Kangso County Party Committee in the field

The Chongsanri spirit, the idea of mass leadership, requires that Party and state leadership should be given on the principle of taking the full responsibility for the national economy and the people's living conditions, giving top priority to the interests of the masses at all times, of rallying all members of society around the Party by educating and reforming them, and of leading them as far as the communist society It also requires that the principle of making all work the work of the masses themselves should be observed

The Chongsanri method, the method of mass leadership, requires that the superiors should help their subordinates, that priority be given to political work in all activities, that general direction and individual guidance be combined correctly, that the effort be concentrated on the main link and that all work should be planned and pushed ahead forcefully

The Chongsanri spirit and method represent the method and style of Party work, work mainly with people   p 301

8   **The Taean work system**—a new form of managing the socialist economy It was established by the great leader Comrade Kim Il Sung in December 1961, when he was

visiting the Taean Electrical Machinery Factory (now the Taean Heavy Machine Complex) It is a system by which, first, the economy is managed under the collective leadership of the Party committee, second, the factory staff, consisting of production guidance, planning, technical, and power supply and maintenance departments, functions under the chief engineer as the chief of staff and gives unified and coordinated guidance to production, third, higher echelons take the responsibility of supplying materials to the subordinate units, and fourth, supply work for the factory workers and the inhabitants of the district concerned is carried out in a responsible manner   p 301